DEVON

A Thematic Study

Brian Chugg

DEVON
A Thematic Study

B. T. Batsford Ltd
London

For Mary

First published 1980
©Brian Chugg 1980

ISBN 0 7134 0417 5

Printed in Great Britain
Redwood Burn Ltd
Trowbridge & Esher
for the publishers, B. T. Batsford Ltd
4 Fitzhardinge Street, London W1H 0AH

List of Illustrations

Contents

Acknowledgments

This book has been the subject of many discussions with my friend and former colleague Richard B. Wright. I thank him for scrutinizing my typescript and for his invaluable suggestions.

I also acknowledge with gratitude my friend Dr R. Newton who read the chapter on history; and Mr J. Lomas RIBA who read the chapter on architecture. I thank: Mr S. Hunt, Curator of Applied Art at the Royal Albert Memorial Museum, Exeter, for assistance with the section which describes the Exeter hall-marks; and my wife for her help with Devon lace. I also wish to thank Mr S. Carr of B. T. Batsford Ltd., for without his encouragement and forbearance this book would not have materialized.

I am grateful: to my friend Don. V. López-Folgado of Madrid University; to my cousins, Major General C. G. Cooper USMC, in the United States and Mr D. Rabley in Ontario; and also to Mrs S. Frazer of British Columbia for providing information which has been used in chapter three.

I wish to thank my colleagues of the North Devon College especially Miss P. Waterer the Librarian and her assistants; Mr G. Morris, Curator of the North Devon Athenaeum; and Mr W. Turner, Town Clerk of Barnstaple, for much help.

I should also like to record my appreciation of the assistance which I have received from: Mrs M. M. Rowe, Head of Devon Record Services; Miss J. Baker, Curator of Fine Art at the R.A.M.M., Miss R. M. Thomas and Mr C. J. Pearson, Keepers of Art at the City Museum and Art Gallery, Plymouth; Commander K. Burns of Plymouth Library of Naval History; Mr J. Barber, Director of Plymouth Museum, Mr J. Manning, Exhibition Officer of the same institution and Mr M. Dowdell of Torquay Central Library.

It is not possible to list all the libraries, museums and other organizations which have helped by supplying information but I wish to mention the staff of the West Country Studies Library; Dartington Hall Record Office; the Lundy Field Society and the Slapton Ley Field Centre.

Whilst not acknowledging them in detail, use has been made of publications such as those of the Exeter and Plymouth Museums, the learned societies and, in addition, the regional newspapers.

Permission to reproduce part of a letter by Thomas Gorges in the archive of the Devon Record Office is acknowledged with gratitude.

The Author and Publishers would like to thank the following for supplying illustrations: Peter Baker Photography: 3, 25; Eileen Cooper Antiques: 13, 15, 24; Leonard and Marjorie Gayton: 11, 23; A. F. Kersting: 1, 9, 10, 12, 16, 17, 18; John Topham Picture Library: 8. The author and publisher are grateful to the following for allowing copies to be made of photographs in their collections: *The Honiton News*: 6, and Torquay Central Library: 7. The remaining illustrations are from the Author's and Publishers' collections.

Introduction

The broad green land known as Devonshire appears to have been conducive to human settlement from the earliest times; some parts of it have probably been under cultivation for over 2,000 years. A marked feature of Devonian life has been the coming and going of its human population. Those centres of activity, the ports, received many people who were attracted from other parts of England by the work available in the sixteenth and seventeenth centuries. In this way the number of indigenous townsfolk became swollen by outsiders whose contribution to their adopted county has been considerable. Today, the London family who go down to Devon for their holidays and the Birmingham couple who come to retire, repeat a process which started a very long time ago. It is pure speculation to suggest that the south Devon limestone caves, which have yielded evidence of early occupation by man, were indeed the first homes of the human species in the British Isles as a whole, but it remains a possibility.

Devon is the third largest administrative region in Britain, being exceeded only by Yorkshire and Lincolnshire; its area is 6715 square kilometres (2591 square miles). The Dartmoor National Park, rising well above the average height of its surrounding hills, forms the most clearly defined of several sub-regions within the county and is 946 square kilometres (365 square miles) in area. Dartmoor's southern slopes form the northern boundary of the so-called 'South Hams' which extend to the South Devon coast. The Exmoor National Park straddles the Devon-Somerset boundary and the larger and higher part of it lies in Somerset. Lynmouth and the steep-sided, wooded valleys which converge on it is situated within the Devon section of the Park together with the south-western shoulders of the moor. In this work the zone is referred to as the 'Exmoor fringe'; it is 200 square kilometres in extent.

The book commences by drawing attention to the features of the terrain within the present administrative boundaries of the county and goes on to describe other areas of knowledge. A few preliminary comments may not be out of place. The many-sided character of Devon is reflected in the themes to which the chapter headings refer. Bearing in mind Devon's geological structure, climate, fauna and flora it is evident that they cannot be entirely separated from those of the adjacent counties of Cornwall, Dorset and Somerset. The same is often true of the subjects discussed in the other chapters. An annotated list or appendix has been compiled to add to the usefulness of each and will be found at the end of the relevant chapter.

The rocks which underlie a region are of paramount importance for the soil and all living species derive from their basic constituents. The Devon rock formations are visually of much interest and the first chapter of this book deals with their structure and disposition under present climatic conditions. Other aspects of environmental study have been excluded through lack of space, but the influence of the rocks on the buildings of the county is indicated in an appendix to the chapter on architecture.

A comprehensive description of the flora and fauna and their habitats could occupy many volumes. Accordingly, in the chapter on wildlife, attention is focussed on the animals and birds which appear at present to be most interesting and which may be observed by a suitably-equipped person with relative ease. Rarities have as a general rule been excluded from the lists which appear at the end of the chapter. For quick reference the species are arranged alphabetically and not according to the natural orders.

Devon's rich history has been described in thorough detail by many twentieth-century authors of repute. In this work attention is centred on a few topics each representative of a different period. The south Devon limestone caves deserve notice not merely for their geological formations but because they provided shelter for the earliest human inhabitants. The starting point of local history is, unquestionably, in these caves. Some new information about Roman Devon has become available as a result of the excavations which have been made since 1950; use has been made of it in the sub-section concerned. Devon's relationship to Spain in the sixteenth century is so important that it must not be omitted in a work of this nature. The challenge of Spain and the adventuring of Devonians in the New World are themes which are inextricably interwoven. In this book the strong links that Devon has with north America are separated, for convenience, at the date of the sailing of the Pilgrim Fathers. Events which occurred before 1620 have a place in the sub-section on 'The Age of the Sea Hawks'; those which took place after that date are placed under the heading 'Devon and America'. The county has played a considerable part in the migration of the European people and the common heritage of Britain and the English-speaking people of north America is destined to endure for ages to come. The history of the first half of the twentieth century too, dominated by wars in which Devonians were much involved, is certain to be the focus of increasing interest in the future when it is possible that it will be seen as a period of change more marked than any other in recent centuries.

The chapter on architecture is intended to relate the buildings of Devon to the generally-recognized styles and periods and to do so in architectural terms. The social and historic associations of some of the examples used are mentioned but it is not the intention to give them in detail. It has had to be assumed that readers are already in possession of some basic knowledge of English architectural development during the periods in question; but it is hoped, nevertheless, that sufficient information is given to enable the newcomer to the subject to understand its main features. Many of the important Devon buildings are mentioned but even so space has permitted neither detailed reference to the remains of monastic buildings nor to the Protestant chapels and the same is true of the farm-houses and cottages. To make reference easy, the names of the periods are used as sub-headings. In the case of localities which are little-frequented the name of a better-known town or village in the district is usually given in the text as an aid to finding them on an Ordnance map. It should not be assumed, however, that the buildings described are open to the public, though many of them may be visited.

Certain crafts, which have at times been important as Devon occupations, are described in the chapter on fine craftwork. In each of these activities Devonian craftsmen and women have produced work having local character-istics the identification of which is attempted. A survey of the craftwork is given; it may be extended by reference to the specialist craft books. The stone-carving of the Devon churches, including architectural ornament but excluding the tomb sculpture of Elizabethan date, has not survived in as good a condition as wood-carving. Stone-carving is included with architecture in Chapter Four whereas wood-carving is discussed in Chapter Five.

The lives and output of workers in the graphic arts as a whole forms the subject of the chapter on Devonian artists. Painters who were either born in Devon or who worked mainly in the county are described and the wider significance of such artists as Nicholas Hilliard and Sir Joshua Reynolds is indicated. In addition the development of print-making as it was applied to the illustrating of the topography of the county has been summarized. The annotated list at the end of the chapter gives a synopsis of the lives of an extended range of artists associated with Devon in the hope that it will be of service to students and collectors.

The topographical chapter is confined to a description of the historic centres of the four principal towns or cities. An attempt is made to relate these to the physical geography of their areas. It is not the intention to deal with all the points of interest; some of the main buildings have been discussed in Chapter Four and it is hoped that the two chapters will be treated as complementary. The post-war planning of Exeter and Plymouth is the subject of comment and, at the end of the chapter, there is an annotated list of an extended number of towns and villages.

This work is addressed to the many who have a more-than-passing-interest in the county of Devon. As footnotes do not form a part of the book, some of the publications which are most relied upon as a ground for evaluation are named in several of the chapters for readers who would like to have more information. There is much material available under the heading of history and it has not been considered to be practical to do this in Chapter Three. However, those interested would find the works of Professor W. G. Hoskins of great value.

The author has endeavoured to produce a summary of knowledge in various fields and when practical the results of recent work have been included. He hopes that he has provided some starting points for further research.

NOTES

Measurements: It should be noted that throughout this work metric measurements are given and are followed by the British equivalent within brackets; the figures have in many cases been rounded up or down and are given as a guide to size and scale and should not be regarded as precise.

Museums: The two major museums are the Royal Albert Memorial Museum at Exeter and the City Museum and Art Gallery of Plymouth. These names are given in full in each chapter when reference is first made to them but subsequently they are referred to simply as Exeter Museum and Plymouth Museum respectively.

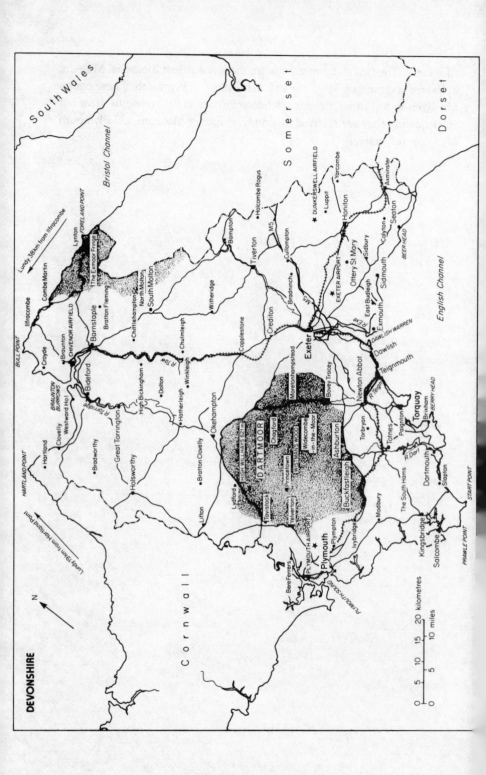

DEVONSHIRE

N

Lundy 38 km from Ilfracombe
Lundy 19 km from Hartland Point

South Wales

Bristol Channel

BULL POINT
Ilfracombe
Combe Martin
FORELAND POINT
Lynton
The Exmoor Fringe
Croyde
Braunton
CHIVENOR AIRFIELD
Barnstaple
Bratton Fleming
Chittlehampton
North Molton
South Molton
Bampton
Holcombe Rogus
Somerset
DUNKESWELL AIRFIELD
Luppit
Yarcombe
Honiton
Axminster
Tiverton
M5
Cullompton
Bradninch
SW
EXETER AIRPORT
Ottery St Mary
Sidbury
Colyton
Seaton
BEER HEAD
BRAUNTON
BURROWS
Bideford
Westward Ho!
R Tor
R Torridge
High Bickingham
Dolton
Winkleigh
Hatherleigh
Chulmleigh
Witheridge
Copplestone
Crediton
Exeter
R Exe
East Budleigh
Exmouth
DAWLISH WARREN
Dawlish
Sidmouth
English Channel
Dorset
HARTLAND POINT
Hartland
Clovelly
Great Torrington
Holsworthy
Bradworthy
Okehampton
Moretonhampstead
Bovey Tracey
Newton Abbot
R Teign
Teignmouth
Lifton
Bratton Clovelly
HIGH WILL HAYS 621m
DARTMOOR
Chagford
Widecombe
-in-the-Moor
YES TOR 618m
Princetown
Ashburton
Buckfastleigh
Torbryan
Torquay
BERRY HEAD
Brixham
Paignton
Totnes
R Dart
Lydford
Tavistock
Yelverton
Plympton
Ivybridge
Modbury
The South Hams
Dartmouth
Slapton
START POINT
PLYMOUTH AIRPORT
Plymouth
Bere Ferrers
PLYMOUTH SOUND
Kingsbridge
Salcombe
PRAWLE POINT

Cornwall

0   5   10   15   20 kilometres
0   5   10 miles

CHAPTER ONE

The Environment

Devon is situated in the south-west peninsula of the British Isles. This means that it is placed on the western edge of one of the world's great land masses which passes back through continental Europe into Asia. To put it another way, Devon lies at the eastern edge of one of the great water masses of the earth, the Atlantic Ocean. It is well to be aware of these facts as one watches the sea from Start or Hartland Point for the maritime climate has helped to mould the character of Devonians and the south-west location has determined their destiny.

If it were possible to proceed south-westerly in a straight line from Start Point the first land reached would be situated south of the equator near the mouth of the Amazon on the north coast of Brazil, an unobstructed sea voyage of 3857 nautical miles. A similar journey in a westerly direction from Barnstaple and Bideford Bay would result in landfall at St John's, Newfoundland, a voyage of 1862 nautical miles. In terms of latitude the fiftieth parallel lies twelve minutes south of Prawle Point, the most-southerly part of Devon, and the fifty-first passes through the village of Clovelly on Barnstaple Bay in north Devon. Within the same band of latitude around the globe are situated Vancouver Island and, on the far side of Asia, the Aleutians. The whole of the United States of America lies, therefore, to the south and so does Japan.

When the first prehistoric people, migrating gradually northwards from the Mediterranean and the Iberian peninsula, arrived on the section of the Normandy coast approximating to the present port of Cherbourg, the part of Devon which is now the site of Dartmouth and Salcombe was a mere 85 nautical miles away. This fact was of much importance from Roman times until the World Wars. Only now, in the late twentieth century, does it appear that the value of the English Channel as a defensive moat is of less concern than its effect as a barrier isolating Britain from her main European neighbours and trading partners.

The impressive variety to be observed in the landscapes of Devon is explained by the different types of rock which underlie it and the forces that have acted on them. The sea cliffs of the north-west have a distinct stratification, the granite of Dartmoor has a quite different composition and a curious red soil dominates the scene in certain parts of the county. The Ilfracombe and Hartland cliffs are composed of the accumulated deposits of the sea bed, the Dartmoor tors are the inner cores of formerly much larger masses of material which were forced up through the earth's crust and from which, during the passage of time, vast outer layers have been removed. The red soils are debris swept down from the mountain range by sudden storms in a generally-arid cycle of time.

This particular part of the earth's surface has seen great changes and upheavals; the record of the rocks gives no cause to regard them as dead or inert. For unimaginably long ages they lay under the sea only to rise as dry land and be submerged again and again in succession. The great beds of Devonian and Carboniferous rocks which form some of the main structures of the county are sedimentary in origin. They were deposited as fine sediments from water and formed the sea bed. At varying times different materials went to form these deposits, and they varied in thickness and sustained differing pressures. The resulting rocks are described today as slates, sandstones, grits and limestones. That they are all of submarine origin is proved by the occurrence of certain fossils within them. Devonian rocks are amongst the oldest formations in the British Isles. Fortunately they now seem to be extremely stable and earth movements such as occur are usually so slight that they pass unnoticed. However, it is worth noting that the *Western Daily Mercury* of the 18 August 1892 reported the following under the title 'Earthquake Shocks in the West':

'The seismic disturbance which seems to have been general throughout the West of England in the early hours of yesterday morning was severely felt in many parts of Devon and Cornwall, some districts in the extreme south, that of Plymouth among them, escaped scot-free, but from the northern portion of the counties reports of subterranean rumblings, earth tremors, rocking houses and agitated crockery ware, are universal.'

The article goes on to describe how after a very sultry day people were awakened from their sleep, at about 30 minutes past midnight. Shock waves and the rattling of windows lasted several seconds and a tidal bore was reported on the Tamar.

An earthquake, confined entirely to Devon, shook the South Hams district at 7.35 p.m. on Christmas Day 1923. R. Hansford Worth carried out a methodical analysis of its effects and found that the greatest shocks were experienced and the loudest noise was heard within an elliptical area stretching from Ringmore in the south to Widecombe-in-the-Moor in the north; this was surrounded by an outer zone where the shocks were less severely felt. Plympton and Torbay mark the western and eastern extremities of this larger area whose southernmost point was Salcombe. Fortunately hardly any damage was caused; but hanging pictures and lamps were set swaying and the accompanying noise was variously described as an explosion, a thud or a rumbling as if caused by an underground wave. The origin of these tremors, which had been preceded by others of lesser intensity, appears to be a north-and-south fault passing through both the sedimentary rocks and the granite somewhere near South Brent.

Modern methods of dating rocks by their radioactivity suggest with some certainty that the Devonian strata were formed more than 280 million years ago. For more than 100 million years before that the sediments had been accumulating to a great depth over the area that is now represented by Devon with the exception of its south-east section. It is helpful to imagine the different sediments as pressurized layers, one upon the other and, in addition, as a result of the forces that were exerted upon them, they should be visualized as forming a shallow trough extending under Devon from Foreland Point in the north to Plymouth Hoe in the south. In such a formation the lowest levels will obviously be the oldest and the uppermost the newest and apart from exceptional circumstances such as those produced by quarrying and mining operations, the only part of the structure fully exposed to view will be the edge of the layers—the sea-cliffs.

The geologist refers to the different layers as 'beds' and divides them into Lower, Middle and Upper. The lowest and therefore the oldest of these Devonian beds are known as Dartmouth Slates; they form the cliffs on both sides of the Dart estuary and continue westwards forming the cliffs of the Erme and Yealm estuaries and they are present on both sides of Plymouth Sound. Extending into the South Hams are the Meadfoot Beds which get their name from Meadfoot Beach at Torquay. These merge in the north with beds named after Staddon Heights which overlook Plymouth Sound. The three beds, the Dartmouth Slates, the Meadfoot Beds and Staddon Grits, form the Lower Devonian in the south of the county.

Certain deposits embedded in the Middle Devonian consist of material of organic origin. They occur as limestones in several different areas south of Dartmoor including Torquay. Some of them are made up of accumulations of coral debris of distinctive shades of grey. The total bulk of these strata suggests that the special conditions required for the development of corals, such as water depth and temperature, must have persisted for a very long time in this region. The limestone areas are significant because, through the percolation of water, caves have been formed in them and, in addition, they are the habitat of certain lime-loving plants which would not otherwise grow in Devon. Volcanic ash in the form of thin bands of tufa occurs at various places along the beds, for instance at Hope's Nose, Torquay; Drake's Island in Plymouth Sound; and in the vicinity of Totnes.

In the south the Upper Devonian beds fill the area between Dartmoor and the Tamar and, on the east of the moor, a smaller area between the high ground and the head of the Teign estuary. Here too, igneous rocks consisting of lavas, probably of submarine origin, occur within the beds. The most impressive igneous outcrop is, however, Brentor, north of Tavistock; it is not as the name suggests a tor but the remains of a small, but nevertheless genuine, volcanic cone.

Returning to the model of the layers, forming a trough-like depression; it should be explained that the centre is filled with rocks of a later date—the Carboniferous Measures. So the Devonian deposits are lost to view and appear to pass beneath these newer rocks. When they emerge again in north Devon they have a dip to the south as would be expected if the supposition is correct. Various differences in character are noticed however; for instance, limestones are very confined, there is no indication of volcanic activity, and, in the Foreland and Hangman Grits, some fine-grained sandstones, which do not correspond with any of the Devonian rocks in the south, are found.

The oldest rocks in north Devon appear to be the reddish Foreland Grits and they form the only prominence on the north coast—Foreland Point near Lynton. The Middle Devonian period saw the return of the sea, the Ilfracombe beds are mainly slates but contain abundant fossil fauna in the patches of limestone in the Combe Martin district. Because of the presence of corals it is reasonable to believe that they are the northern counterpart of the more widespread limestones of the south. On top of these Ilfracombe beds are the smooth, flaky Morte Slates and the blue-grey Pilton Beds of the Upper Devonian period.

These Devonian strata, both in the north and south, merge into the Carboniferous rocks which are known by the local name 'culm'; in fact they bear little resemblance to the Carboniferous rocks of other parts of the British Isles and though they may contain some deposits worth mining, such as the black pigment formerly extracted at Bideford, and the coal mined at Bovey Tracey and used for firing the kilns of the potteries, good quality coal is not present. The Carboniferous rocks extend over a large area of north and central Devon amounting in all to about 3100 square kilometres (1200 square miles). If the model of the layers is correct, younger and younger rocks would be expected to outcrop successively towards the centre of the area and this is indeed what happens. The oldest Culm Measures are found adjacent to the Devonian rocks in two narrow zones in both the north and south of the county.

Dartmoor, the main physical feature of Devon, rises as a distinct subregion above the surrounding farmlands and covers a tenth of the land surface; it indicates a forcible upwelling of material beneath the Devonian and Carboniferous rocks. The upward movement of the granite may have been conditioned by the existing bedding planes of the sedimentary rocks which would have tended to rupture. During the intervening ages the sedimentary layers originally resting on top of the Dartmoor granite, have been worn away by the forces of erosion leaving the granite exposed. Where the granite is in close contact with the Devonian and Carboniferous they have been altered so completely, through the effect of high temperature, that they are known as the 'metamorphic aureole'. This zone of resistant rock encircles Dartmoor; where rivers flow across it such features as Lydford Gorge and Becka Falls have been formed. The most-southerly part of the county, the coastal strip between Start Point and Bolt Tail, also consists of an outcrop of metamorphic rocks. These are mainly schists, that is to say, they are fine-grained and their mineral content is arranged in more or less parallel layers; their age is similar to that of the Dartmoor granite.

Lundy, meaning Isle of Puffins, situated in the Bristol Channel off the north Devon coast, also consists of granite and, it has been suggested, owes its formation to processes similar to those responsible for the formation of Dartmoor; but it was not necessarily created at the same time. The sedimentary rocks seen at the south-east tip of Lundy rest at an angle which confirms that they were indeed tilted by an upward force exerted from below. This corner of Lundy is similar in appearance to some of the north Devon mainland cliffs. The remainder of the island consists of a tableland surrounded by a remarkable range of granite buttresses not to be found elsewhere in Devon.

The whole orientation of the impressive north Devon cliffs appears to be related to the east-west strike of the sedimentary rocks. From Bull Point to the Somerset county boundary and beyond the coast follows a remarkably straight line which, incidentally, nearly follows the line of latitude; it is a good example of a 'concordant coast'. At Bull Point the coast turns almost 90 degrees. This distinctive angle occurs also at Hartland Point where the north-south orientation is taken up again. As one would expect, the cross-section of the structure revealed in the sea-cliffs has much of interest. South of Hartland Point in particular, it is clear that the layers have been subjected to movements of cataclysmic intensity. Forces applied from north and south have had the effect of folding and breaking the layers so that they are no longer arranged like a sandwich but resemble a concertina; these famous 'synclines' and 'anticlines' take the full force of the Atlantic storms. The folded structure does of course extend beneath the surface of the adjacent district.

The general direction of the south Devon coast changes in the neighbourhood of the southern headlands, Prawle and Start Points. From Prawle to Plymouth it faces south-west. From Start to Axmouth, near the Dorset boundary, the general direction in which it faces is south-east. The result is an angle at Start as marked as that at Harland in the north. But the south Devon coast is of an altogether more involved outline and more sheltered character. A fine series of drowned-river-valleys or 'rias', the result of a lowering of the coast in comparatively recent geological time, penetrate the shoreline between Berry Head and the Cornish border and create the well-known, lush valleys of south Devon. They carry the climatic influence of the sea inland and provide the seafarer with anchorages at all states of the tide, and, they were the cradle of the Devon maritime tradition. All the way from Dorset to the Cornish borders the coast is visually enhanced by a succession of headlands of a variety of rock types.

Both Start Bay in the south and that part of Barnstaple Bay that lies between Abbotsham and Bull Point in the north, have a hinterland whose hills run roughly at right angles to the shore. These are fine examples of 'discordant' coasts. Each headland represents the seaward end of a bed of rocks running east to west. Beside Barnstaple Bay extensive ranges of sand dunes have been built up at Saunton, Croyde and Woolacombe between the imposing headlands of Downend—consisting of Baggy Beds, Baggy Point—consisting of Marwood Beds, and Morte Point—consisting of Morte Slates. In Start Bay between the headlands the sea has thrown up sand and shingle bars behind which freshwater lagoons have been impounded. These localities, in both north and south, are ecologically important.

The earth movements which brought about the crushing of the Devonian rocks and the upwelling of the granite created a mountain range and were almost certainly accompanied by climatic change. The south-west is thought to have become part of a desert having a hot climate. Occasional downpours caused flash floods to sweep down the steep mountain valleys into lakeland areas where sedimentation took place. In the 'Bovey Basin', south-east of Dartmoor, deposits have been found to have the awesome depth of 915 metres (3,000 feet); similar deposits occur on a smaller scale near Peter's Marland, south of Great Torrington. Aridity prevailed through two geological ages, the Permian and Triassic; these were periods when the existing rocks were shattered and broken down. Large angular fragments would have accumulated as scree but some would be swept to lower ground. Many of the deposits formed in this way still exist in parts of Devon in the form of 'breccias' and sands.

The rocks so far mentioned: the Devonian, the Carboniferous and the granite, are usually referred to as the 'old rocks', but in the south-east part of the county newer rocks appear. A line drawn roughly from north to south through Exeter marks the approximate division between the old and the new, but some older rocks are found to the east and some new rocks occur to the west of it. Though it is difficult to establish a firm dividing line the fact that the colour of some of the new rocks and the soils that they have yielded, is red immediately identifies them in the field. The pigment is in fact red oxide of iron and it will be noticed that it occurs on the south coast between Budleigh Salterton and Paignton and it extends inland from the foot of Woodbury Common east of the Exe estuary to the Haldon hills on the west. A long tongue of red soil reaches up the Creedy valley to Crediton and North Tawton and spreads as far as Hatherleigh. Another tongue extends to Tiverton and there are small outlying patches as far away as Portledge on Barnstaple Bay. Where it is juxtaposed with the varied colours of vegetation this soil pigmentation produces exceptional visual interest.

The fragments which formed this reconstituted rock, the New Red Sandstone, were obviously composed of the disintegrated outer layers of the Devonian and Carboniferous. The new rocks have a north-south strike almost at right angles to the older. Volcanic debris occurs within the area of new rocks in the form of outcrops, especially in the Exeter region where over 50 sites have been listed. Moving into east Devon the sandstones of the Permian age are overlaid by Triassic marls and sandstones. It is usually assumed that the earliest of these strata make up the pebble bed forming the ridge of Woodbury Common. The marls which occur over an extensive part of east Devon probably originated as a blown dust. Since it was first deposited the surface has been dissected by the action of the rivers Axe, Sid, Otter and Culm leaving, between their valleys, a series of distinctive standing plateaux surrounded by escarpments. They dominate the landscape between Sidmouth, Honiton and Axminster with their more or less horizontal ridges which are not like other Devon hills.

A bed of pebbles from 21 to 24 metres (70-80 feet) in depth which commences at Budleigh Salterton and, in a diminishing form, can be traced northwards into Somerset has attracted much attention. Sometimes known as 'Bunter Pebbles', a term derived from the German name for New Red Sandstone, the deposit is thought to be debris brought down by a major river fed by rainfall on distant peaks. No local source of such pebbles exists today nor does a river capable of moving a mass of this bulk fit the scale of the present landscape. Towards the south-eastern corner of Devon the rocks, consisting of chalk and greensand, are of younger age. The lowest deposit of all is the gault clay which may be seen on the coast near the Dorset boundary.

The newer rocks occur west of the Exe in the form of the Haldon hills. This greensand plateau, surrounded by escarpments, is a reminder of the similar features in east Devon. Considerable interest arose following the discovery in 1808 of a deposit of Tertiary gravels at Orleigh Court, near Bideford. It led to speculation that little of the region remained above water during the Upper Cretaceous period; if this is correct then very large quantities of the greensand have been eroded and removed because today the only other separate remnant is the Haldon hills. Removal of the chalk must have been even greater for all that remains today is the outcrop which includes the attractive Beer Head—the most westerly extension of the Upper Chalk visible in England.

One of the more complex features of the Devon scene is the remnants of the 'planation surfaces'. Numerous observers have become aware that, though the land surface is very hilly, the hills have a certain regularity; over large areas of the county their heights are very similar and the tops tend to be flattened. Only rarely does a Devon hill rise head and shoulders above its surroundings as Cawsand Beacon rises above the South Tawton area and Yes Tor above Okehampton; over the greater part of the county there is considerable uniformity. It has been postulated that 70 million years ago, at the beginning of the Tertiary period, a level plain was established following an uplifting of the land surface; it is now thought to be represented by some of the high-level flat areas of Dartmoor. Erosion would have continued and, after a considerable time, tilting and faulting of the surface took place. The curious fact that almost all of Devon's rivers are south-flowing may be explained by the tilting; to the faulting is attributed the formation of a large lake south-east of Dartmoor, the 'Bovey Basin'. The sea-level continued to fall in relation to the land and in the course of time three further planation surfaces were created at heights below that of the early Tertiary surface. The remains of these planes may now be perceived in the form of hill-tops of more or less regular height in various areas of the county. Only such clues indicate the former existence of extensive flat-lands.

About two million years ago during the Pleistocene period the planation surfaces were converted by river erosion, in a sub-Arctic climate, into a landscape somewhat similar in its broad outline to the present. Due to the southerly location glaciation as such did not occur in Devon during this comparatively recent geological period known as the Ice Age. Consequently there are no natural lakes to supply water needs and this has led to the construction of reservoirs. The Ice Age is also considered to be the period when the Dartmoor tors and their 'clitters' were formed and current thinking has suggested that some of the features of the north Devon coast, and the adjacent Exmoor fringe, may be attributed to forces applied by the ice-sheet banked up against the cliffs; it was not massive enough to surmount them, though certainly large enough to divert the 'melt-water' along certain channels. The presence of several erratic boulders near the north Devon beaches, and boulder clay at Fremington, lends some weight to this theory. The locking-up of vast amounts of water in the form of ice led to a south-westerly extension of the peninsula known as Devon and Cornwall and, debatably, to the formation of a land-bridge to Europe. This had a bearing on the plant and animal life of the region when the waters returned.

Devon occupied a central position in relation to the successive advance and retreat of warm and cool conditions during the Ice Age. One outcome of these contrasting periods was that different species of plants and animals flourished at different times. Dramatic evidence of the reality of the warm interglacial periods was produced in 1965 when, during excavation work for the Honiton By-pass, the remains of hippopotamuses and straight-tusked elephants were discovered in a bed of peat. Some of the bones may now be seen in the Allhallows Museum at Honiton.

The structure of Devon is complex and it is impossible to separate it from that of Cornwall and the part of Exmoor which lies in Somerset. It is, there-fore, not surprising that most of the published information on the geography and geology of Devon is to be found in the relevant chapters of works that treat South-West England as a whole. Outstanding among the more recent books in this category are *South West England* by Shorter, Ravenhill and Gregory, published in 1961, and *The South West Peninsula* by Millward and Robinson, published in 1971. The papers published to mark the occasion of the annual meeting of the British Association, held at Exeter in 1969, and published under the title of *Exeter and its Region*, edited by F. Barlow, also contains major contributions to the study of Devon. The handbook of regional geology *South West England*, first published by the Geological Survey and Museum in 1935, is an essential source for the systematic study of rock types; the geology of the north coast received detailed treatment in *The Coast Scenery of North Devon* by Arber, 1911, the nearest south coast equivalent is *The South Devon Coast* by Burton, published in 1954.

In this chapter generalizations have of necessity been inevitable. Many geologists and geographers have put a great deal of thought into explaining the physical structure of Devon and much has been achieved, but ultimately there is much which human reasoning cannot explain. Whether or not these complexities have moulded the character of the local inhabitants is a matter for the outsider to consider but certainly, as history proves, Devon's position has given the county an important place in the affairs of the nation.

Climate

The weather of Devon in common with that of the rest of the British Isles is dominated by the prevailing westerly winds. The large, continental land masses, lying to the east and south are also a major influence. As the county is situated at a point where large land and water masses meet, the climate tends to be dynamic. The idea, often put forward, that the south-west is mild is not strictly correct although according to the records it is true of its coastal areas. Some parts of the county are wet, cold and windy for much of the year. Devon is second only to the extreme north-west of Scotland as far as wind speeds in the British Isles are concerned, and Dartmoor is one of the places most susceptible to fog. When reading through the records, the recurrence of exceptional natural events is surprisingly evident and can be explained by the complexity of the influences to which the region is subject. The most remarkable of these events are given in the list at the end of this chapter.

In view of these remarks it is still revealing to note that the prevailing winds do frequently bring mild maritime air over Devon. A northerly shift of their area of origin, in the central north Atlantic, brings polar air from the Greenland region of the north-west. When the pattern of westerlies breaks down Britain is influenced by the continental air-stream and in winter when the wind comes from the east or north-east the temperature can be expected to fall; solar radiation making little difference owing to the slanting rays of the winter sun. Devonians have reason to remember the bitter winds from the east, particularly so when they have passed over an ice-bound England. But it is also true that places sheltered from the east or north by hills are able to enjoy more clement conditions than other places situated not far away; and it must not be forgotten that the prevailing westerly winds do give the British Isles winter temperatures unusually high considering the latitude.

The southern position of Devon in relation to the rest of the country is important; so too is the influence of the sea, both the south and north coast being marginally affected by the Gulf Stream Drift. But of greater importance is the considerable change of height within the county. Atlantic air is rapidly cooled as it moves across Devon especially when it is forced to ascend the Exmoor fringe or western Dartmoor. This rate of change of temperature with height, known as 'environmental lapse rate', tends to be higher in the south-west than the national average of 0.6 degrees centigrade per 100 metres. Conditions on the high moors are similar to those prevailing in southern Iceland. The American naturalist Edwin Way Teale, visiting Devon as part of his journey through Britain in search of spring, wrote: 'The wind and the rain and the cold—these are inseparable in memories of Dartmoor. The earliest snow in England falls on these high moors. Even though April had come, we noticed coatings of ice on the smaller bogs.' The uplands of Britain produce much more rapid reduction in the potentialities for plant growth than land of a similar height in continental Europe.

In comparison with Britain as a whole the south-west can be regarded as one of its wetter regions. There is a very close relationship between height above sea-level and rainfall. The whole of Dartmoor and the whole of Exmoor receive over 1524mm (60 inches) of rain per annum. On Dartmoor the area affected coincides roughly with the 305 metre (1,000 foot) contour. The Exmoor fringe, lying in Devon, is slightly wetter than the higher parts lying farther west in Somerset. The wettest month of average is December. The driest periods are May and early June; and June on average has most sunshine; July and August are usually wetter, but it needs to be emphasised that it can rain heavily in any month. The August rain on Exmoor which produed the Lynmouth flood disaster in 1952 measured 228mm (9 inches) in 24 hours. This is one of the heaviest falls ever recorded in the British Isles and it is interesting to note that the two other great rainfalls happened in adjacent Somerset. The Devon River Board considering the Lynmouth deluge reported that: 'As assessed by preliminary investigations the flow could be included in the list of extreme flood discharges of the world.' In *A History of the Parishes of Lynmouth and Countisbury*, 1907, J. F. Chanter gave reasons for supposing that there was an acute flood at Lynmouth in 1769.

The driest parts surround Exeter where the annual total drops to 825mm (32.5 inches) per annum. A band almost as dry follows the south coast from the Exe estuary to the Dorset boundary. A similar band extends north-west from Exeter and joins the middle reaches of the river Taw and continues as far as its estuary.

The susceptibility of the south-west to heavy snowfalls has been demonstrated many times. In the Great Blizzard of 1891 snow drifted to a depth of 61 metres (200 feet) in Tavy Cleave; in 1963 it lay for three months on the Exmoor fringe and for six months on the highest parts of Dartmoor. Hard frosts do occur even in the protected coastal strips of the south coast and Barnstaple Bay. To quote Robert Langdon, one-time Town Clerk at Barnstaple:

'In the year of Lord God 1607, in January, the river of Barnstaple was so frozen, that many hundred people did walk hand in hand, from the bridge unto the Castle Rock with staves in their hands as safe as they could go on dry land'.

In Devon with its strong breezes, high rainfall and spectacular thunderstorms one is very much aware of a sky which can often change. Drifting cloud formations, full of moving patterns and surprises, appear and disappear —giving long sunny days. The coasts of Devon are among the sunniest places in England and receive on average 1600 to 1700 hours of sunlight per year. Only farther east on the south coast are higher amounts recorded in this country. Thus climatic conditions in Devon take the form of an extraordinary duality; on one hand there is mildness and sunlight on the coasts, on the other the harsh conditions of the high moors.

Some exceptional natural events affecting Devon

1412	Severe storm destroys Down St Mary church.
1593	Drought in north Devon (Philip Wyot's journal).
1607 January	The river Taw froze at Barnstaple.
1638 21 October	Thunderbolt at Widecombe-in-the-Moor.
1703 26-27 November	Winstanley's lighthouse swept off the Eddystone.
1769	Acute flood at Lynmouth.
1776 January	Extraordinarily mild (D'Urban and Mathew).
1814 11 January	Great Snow Storm.
1824 21-22 November	Gale at Plymouth, 12 ships wrecked 18 more damaged.
1859 25-26 October	'Royal Charter Storm' damages Torbay seafront.
1866 10 January	The Great Gale, 40 ships wrecked at Brixham.
1881 20 January	A Great Snow Storm in Devon.
1891 9 March	The Great Blizzard in the West.
1910 16 December	North Devon Storm, 'tidal wave' at Ilfracombe, 200 sheep drowned on Braunton Marshes.
1917 January	Hallsands destroyed by the sea (N.B. Half a million tons of shingle removed between 1897 and 1901).

1929 16 February	Exceptional snowfall over eastern Dartmoor.
1952 15 August	Acute catastrophic flood at Lynmouth.
1960 28 September- 8 October	Serious floods in various parts of Devon.
1963	Unusually cold January and February.
1968 10 July	East Devon Flood.
1976 July-August	Drought throughout Devon.
1978 February	Severe blizzard cuts Devon off from England.
1979	Unusually cold January and February.

CHAPTER TWO

Wildlife in Devon

From the point of view of its natural history Devon has many interesting and special features. It is an established fact that the physical structure and geological composition of a region affect both its flora and fauna. A recognized dividing line, the so-called 'Highland-Lowland line' passes through Devon. It is traced from the mouth of the river Tees in the north to that of the Exe in the south. This line roughly divides the higher hills of Britain from the lowlands and the harder, acid rocks from the calcium-rich south-east. It follows that by this definition much of Devon comes within the highland category, and plants adapted to bleak upland situations such as purple moor grass, bog cotton and the heathers, do indeed flourish in parts of Devon. The south-east of the county, beneath which lies the newer rock, supports different plant communities which are less common or even rare to the north of the line. This may be verified by looking at the plant distribution maps contained in the *Atlas of the British Flora*. The rocks of the county as a whole, being mainly old and predominantly acid and limestone being of local significance only, around Torbay and Plymouth, chalk and lime-loving plants are restricted; Devon for instance is not a cowslip county. On the other hand one of the plants which does well on the coastal limestone is the rare rock-rose, *Helianthemum appenninum*, a variety which is familiar in Mediterranean lands from Spain to Greece, whose presence can also be attributed to the mildness of the weather.

Climate is indeed a great influence on plant life. At its most obvious it allows many Mediterranean and sub-tropical species such as the acacias, the eucalyptus and gigantic members of the viper's bugloss family, usually considered to be incapable of withstanding severe winter conditions, to be grown in sheltered gardens in south Devon. In several coastal areas the holm oak of the Mediterranean is well-established and even regenerates from its seeds. The red valerian and the *Senecio cineraria*, a tender plant of the ragwort family which has no English name as far as is known, are locally common on both coasts. Even in north Devon some sub-tropical plants are grown on the coast, for example in the Clovelly area the fuchsia appears as a hedgerow plant and the tamarisk is quite well established in several localities. The present climate, being generally damp and mild, does not favour species that are adapted to extremes of heat and cold. A succulent, the wall-pennywort, and the hartstongue fern, both having a limited range in Britain as a whole, are common almost everywhere in Devon and are good examples of plants which flourish in the mild, moist climate. Woodland plants such as the bluebell and primrose grow freely in the hedges and even on open moorland and cliff-tops for the same reason.

One of the characteristics of the landscape is that it was free from glaciation in the Ice Age. Modern studies suggest that, at its greatest extension, the ice sheet and glaciers reached the Bristol Channel coast. Though there is no evidence in the form of moraines or rock surfaces that have been scraped by the movement over them of masses of ice, which would mean that glaciation had occurred, it does follow that at times Devon would have been subject to a degree of coldness sufficient to produce the conditions known as tundra — with the drastic restriction of flora and fauna which that term implies.

It has to be realised that much of the present flora and fauna of the South-West could not have survived at all in Britain during this period. How then is its presence today explained? A simple answer might be that some plants quickly adapted themselves to the harsher conditions and maintained a foothold. But the expansion of the cold polar regions produced several important side-effects including, as mentioned in Chapter One, a considerable lowering of the level of the sea due to the locking-up of vast quantities of water in the form of ice. This led to extensions of dry land to the south and west of Devon and Cornwall and north of France and Spain. Just as in America plants and animals were able to retreat southwards before the advance of the ice so, the theory goes, there was a southern refuge which pre-glacial species of south-west Britain might colonize as the ice advanced. From this region recolonization could eventually have taken place as the climate became warmer again. The important point is that, as the waters rose, varieties that had used this land-bridge connecting southern

Britain to the continent would have become isolated again. Thus a group of animals and plants found in south-west Britain are referred to as 'Lusitanian' from the Roman name for Portugal. These species also occur on the west coasts of Portugal, Spain, France and Ireland and nowhere else. However, this is a highly specialized subject and the identification of the small mammals, insects and plants concerned is a matter for the expert.

Some plants and animals which are scarce or absent in the north and east of the British Isles are to be found in the South-west. On the other hand just as some northern birds have the southern boundaries of their ranges in Devon and the South-west as a whole, so do some mountain plants. Both the crowberry and cowberry have their southernmost habitat on Dartmoor; the latter has not, however, been reported since the early part of the century. In the case of the lesser twayblade, an orchid, Exmoor is the southern limit and, once again, its occurrence is rare. In the mountains of Scotland and north Wales the fir clubmoss is common; it occurs on the higher parts of Dartmoor too but, as a rule, true mountain plants are not found in Devon. Owing to the absence of lakes, Devon is not a good place in which to see the water-lily or other large aquatic plants at their best. Much of the vegetation, such as the dwarf, western gorse and bell heather, which, by its strong colour dominates the uncultivated moorland and coastal areas, is typical of the Atlantic coasts of Europe. At the small end of the scale the diminutive ivy-leafed bell-flower, which is found occasionally on Dartmoor, is, in the rest of Britain, confined to a few isolated sites.

A favourable factor from the point of view of its natural history is the absence in Devon of large-scale industrial undertakings of the type that cause severe pollution of the environment. A direct result is that the sensitive lichens grow prolifically in much of the region; the *Usnea articulata* which trails from the branches of oak trees, and is sometimes wrongly described as Spanish Moss, is probably the best known. The county is fortunate too in that the nature of the land does not lend itself to the intensive application of pesticides in the practice of agriculture. Farming policy tends to be traditional and Devon's network of fields and lanes still form a splendid wildlife reserve even though many hedges have been removed in recent years. Species such as the large royal fern which used to be mentioned in the guide books are, however, now restricted to a few remote localities.

The highest parts of the moors should not be regarded as rich in natural history interest but rather as restricted habitats dominated by blanket bog to which certain specialized plants are adapted. Around Dartmoor and in the Exmoor fringe zones of considerable natural history interest and scenic beauty occur where the wild and tamed land meet. In one such area on the edge of Dartmoor, Yarner Wood, a National Nature Reserve having some indigenous woodland, some under intensive management, and interesting bird life, is situated. Dunsford Wood, similarly placed, is famous for its wild daffodils and, like Yarner, it is at present the site of a nature trail which is open to the public. On the opposite side of Dartmoor the river Lyd has cut deep into the rocks of the metamorphic aureole at Lydford Gorge; this has produced some fascinating rock forms which are veiled by oak woods.

One of the most famous botanical sights of Dartmoor is Wistman's Wood which is to be found in the West Dart valley north of Two Bridges. It is a small oak wood growing almost entirely from between the boulders of a 'clitter'. The gnarled and stunted growth of the boughs, on which grow epiphytes, has captured the imagination of visitors ever since it first became accessible. A similar, though less-abnormal scene occurs at Piles Copse in the Erme valley near Harford; Black Tor Copse which is situated in the upper West Okement valley, is yet another example. Each small wood grows near the limit of conditions that can be tolerated by the pedunculate oak and has suffered little from human interference until modern times. Wistman's Wood and Black Tor Copse are now afforded some protection by the Nature Conservancy which has classified them as Forest Nature Reserves. Whether or not these woods represent fragments of an oak forest which once spread over a much larger area is debatable. On the Devon side of Exmoor, Badgworthy Wood consists of similarly situated oaks and is a remnant of a much larger area of natural woodland, but, being less handicapped, the shapes of the trees tend to be more normal. The deep wooded-valleys of the east and west Lyn rivers constitute varied habitats including mountain streams. Devon's larger coniferous plantations, other than those on Dartmoor, include Eggesford Forest which was the first in England and Wales to be planted by the Forestry Commission; this occurred in 1919. It is now the site of Forest Walks open to the public. Another large area is Haldon Forest which has proved to be attractive to roe deer.

Many of the more interesting ecological features are to be found in or near the coastal areas of Devon. Both Braunton Burrows in the north, a National Nature Reserve, and Dawlish Warren in the south, managed by the Devon Trust for Nature Conservation, are outstanding in this respect.

The Burrows and similar places where rapid sand drainage ensures comparatively dry and warm local conditions are more conducive to the growth of sun-loving plant species than the rest of the county. Dawlish Warren still retains some of its botanical interest in spite of the inroads of the sea and its popularity as a recreational area. The famous 'undercliffs' between Axmouth and the Dorset boundary, the result of a landslip in 1839 and at other dates, make up a National Nature Reserve 8 kilometres (5 miles) in length and from 180 to 640 metres in width.

Because the use of pesticides has not been excessive and marginal-land, particularly along the coasts, is sometimes so steep and intractable that it has been impossible or uneconomic to plough it, the insect life of many parts of Devon can still be described as rich and varied. In one coastal locality the lovely large blue butterfly with its almost incredible life history which is dependent on several secondary factors, including the presence of wild thyme and an ant of a particular species, used to maintain a precarious hold whereas it had ceased to exist in its other English sites. Now, in September 1979, it is regarded as officially extinct in Devon too. Among the more spectacular lepidopterous insects some of the hawk moths are not uncommon; even the death's head and the oleander hawk moth are seen on rare occasions. Dragonflies are well represented in Devon; along the moorland streams the *Cordulegaster boltonii* one of our largest examples, the bodies of which are ringed with black and yellow, is quite common in the summer. The entomological section of the Devonshire Association has compiled records of all the larger orders of insects found in the county.

All the British amphibians except the natterjack toad and the crested newt are reported from Devon. The common frog and toad are, indeed, still quite common in spite of the obvious reduction in the number of frogs which may be attributed to the loss of suitable habitats through drainage schemes and possibly to the use of persistent pesticides. There are reports of edible frogs and marsh frogs having been seen in south Devon; if these sightings are correct then they probably refer to introduced specimens. In the case of reptiles neither the sand lizard nor the smooth snake is present in Devon though there are records of them having been seen some time ago, and it is known that an attempt was once made to introduce the smooth snake. The status of the four other British reptiles may be described as common. Some details of these amphibians and reptiles are given in the chapter appendix.

The seas around Devon are the meeting place of two classes of marine species, those adapted to existence in cold water and those requiring warmer water. The latter are rather more common than elsewhere in Britain, whilst cold water types are near their southern limits. Not only that but the north Devon coast and the south have slightly different faunas due to the north being both cooler and subject to greater disturbance by the sea itself. The result is that the southern coast has a more varied fauna. It has been suggested that the Victorian biologists who stayed at Ilfracombe and Torquay depleted the local coasts of varieties such as the little Devonshire cup-corals; they are seldom seen today though they still occur around Lundy, which is an exceptionally good place for the study of marine biology. Near the coastal towns pollution of the sea is an adverse factor which has to be borne in mind, especially in south Devon.

An unfortunate change in the marine life of Devonian coastal waters occurred in the 1930s — the decrease of the herring shoals which, until then, had supplied a considerable herring fishing industry in south and to a lesser extent in north Devon. The last good catches were made in 1925-26 and there was then a sudden collapse. The reason may have been that there was a slight warming-up of the water. The Marine Biological Association of the United Kingdom established its laboratory and aquarium at Plymouth in 1888 with the object of studying the lives of sea fishes. As a result knowledge of the marine life of the area is extensive. The aquarium which is open to the public is well-stocked with fish from Devon seas.

The British Isles as a whole is not rich in mammals, there being about 40 species; to these must be added about 10 established aliens. In British coastal waters there are known to be some 20 marine mammals; two of these are seals, the remainder being of the whale family and are merely visitors. The total comes to about 80 at the most. Devon, with its varying terrain in the form of woodlands and moorlands, coastline and estuaries, farmland and streams is well provided with natural habitats and probably possesses as varied a fauna as any county in England. In fact, most of Britain's remaining native-born mammals may be seen in Devon. However, they are hardly a feature of the landscape; even the largest of them, the red deer, is seldom visible in the open and the rabbit, which one could expect to see on any Devonshire farm or common until the 1950s, has been catastrophically reduced since then, except on Lundy, by myxomatosis. Although the species are comparatively few compared to the birds there are nevertheless large numbers of some of them. Even wild deer live within a few miles of several of the towns of Devon and on any cross-country walk, mammals, which are either asleep because they are nocturnal or are exercising their exceptional powers of concealing themselves from their enemies, are passed without being seen.

The changes, in recent decades, among the mammals of Devon largely coincide with those which affected other English counties. The decline of the red squirrel evidently started early in the century. The American grey squirrel, when it was released at Exeter in 1915, found its red relative already in retreat and it was not a case of the grey over-running the red though the grey now inhabits the whole of Devon. The rabbit had been introduced into Britain as early as the end of the twelfth century and by the first half of the twentieth it was the mammal most likely to be seen in the Devonshire countryside. In fact it had become a pest and was the principle animal problem. To many it was a source of meat and large basketwork crates of dressed rabbits, destined for city markets, were a daily sight at the railway stations until 1953. The outbreak of World War II had coincided with the passing of the law prohibiting the setting of gins, thus providing the opponents of the law with an excuse to circumvent it. Formerly, stoats, weasels and polecats, the last of which is said to have been killed at Spreyton just north of Dartmoor in 1925, provided a natural system of control. But weasels and stoats were themselves being reduced. Good farmers continued to protect their crops by shooting rabbits, especially in the early winter before the young wheat appeared. All this changed when the myxomatosis epidemic decimated the rabbit population within a few months.

Another alien, the mink, began to be noticed on some of the Devon rivers in 1953, having escaped from mink farms in the late 1940s. It was first noticed that it was breeding in the wild in the Teign valley in 1956 and inevitably it posed a threat to local wildlife. This was pointed out by naturalists when the problem was a small one. Now, though it is hunted by otter hounds, erradication is impossible and it is accepted as part of the British fauna. Mink have taken innumerable game birds and song birds. More exotic but, perhaps, not ultimately such a threat as the mink are the Hodgson's porcupines which, unfortunately, escaped from a Wildlife Park near Okehampton during 1969. The original pair certainly bred, probably in an old badger set, for six have been captured by the Ministry of Agriculture after, apparently, causing the deaths of a couple of domestic pets and producing some consternation in the neighbourhood. As late as the end of 1978 evidence of damage to the bark of trees suggests that a few may still be active.

The existence of a large number of red deer in a truly wild state in a highly agricultural county such as Devon is remarkable. Though the haunts of the Exmoor deer lie mainly in Somerset smaller herds have now established themselves at various places in north, east and west Devon. These deer differ from those of the highlands of Scotland in that they are essentially woodland creatures and have to a certain extent become dependent on cultivated crops for their food; their body and antler structure is therefore greater than that of their northern relatives. They often lie up in dense woodland during the day and indeed for much of the year they are able to feed quite well on the plants, herbs and shrubs, such as shoots of blackberry, that are readily available. However, when the natural supply of food is reduced in the winter, root crops such as swedes, turnips and potatoes are liable to receive their attention. Corn is damaged not so much by attempts to eat the grain as through the use of fields as 'dormitories', a habit that causes damage to the crop and annoyance to farmers. There is no doubt that the anomalous survival of the red deer is due to the high sporting-value and general interest found in them by the farming community; if they were not controlled, they would increase very rapidly.

Both our largest bat, the noctule and our smallest, the pipistrelle, occur in Devon. The smaller bats are most difficult to identify but there is an almost complete collection of the British bats at the Ilfracombe Museum; they were taken in north Devon during the 1930s by M. Blackmore.

Rather more than 200 types of birds breed regularly in the British Isles but of these a quarter are summer visitors only. A few of these, such as the pheasant and the Canada goose are aliens which have become established in the British Isles. In addition there are 90 to 100 more or less regular winter visitors or passage migrants. Both come from the sub-Arctic regions and whilst the visitors remain for the winter, the passage migrants pass on to regions farther south and so are seen in the British Isles only briefly whilst travelling in spring and autumn. More than 150 occasional or irregular bird visitors have been recorded. About 336 species of birds have been recorded in Devon of which about 112 breed regularly. For comparison Somerset lists 294 of which about 116 breed regularly. Devon's geographic position is an important influence on its birds; so too is its large size in relation to that of other English counties. The varied habitats within the area satisfy the requirements of different birds and, in this connection, the high proportion of sea-cliffs and the extent to which marginal and hill land survives should be particularly noted.

The size of Devon leads to some variation of distribution within the area. Strays from Europe are more likely to occur in the south than the north. Similarly, American wanderers are more likely to turn up in the north than in the south. But there are also variations of a more local type, and many changes in the environment since the beginning of the present century, such as the intensification of agricultural methods, have had a marked effect on bird life. It is now recognised that the 13 coniferous plantations established in Devon by the Forestry Commission during the course of the present century, have had the effect of increasing the population of certain varieties of birds. The forests of Dartmoor are situated on moorland rising to 457 metres (1500 feet) and several birds, including Montagu's harrier, the merlin, redpoll and siskin nest only in them. Likewise, the habitat of the nightjar, coal tit and goldcrest is almost entirely confined to the conifers in that area. The sea-cliffs offer nesting sites which are attractive to birds such as the auks and kittiwakes, but they also present opportunities for observation and this is inevitably disturbing to them. These birds suffer, too, from the effects of oil pollution. Quite apart from the results of accidents such as that involving the *Christos Bitas*, whose long-range effect was felt on the north Devon coast in 1978, a slight degree of oil pollution has been evident since the second World War.

Resident birds are of course augmented by summer migrants from the Mediterranean and Africa and by winter migrants which come from the north. The great majority of African migrants approach the British coasts on a broad front across the English Channel. There is, however, a tendency for certain routes to be followed, which indicates a marked preference for the shorter sea-crossings. In Devon the coast between Start Point and Slapton Ley is one of the main points of entry. Estuaries such as the Exe are also good places at which to watch migration taking place. To the north of the Devon mainland Lundy is situated in the Bristol Channel 19 kilometres (12 miles) from Hartland Point between the Atlantic coast of Devon and that of south Wales. The reports of the Lundy Field Society provide evidence that the island is used by migrants as a stepping-stone both in the spring and autumn. The coast is not the only place where migration may be seen taking place, but it does usually have the advantage of a wide, uninterrupted view of the sky.

Winter migrants from Iceland, Greenland and the high Arctic, such as the white-fronted geese and Brent geese, reach northern counties first and Devon later in the year. Some, the barnacle and pink-footed geese for instance, only occasionally extend their range to Devon. The same applies to the migration of blackbirds, fieldfares, redwings and goldcrests from Scandinavia in October. They are more familiar in our eastern counties than in Devon. Sometimes in exceptionally severe weather conditions a local migration occurs and redwings and fieldfares flock to the meadows of Devon in an attempt to avoid the worst effects of the colder climate elsewhere in the country.

The estuaries attract ducks and waders as passage migrants. Few of the birds can be classified as residents, but large flocks remain as winter visitors especially on the Tamar, Plym, Yealm and Exe in south Devon. The Taw-Torridge estuary on the north coast, being the only estuary in long ranges on cliffs, usually has an average peak count of waders over 15,000, which means that it is fourth in importance in the south-west.

One of the satisfactory tendencies of the present day is the recovery of the buzzard after the crisis of 1953 when one of its main sources of food, the rabbit population, was greatly reduced by myxomatosis, followed, a decade later, by a severe winter. Another bird, regarded as almost symbolic of the fresh, clear streams of Devon, the dipper, has also maintained its numbers well.

The county has been fortunate in having considerable interest shown in its natural history in the past; J. C. Bellamy's *Natural History of South Devon* appeared in 1838. A considerable impetus was given when P. H. Gosse stayed at St Marychurch, Torquay, and at Ilfracombe in 1852; he published *A Naturalists Rambles on the Devonshire Coast* in 1853. He settled at St Marychurch in 1857 and lived there until his death more than 30 years later. He spent his time studying marine biology; his *Manual of Marine Zoology* alone contained nearly 700 of his drawings, and *Land and Sea*, in which south and north Devon together with Lundy are featured, was published in 1865. Such records as these created useful foundations for later studies.

Colonel Montagu, one of the earliest British ornithologists, after whom Montagu's harrier is named, lived for some years at Knowle, a house near Kingsbridge in south Devon. He made many of his most pertinent observations in the district. Early work by Montagu and other ornithologists of regional repute was gathered together and expanded in the nineteenth century by W. S. M. D'Urban, one time curator of the Royal Albert Memorial Museum at Exeter, and the Reverend M. A. Mathew and published in 1892 as *The Birds of Devon*. In the *Victoria County History of the County of Devon* published in 1906 there is a section written by D'Urban which summarizes his earlier work. In the first half of the present century a number of books dealing with the natural history of particular districts of the county were published. These works include *Braunton: a few Nature Notes* by Dr F. R. E. Wright, 1932; *Ilfracombe, Flora and Fauna* by M. G. Palmer, 1946; and *Lundy Isle of Puffins* by R. Perry published in 1940. *Dartmoor* by Professor L. A. Harvey and D. St Ledger-Gordon followed in 1953.

During this period the observation of birds grew in popularity and in 1929 the Devon Bird Watching and Preservation Society, which had been founded in 1928, published the first of its interesting Annual Reports and in 1960 established the Slapton Bird Observatory. The Slapton Ley Field Centre of the Field Studies Council was established in 1959. The Lundy Field Society had been founded in 1946 through the efforts of Professor L. A. Harvey of the University College of the South West and Martin Coles Harman who then owned the island; publication of the society's annual reports commenced in 1947. By this means the two localities considered to be most sensitive from the point of view of bird migration have now been kept under observation for a number of years. In 1969 in his *Birds of Devon*, which is regarded as the standard work on the subject, Robert Moore brought the work of D'Urban and Mathew up to date. The Devon Bird Watching and Preservation Society published in 1974 the *Atlas of Breeding Birds of Devon*, which is a valuable aid for those seriously interested in the ornithology of the county. This publication shows the distribution of breeding species in each of the 96 ten-kilometre squares into which the map of Devon is divided for the purpose. The work forms part of the *Atlas of Breeding Birds in Britain and Ireland* published in 1976 by the British Trust for Ornithology and which represents the teamwork by field workers on a large scale.

The chapter appendix does not attempt to include all those birds which live in or visit Devon but it contains the most significant as far as the county is concerned. Whenever the status of a species has changed or appears to be changing in relation to the position in the country as a whole it receives attention. It is hoped that the bird list will be of assistance to the general ornithologist on his way around the county. In the same way the notes on mammals, reptiles and amphibians cover only those kinds that seem to be most interesting or which there is a reasonable chance of seeing.

When the weather discourages the study of natural history in the field the civic museums of Exeter and Plymouth and the museum of the Natural History Society of Torquay each house major displays of specimens collected in the county. Several small museums, such as those at Tiverton and Ilfracome, also have a number of exhibits which reflect the considerable richness of the wildlife of Devon.

Mammal list

BADGER: Badgers are widespread, though not necessarily numerous, inhabitants of Devon. The sets are sometimes of a size and complexity that suggests use over a very long period of time. This is especially true of those situated in the precipitous 'chines' and sandy ridges of the south-east of the county. Like the foxes, badgers find that the 'clitters' of Dartmoor, particularly those on the edge of the moor, offer a greater natural protection. The nature of this terrain means that excavation of the sets tends to be limited by the very presence of the granite and food may be short in the periods following partial-hibernation. Badgers frequently live near cliff-tops and, it would seem, prefer a sloping site. They also like to live close to a supply of 'bedding' such as bracken and, being especially clean, will sometimes bring out their bedding to give it an airing. The main item of food is the earthworm. Unfortunately there has been much needless molestation of the badgers in Devon—a situation which it was hoped that the Badger Act, 1973, would help to put right. It is therefore ironic, to say the least, that the animal has become suspect of spreading bovine tuberculosis in the south-west and at present, in certain areas, official policy is to exterminate it. In the region as a whole 9,000 are estimated to have been gassed by 1980.

BAT, GREATER HORSESHOE: The number of the greater horseshoe bats which formerly existed in many parts of Devon has been considerably reduced. A cave at Buckfastleigh is thought to be used for hibernation by about a quarter of the present British population and it is now protected by the Devon Trust for Nature Conservation.

DEER, FALLOW: There are several parks where fallow deer were kept in the south and east of the county and 'escapes' have resulted in this variety being quite well distributed in that area. Small herds have also been noted in the wooded parts of the Teign valley and near Plympton.

DEER, RED: The domain of the red deer was formerly confined to the eastern part of Exmoor which lies in Somerset. The Devon part of the moor has not proved to be so attractive to them in modern times, although several of the larger areas of woodland in north Devon harbour the animal. The herds of red deer now reported in east and west Devon woods are recent and interesting arrivals in what is new territory.

DEER, ROE: This species is now present and perhaps common in a number of localities. The protection afforded by the growth of the new coniferous forests must certainly contribute to the recent tendency of deer in general to increase their habitat. Roe deer have for some considerable time been plentiful on the county's eastern fringe in the Axminster district and it is reasonable to suppose that this represents the westward spread of the Dorsetshire population. The roe now lives in many woodland areas in north and south Devon and is moving westwards but, being small

in size and of furtive disposition, it can only be seen with much effort.

DEER, SIKA: An introduced Japanese relative of the red deer, though smaller, is the sika, which is reputed to be well-established in east Devon woodlands. There is also a herd on Lundy which, given care, is a good subject for the stalker armed with a camera.

DORMOUSE: The large mouse with the squirrel-like tail and the only British mammal which truly hibernates--is a nocturnal creature. It was never as common in Devon as in some south-eastern counties and today is certainly less common than formerly.

FOX: Thanks to the hunting fraternity the fox is widespread in Devon. It declined numerically during World War I and it used to be controlled by gin traps. It is now well known that the fox has adapted itself in a very clever way to modern conditions by living anywhere and eating anything. It scavenges along the shore and also in urban areas from which it may well return to the country again. Hill foxes, with territories on Dartmoor or the Exmoor fringe, feed well on other animals that die there; this is particularly true during periods of hard weather. In reports of foxes killing lambs it must be borne in mind that attacks are usually on sick lambs.

HARE: There seems little doubt that the hare population has decreased in Devon during the last half-century. Those that remain seem to show a preference for certain areas, for instance, the Exmoor fringe.

MINK, AMERICAN: This relative of the otter and skunk was first noticed on some of the Devon rivers in 1953. Many attacks on birds such as pheasants and turkeys have been reported in the local newspapers during the last decade. It is perhaps fortunate that mink have only one litter, of about four kittens, per year.

OTTER: Earlier in the present century the numerous streams, rivers and estuaries of Devon were comparatively free from pollution and so provided a good habitat for the otter. Without too much difficulty it was possible to view an otter family at play at twilight, provided that one knew where to look. It will be recalled that Henry Williamson based his famous work, *Tarka the Otter*, on observations made on north Devon streams in the early 1920s. The environmental conditions have changed during the last 50 years but not so drastically perhaps in Devon as elsewhere. A population of one otter for every eight kilometres (five miles) has been suggested for typical Dartmoor rivers. Pollution of rivers is possibly responsible for a general decline in the number which certainly has nothing to do with the arrival of the mink—a much smaller animal. The otter no doubt can take both trout and salmon, but it has been pointed out that they could pick off the sick fish, frogs and eels in a river, thereby leaving a healthy fish population. In Devon, until the decline in the population, the otter was kept in check by otterhounds. Two packs, the Culmstock and the Dartmoor, survive though the otter is no longer hunted.

RABBIT: The myxomatosis epidemic of 1954 rapidly decimated the population and, fortunately, recovery has been very slow. Upsurges seem to have been checked by fresh outbreaks of the disease. As widely reported, the rabbit has sometimes adopted the habit of living above ground in, for instance, dense thickets of gorse.

SEAL; GREY OR ATLANTIC: There is a colony of Atlantic seals at Lundy, but none on the mainland coasts of Devon. Recent research has shown that at least some of the Lundy seals may be classed as resident and that the birth of pups occurs annually. This modifies an earlier supposition that the island was mainly a maturing-ground for young seals.

It appears unlikely that more than 50 individuals at the most are present at any one time. From time to time single seals are noticed on the north Devon coast, at Hartland Point, Baggy Point and Combe Martin for instance. These sightings are not common and it seems reasonable to suppose that the seals concerned come from Lundy.

SQUIRREL, GREY: It is now present in all parts of Devon damaging trees and destroying the eggs and young of small birds.

SQUIRREL, RED: This species was described as abundant in Devon until about 1910, when it began to decline in number as it did in other parts of the country.

WHALES: This group of animals includes whales, porpoises and dolphins. Some two dozen types are known in British waters, but only about half a dozen of the smaller ones are common in inshore waters where they sometimes approach the coast in pursuit of mackerel. Sightings off the Devon coasts are, therefore, occasional and usually involve the porpoises and dolphins, including the largest of the dolphins known as the killer whales. As is generally known, much information about the distribution of whales has been accumulated through the scheme whereby, since 1913, any member of the whale family stranded on the British coasts is reported to the British Museum of Natural History by coast guards and receivers of wrecks. In fact whales are most familiar in Devon because of the many strandings which have occurred and are proved by the existence of the jaw-bones of some of the toothless whales, erected at various points on the coast as trophies. They testify to the fact, borne out by the records, that during the early years of the century there was quite a significant number of strandings of the larger whales and they have not been repeated since. An 18 metre (60 foot) common rorqual, for instance, was cast up at Croyde Bay in 1916, and a 19.5 metre (64 foot) common fin whale came ashore at Westward Ho! in 1921. The apparent cessation of such strandings may be an expression of the reduction of total world stocks; or it could merely reflect the fact that, since the 1920s, the whaling stations in Ireland and Scotland have ceased to operate. It is possible that some of the specimens which came ashore had been wounded in whaling operations. Today, a stranding on one of the Devon coasts is most likely to be the common porpoise, the bottlenosed dolphin or the pilot whale.

Amphibians and Reptiles

FROG, COMMON: The tadpoles of the frog may be found in suitable habitats throughout the county, including the high moors, in the early months of the year. In the valley bogs of the moors they are sometimes prolific. The mass-spawning of the males and females which recurs, from year to year, in favoured pools and streams is a memorable sight.

LIZARD, COMMON: The most common reptile in Devon, it occupies a wide variety of habitats but loves south-facing drystone walls, where it can easily dart to safety between the stones.

NEWT, PALMATE: The favourite haunts of this creature are pools and ponds throughout the county, including those on open moorland.

NEWT, SMOOTH: This is the least common of the newts in Devon.

TOAD, COMMON; Unlike the smooth moist skin of the frog the toad has a warty skin. However, herpetologists identify the two species by a structural difference in their shoulder girdles. Another characteristic of the toad is that it only takes to water for breeding activity. It is fairly common throughout Devon.

SLOW-WORM: The lizard without legs which thrives on slugs and snails, is second only to the common lizard in the frequency with which it is observed. It is found in farmland, woodland and in gardens throughout the county.

SNAKE, GRASS: This harmless reptile is said to be on the decline in Devon and this may be linked to the destruction of habitats by drainage. Mainly to be seen on the banks of ponds and streams it grows to between one and one and a quarter metres (three and four feet) in length and is longer than the viper. The sight of one of these snakes, swimming strongly, contains a hint of primeval life.

VIPER: The viper lives all over Devon, including the clitters of Dartmoor, parts of the Exmoor fringe and the cliff-tops. The discarded skin of a viper will sometimes be found. Unlike the grass snake, which lays eggs, it brings forth its young alive. Unfortunately, Devonians have what amounts almost to an obsessional fear of 'adders', as local people prefer to call them, and they are unnecessarily killed. A bite from one of them is a rare occurrence and should receive hospital treatment. Although the victim is likely to be seriously ill he should find comfort in the fact that fatalities from this cause are almost unknown.

Birds

BUNTING, CIRL: This species was first discovered in the British Isles by Colonel Montagu near Kingsbridge in Devon and it still favours the south Devon coastal strip but there are a few isolated records from central and low-lying parts of north Devon. The cirl bunting is usually associated with elms. South Devon is the birds' main breeding territory in the British Isles. The hundred of so breeding pairs concerned are the most northerly of a population which is widespread in France, Spain, Italy and Greece.

BUZZARD: It appears that the number of this soaring bird has increased markedly since the last century, though its history has not been one of even development. From information given by D'Urban it would appear that it increased significantly in the first two decades of the present century. Unfortunately myxomatosis in the wild rabbits deprived it of one of the main items in its diet and there was a noticeable and sudden decrease which was not helped by the severe winter of 1963. Now, happily, the population is increasing and the buzzard is almost certain to be seen somewhere within every square kilometre of the county except the towns. It is even possible to see three or more soaring together as a group: a reminder of the larger groups that were sometimes seen during the 1930s.

CHOUGH: In the last century, according to D'Urban and Mathew, the chough could be observed along the north Devon coast including Lundy and also on the south coast. But it was already losing ground and during the first half of the twentieth century there were only a few reports of the bird having been seen and only a single report in the last decade. The nearest areas where it is resident are west Wales and Britanny.

CORNCRAKE: The male bird reveals its presence by its often-repeated rasping call-notes, but otherwise it is extremely secretive. The Devon population has greatly decreased and it must now be regarded as reduced to the status of a rarity.

CUCKOO: The familiar call of the male bird makes its presence known all over Devon, including the high moors, though the occasions on which it is heard have decreased in recent years. Breeding is naturally much more difficult to prove, but, through the 'Atlas' project, organized by the British Trust for Ornithology, it was established that breeding takes place in much of Devon.

CURLEW: A numerous inhabitant of the estuaries and surrounding farmlands during the winter months. Some of its former nesting sites have been ploughed up and there is, no doubt, pressure on the bird as a breeding species.

DIPPER: The habitat of the dipper is fresh flowing water and its adjacent banks and this is well demonstrated by the fact that it is seen along streams and rivers almost everywhere in the county. The only places where it is not seen are the drowned-river-valleys of south Devon and the estuary of the Exe. It nests in holes in the banks and under bridges where it builds a large nest, usually domed in form.

DOVE, COLLARED: As everyone interested in ornithology will know this bird was not present in Britain until 1955, when it began to breed in north Norfolk. In 1956 there were only three known nesting sites in that county. The spread of the species since then can only be described as explosive. By 1960 breeding was occurring in nine counties, one of them being Devon. During the following decade it spread from Plymouth to all parts of the county.

FLYCATCHER, PIED: This species, which winters in tropical Africa, nests in holes in oak trees in the woodlands of the Exmoor fringe. More interesting has been the oc-cupation of nest boxes in the National Nature Reserve at Yarner Wood. This has occured mainly since 1955 and recent breeding in other areas adjoining Dartmoor has been directly related to the original colony at Yarner.

FULMAR: In extending its range from the north-west, during the first half of the twentieth century, the fulmar was similar to the collared dove which spread from the south-east in the 1960s. In 1900 it occupied the extreme north of Scotland. Lundy was reached in 1939 and the first breeding occurred there in 1944. The graceful birds may now be seen along cliffed parts of both the north and south coasts of Devon where nesting takes place at various places.

GANNET: The gannet bred on Lundy until about 1900 and its disap-pearance from that island coincided with the establishment of the colony on Grassholm. The bird is seen searching for food in north and south Devon coastal waters.

GOOSE, CANADA: This goose was first introduced into England over 250 years ago. In Devon it was released at Shobrooke Park near Crediton in 1949 and it has spread to favourable habitats in central

Devon and the Exe estuary.

GROUSE, BLACK: Several attempts have been made to reintroduce this species to Exmoor and Dartmoor in the last century and the present. It survives in small numbers on Dartmoor, on the Exmoor fringe and also in the Somerset part of Exmoor. The red grouse, a bird of the same family but belonging to a different genus, breeds more successfully on Dartmoor; apart from that its history and status is very similar.

GUILLEMOT: The distribution co-incides almost exactly with that of the razorbill, that is to say there are colonies on Lundy and smaller ones on the north and south mainland coasts of Devon. The guillemot usually congregates in groups of a larger size than does the razorbill.

GULL, BLACK-HEADED: The breeding colony at Braunton, which became established during World War I, survived great disturbance during the second World War when the armed services exercised in the vicinity. Due to increased civilian interference the site was finally given up.

GULL, GREAT BLACK-BACKED: Unfortunately this predator of other birds has extended its range since D'Urban and Mathew's day. It now occupies nesting sites along both coasts and, notably, on Lundy where its effect on other seabirds is detrimental.

GULL, LESSER BLACK-BACKED: This species is less numerous than its larger relative. Though it does breed at certain places on both coasts it is not numerous except on Lundy. The Scandinavian form occurs as a passage migrant.

HERON, GREY: There are between 20 and 25 heronries scattered throughout the county. They are situated not only near the estuaries but also in central Devon. The bird may be seen on all rivers and streams, including those on the moors.

HOBBY: A falcon with rapid flight like a peregrine but with longer wings and shorter tail suggesting, in flight, a large swift. It is found throughout continental Europe. The few breeding pairs in Devon constitute the edge of the bird's range. D'Urban and Mathew classified it as a scarce summer migrant; it still retains that status but breeding has been proved.

HOOPOE: The hoopoe is a bird of exotic appearance and though it must be termed a rare stray it is not to be mistaken. Hardly a year passes in which it is not observed somewhere in north or south Devon, Dartmoor or Lundy.

KITTIWAKE: Lundy has been the site of a large breeding colony for as long as records exist. The bird may also be seen from time to time at various places on the mainland coasts, but it nests only at Torbay and Woody Bay.

LARK, WOOD: Southern England is the north-western edge of the range of this bird. South Devon, especially parts of it in which there are scattered trees, provides breeding ground for quite a large proportion of this country's nesting-pairs. It is now, unfortunately, a declining species.

MERLIN: This little falcon has been seen, but not often, on Dartmoor and the Exmoor fringe.

NIGHTINGALE: Devon is the western extremity of the bird's range in southern England and though there are occasional reports of it from other parts of Devon, including Lundy, it is only truly established in east Devon. The songs of blackcaps or late-singing thrushes are sometimes confused with that of the nightingale.

NIGHTJAR: The long-sustained 'throbbing purr' of the nightjar reveals the presence of the bird in certain parts of west and east Devon, on the eastern edge of Dartmoor and around the lower Exe.

OUZEL, RING: This member of the thrush family, a black bird with a broad white crescent on its breast, is an early migrant. The general opinion seems to be that its numbers are few, but pairs of the birds are usually to be discovered in the high combes of the Exmoor fringe and Dartmoor—its main habitats in southern England.

OWL, LITTLE: This species was introduced into eastern England in the late nineteenth-century. The first appearance recorded in Devon was 1911 and the bird is now found in numerous places except the highest moorland and the extreme west.

PARTRIDGE: The decrease of this bird is no doubt related to the removal of hedges, the use of pesticides and the general intensification of agricultural practice; it is, however, still widely distributed.

PEREGRINE: During the last century the peregrine bred on both coasts of Devon, on Lundy and in many inland parts of the county including Dartmoor. In winter months the bird was active in the river estuaries where it harried the waders and plovers. It is stated that it was not uncommon to see one of these fine falcons, whose flight behaviour has been described as one of the supreme sights of the natural world, from the quays of Barnstaple. The situation has changed very much. Firstly, the threat they posed to carrier pigeons during World War II resulted in them being killed on that account. Then, in the 1950s, the widespread use of toxic chemicals in agriculture led to the accumulation of sub-lethal doses in field birds. As these same birds were devoured by the peregrines, so more dangerous levels of the poisonous substances became concentrated in their digestive organs. Today it is still possible to observe the bird in Devon but the number of pairs is so small that the least said about their habitat the better.

PIPIT, TREE: Found in the fairly widespread, thinly-wooded, wild areas that it favours. It is not present in the South Hams or in a zone of central Devon extending eastwards from Bideford.

PLOVER, GOLDEN: Present on the moors and the estuarine sand banks in the winter. There is evidence of breeding on Dartmoor.

PUFFIN: The place name, Lundy, is Norse for 'Isle of Puffins'. A colony of the birds existed there until World War I but it has gradually shrunk and, unfortunately, it appears that, due to various adverse factors, few birds are now breeding successfully. A recent tendency for a small number of birds to nest in inaccessible places on the cliffs, rather than in holes in the adjoining grassy slopes, could perhaps improve the chances of it becoming firmly established again.

RAVEN: For unknown reasons the bird has expanded its population in Devon within living memory. It nests on the sea-cliffs of both coasts and also in trees and quarries throughout the county. On Dartmoor and the Exmoor fringe large flocks of ravens may be seen congregating and foraging.

RAZORBILL: The large colony that used to exist on Lundy has now decreased. Fortunately there are growing colonies on both the north and south coasts.

REDPOLL: In the past quarter of a century the redpoll has spread in Devon. It appears that this westward extension of its range is closely related to the new coniferous forests which it favours as its nesting place. Although a small number of reports of breeding pairs occur before 1950 they are the exception.

REDSHANK: A wader which has had a varied history. Quite numerous in earlier days, but it decreased towards the end of the last century. In this century it gradually recovered its former status as a passage migrant and it began to breed on the estuaries. This was the situation until the severe winter of 1963 which seriously depleted the breeding stock. It can now be classed only as a bird which formerly bred in Devon.

REDSTART: Arriving in Devon from tropical Africa in April the range of the redstart covers almost the whole county with the exception of part of the South Hams and the part of west Devon adjacent to the Cornish boundary. This then is another case of a variety which has improved its status during the present century.

REEDLING, BEARDED: A rare visitor to be found only in extensive reed beds, it has been reported in Devon in the past and was positively identified at a number of localities during the 1960s.

SHEARWATER, MANX: This essentially oceanic bird occurs commonly off the coasts of Devon. Small numbers come to land on Lundy and have attempted to breed— usually unsuccessfully as far as can be ascertained. It is pleasing that the strange, nocturnal cries of the shearwaters as they come in to land on the grass-covered clifftops, have, in recent years, been heard on both the north and south coasts of Devon.

SHELDUCK: Since the reportings of D'Urban and Mathew in 1892 this variety has strengthened its position and now breeds on every Devon estuary. It is thought that most of the adult birds migrate to Bridgewater Bay in order to moult in June and July. They appear to leave groups of young under the care of single pairs of adults which migrate later.

SISKIN: The species has, without doubt, been attracted to the massive coniferous plantations which are now reaching maturity on and around Dartmoor and it is thought that it breeds occasionally. This constitutes an improvement in its status since D'Urban described it.

STONECHAT: On rough ground, where the wild gorse grows near the coasts and also in the Exmoor fringe and large areas of the south including Dartmoor this resident chat is quite a common sight. It undoubtedly suffered during the severe winter of 1963 when it is known that a small group on Lundy perished.

TIT, WILLOW: When D'Urban and Mathew made their comments on the marsh tit, the willow tit had not been differentiated from it and it did not appear on their list. The two birds are very much alike. The willow tit may be identified by its dull sooty-black crown and distinctive call-notes. The marsh tit has a black cap and chin and a loud distinct call in contrast to the repeated monosyllables of the willow tit. The marsh tit may be observed almost anywhere in Devon, but the willow tit is confined to the north, the north-west, and on Dartmoor the two species co-exist.

WAGTAIL, GREY: Beside streams and rivers throughout Devon this beautiful yellow-breasted bird is found. The yellow wagtail is less common and breeding is restricted to a few pairs near the south coast.

WARBLER, GRASSHOPPER: Once the almost mechanical 'churring' song of this warbler has been heard in the field little further difficulty is experienced in identifying the bird, which spends most of its time in dense cover. It may be heard almost everywhere in Devon and it probably breeds in many places, but this is difficult to prove.

WARBLER, REED: There has been a westward spread of this species during the present century. The Devon population represents the most-westerly edge of the breeding range. The bird now nests in most of the estuarine marshes, but seems to favour those of the southern part of the county. Its relative the sedge warbler is much more common in both north and south.

WARBLER, WOOD: Arriving in late April from central Africa, this retiring warbler is identified in the leaf-canopy of large, deciduous woodlands throughout Devon by its song, which includes a distinctive accelerating trill.

WHEATEAR: An early migrant arriving before the end of March, the wheatear is quite a common sight in the summer months on the Exmoor fringe, along the north Devon coast and also on most of Dartmoor. Its quietly contrasting colours and white rump are features by which it may be identified. In spring and autumn some elegant, richer-coloured specimens sometimes observed are likely to be members of the Greenland race which passes through Devon and the South-west on passage between Greenland and north Africa.

WHINCHAT: Arriving from tropical Africa in the month of April, this species occupies hill-country such as western Dartmoor, the Exmoor fringe, the Culm-measure country and the east Devon commons. At present this is another bird which is quite numerous. It appears to have become more numerous since D'Urban described it as a rare bird in north Devon.

WHITETHROAT, LESSER: Whereas the whitethroat breeds throughout the county, the lesser whitethroat is confined to the south and east of the region. It may be that this variety is gradually spreading westwards from its haunts in eastern and Midland counties, but Devon is on the edge of its range. It winters in north-east Africa.

WOODPECKER, LESSER SPOTTED: Unlike the greater spotted and green woodpeckers which are found in all the large deciduous woods this small shy bird is thinly distributed in Devon. It does not frequent the woods on Dartmoor, the Exmoor fringe or other upland areas.

CHAPTER THREE

Episodes from Devon's History

A hyena's den

Underneath a residential district of modern Torquay lies one of the most remarkable historic sites in Britain—Kent's Cavern. It consists of a series of chambers and connecting passages having a combined length of 800 metres (nearly half a mile). Situated in Ilsham valley it is worth visiting on account of its anthropological and geological interest. A path has been laid down and steps are provided where necessary, so though a visit is robbed of some of the excitement of potholing, it is dry and comfortable enough for people in ordinary clothing to find the experience enjoyable. The whole complex is unobtrusively floodlit and the strange forms of the water-dissolved limestone and the strong local colours, produced by the presence in the water of iron and copper, are seen under ideal conditions.

Kent's Cavern is, however, much more than an ordinary cave. It is thought to have been one of the earliest homes of humankind in Britain and for this reason is significant in an historic context. The cave has probably been known to man almost continuously since the Early Stone Age, and in the northward migration from the Mediterranean it was, perhaps, somewhere in this south Devon region that men and women first set foot in what we now call the British Isles.

The cavern burrows into part of the Torquay limestone, which is itself embedded in the Middle Devonian rocks; like most limestone caves it was formed by the percolation of water over a long period of time. The temperature of the cave remains a constant 10.5° C (53° F) all the year round and this may have been an attraction to early man. The actual origin of the name is uncertain but it has been called Kent's Cavern at least since 1659.

Here in the year 1825 a flint knife was discovered and this is reckoned to be one of the earliest findings of a human artefact in any cave. As time passed more flint implements were unearthed. In 1867 parts of a human jaw were found embedded in stalagmite. When an undisturbed stalagmitic accretion of great age was removed and flint implements associated with prehistoric animal remains were revealed beneath it was realised that, without doubt, the two had co-existed. This may not seem very remarkable now, but in the nineteenth century fierce arguments developed because discoveries such as these refuted the implications of Creation as described in the Bible and led to a full understanding of the fact that animal life had existed on earth long before written history.

The mammalian bones which have been found in the cavern have been described and classified by many investigators, resulting in a large number of publications on the subject. A total of 36 species has been identified, including man, the straight-tusked elephant, wild boar, fallow deer, mountain hare, pine marten and lemming. These were found lying above thousands of teeth and bones of the horse, hyena, rhinoceros and elephant. The lowest deposits are apparently of a very much greater age than those of the upper layers. This poses a question which could perhaps be explained if, for a certain period, the entrance of the cave had become sealed. The very existence of bone deposits as concentrated as these is the cause of considerable interest in itself. Under ordinary conditions as we understand them the time-span necessary for such an accumulation to form must have been of very great length and special reasons have been sought to explain it. One suggestion is that floods, or the waters of a river, entering the system through entrances now closed were responsible for gathering together some of the deposits, and it is obvious, as almost every large bone bears the tooth marks of the species, that for long periods of time the cavern was a den of the hyena. Many of the larger carcases are assumed to have been dragged into the interior in a dismembered state, the entrances to the cave being so narrow that it is difficult to believe that it could have been otherwise.

One significant fact is that some of the animals represented are types that are adapted to a cold climate and some to warm. This is further proof of Devon's central position in the overlapping cold and warm zones which advanced and retreated in succession during the Ice Age. Northern species spread southwards then, in the interglacial periods, others such as the straight-tusked elephant, the narrow-nosed rhinoceros and the hippopotamus spread north as the climate became warmer. Evidence of these fluctuations is preserved in the mammalian remains.

Kent's Cavern is by no means the only south Devon bone-cave, it is not even the only one in Torquay itself, but of the others only Brixham Cavern, sometimes known as Windmill Hill Cavern, may be visited with similar ease by the general public. The sites of the rest of the caves range from Plymouth in the west to Chudleigh, only 13 kilometres (8 miles) from Exeter, in the east. Even in the present decade two schoolboys have stumbled on another previously-unknown cave at Oreston, Plymouth. At Torbryan the Tornewton Cave is of great interest because of the long-undisturbed series of deposits which have been discovered there. They represent a clearer time-sequence than do those of Kent's Cavern and include two so-called 'cold layers', with reindeer remains, between which there is an 'inter-glacial layer' containing the remains of hippopotamuses.

An informative display of objects from Kent's Cavern may be seen at the Museum of the Torquay Natural History Society; other specimens are displayed in the building through which admission to the cave is gained, and more may be seen at the Royal Albert Memorial Museum at Exeter.

Romans in the rain

A glance at a map of the type which shows the remains of Roman civilization in Britain makes it obvious that, compared with the south-east and the Midlands, Devon was of secondary interest to the invaders. The exception was Isca Dumnoniorium, the modern Exeter, which represents the western limit of the Roman advance; the town was linked by road to Ilchester in Somerset, though the exact route taken by it has not been determined along the whole of its length.

In recent years much fresh evidence of Roman Devon has come to light as a result of archaeological excavations. In the Cathedral Close at Exeter structures of considerable historic and architectural importance have been revealed. On the remote north Devon coast two outposts, at Old Burrow and Martinhoe, have been positively identified as Roman observation posts; and an awareness of a fortified camp near North Tawton is now reinforced by the discovery of another at Okehampton. Apart from these there are the remains of two villas, both of which are situated in south-east Devon. One of them, the Seaton site, has recently been shown to consist of a greater range of foundations than was earlier believed to be the case. There may also have been a Roman building at Stonehouse, Plymouth, but the area has seen so much human activity that the discovery of foundations which might prove that it had existed is now unlikely. The thin pattern of Roman occupation in Devon was unlike the settlement which took place in south-east England; either the area held only slight interest for the invaders or the inhabitants gave them little trouble. It is possible, too, that there are other sites awaiting discovery in parts of Devon hitherto believed to lie outside the Roman sphere of influence. There seems little doubt that further studies will produce additional information and probably a need to revise our present knowledge.

Julius Caesar landed with an expeditionary force on the coast of Kent in 55 B.C. and remained for about a month. In the following year he returned and penetrated as far as Hertfordshire, but, once again, as the autumn weather set in he decided to withdraw, leaving most of the country and certainly the south-west unexplored. It was almost a hundred years later, in A.D. 43, that the Emperor Claudius landed an invasion force of over 40,000 on the Kentish coast and marched north to cross the Thames and take Colchester. From this point three legions fanned out and gradually occupied the territory behind a more or less straight line drawn from Lincoln to Exeter. The conquest of the West Country was probably complete by A.D. 47-48. The Fosse Way, a military road manned by detachments of troops, then marked the frontier-zone between occupied and unoccupied Britain with Lincoln at one end and Exeter at the other. During this stage of the conquest Isca Dumnoniorium became the strongpoint of Roman Britain in the south-west. It would appear that a fort was established just to the east of the present remains of the city wall; the western angle of this fort would have coincided with the position of the medieval south gate which can still be identified. Most of England was occupied when in A.D. 122 the Emperor Hadrian ordered the construction of his famous wall to defend the north and by this date Isca was beginning to change from a military base into a civic centre.

In the south-west Exeter represented the only substantial example of the planning ideas and building methods which were employed by the Romans; the evident lack of remains in Devon as a whole leads to the conclusion that their influence did not extend much farther. It has been suggested that the native tribe, the Dumnonii, came to an arrangement with their overlords; apparently, no surviving records mention them being conquered. The hill-country of Devon with its thick oak forests and wide valley marshes, coupled with the weather, which was probably as damp and blustery then as it often is today, did not present the ideal territory in which to implant Latin culture. Only where the climate and terrain approached the conditions prevalent in lowland Britain generally would the Romans feel confident in establishing permanent structures and only south-east Devon met these requirements. The remainder of the county had little to offer and was of minor strategic importance. It has been established that the Second Augustan Legion arrived at Exeter about A.D. 47 and remained there until it was moved to Gloucester in A.D. 67. A legion was a formidable force consisting of 6,000 trained men, probably more than enough, if necessary, to overwhelm opposition in Devon.

Whilst the legion was stationed at Exeter the northern flank of the occupied zone in Somerset may have been threatened by the Silures, the Celtic tribes of south Wales who were led by Caractacus. It is likely that to meet some such threat the frontier was extended westwards from the Fosse Way in the section adjacent to the mouth of the river Severn. In association with this move and in order to check any seaborne movement on the part of the Silures observation posts were established on two high points of the north Devon cliff-edge, one to the east and one to the west of Lynmouth. The south Wales coast is usually visible from these points.

Evidence of accommodation in the form of wooden barracks divided into cubicles, for about 80 men in each fort, was found when, in 1960-61, Lady Aileen Fox and Professor W. L. D. Ravenhill excavated the sites for Exeter University in conjunction with the Devon Archaeological Society and the Devonshire Association. The buildings were proved to have been rectangular in plan and protected by a rampart, square in plan, and topped with wooden stockades. These defences were further strengthened by outer embankments about 21 metres (70 feet) beyond the inner rampart. Evidence of fires was found near the edge of the cliff.

The crews of Roman ships in the channel could have observed the smoke signals and acted accordingly. The sea may also have been the route by which the fortlets were kept supplied. The Martinhoe site was occupied from about A.D. 64-74, the period when the military occupation of Exeter was at its height; it has been suggested that it was built to replace Old Burrow. Do these fortlets imply a stronger presence in the area than has usually been assumed and were they supplied overland? The full details will probably never be known.

At Exeter the site chosen for the establishment of what was, at first, mainly a military base had many features to recommend it. Though it is not immediately apparent in the modern city, its centre lies on a hill surrounded on three sides by fairly steep inclines offering a good defensive position. Three kilometres away to the north Stoke Hill rises to 158 metres (519 feet) and provided the Romans with a site for their signal station. The river Exe in those days was naviagable as far as the point, at the bottom of Fore Street, at present occupied by the road bridges. Downstream from Exeter in the vicinity of Topsham it would have been possible to land heavy equipment. Indeed, it is probable that Topsham was first established as a Roman port. From the point of view of defence the river must have been reassuring to the Roman commanders for it provided a clearly-defined barrier on their western flank.

Until recently the only visible evidence of the Roman occupation west of the Exe was a road, with side ditches, passing over Haldon Hill towards Newton Abbot; its position is marked on some editions of the Ordnance Survey map. It may have been part of an overland route to Mount Batten, Plymouth, where a trading settlement had been in existence since about 1,000 B.C. Roman coins have been discovered there. Another road skirted northern Dartmoor, providing the most direct route from Exeter to Cornwall. Beside this road, near North Tawton, is the imprint of a fortified camp which seems to be laid out on the standard Roman proportions. On the Exeter side of this site five kilometres (three miles) of straight hedge-banks, most of them being parish boundaries, are aligned along a route now believed to have been that of the road. Exciting new discoveries are still being made. The point at which this route north of Dartmoor crossed the river Okement has recently been established and the site of another fortified camp has been located in the vicinity. The identification of a temporary camp site at Alverdiscott between Barnstaple, Bideford and Great Torrington is of equal interest for it suggests that at times the Roman presence was very real even in comparatively remote parts.

Only in the present decade has an opportunity arisen to apply modern archaeological techniques to the remains of Roman Exeter. Until the 1960s a large unattractive Victorian church, St Mary Major, stood in the Close not far from the west front of the Cathedral. It had been built on the site of a Norman church of the same name. After the church was demolished excavations were carried out on and near the site in 1971 and 1972 and as a result people of Exeter witnessed the uncovering of a layer of elaborate sub-structures well below the present ground level. The main building which was revealed can be described as a legionary bath-house; it consisted of three large rooms, two of which, the caldarium and tepidarium, were fully excavated. These were equipped with the under-floor heating arrangement known as a hypocaust. Adjoining the bath-house there were, as might be expected, indications of a palestra or open-air courtyard used for exercising. Through the evidence of coins and pottery found on the site it was established that the building had been in use from about A.D. 50 to A.D. 75. When the legion was moved to Gloucester a small holding-force was probably left at Exeter and there are signs that the bath-house was reduced in size at about this date.

Later still, the building became a basilica and the area occupied by the palestra was converted into a forum surrounded on three sides by arcaded shops and offices of a type which still exists at several ancient sites in Italy itself. In such ways the transition from a military base to a civilian town took place. These recent findings indicate a Roman involvement in Exeter on a scale that had not previously been conclusively proved by visible remains of buildings, although until recent years a mosaic pavement of inferior quality existed in Waterbeer Street behind the Guildhall. Exeter reached its maximum size in the third century when a stone wall was erected on the line of an earth rampart of the second century to encompass about 0.4 of a square kilometre. This wall defined the limits of the built-up area until the late medieval period; considerable lengths of it survive even today.

Britain was completely severed from the Roman Empire in A.D. 410, when the Emperor Honarious sent messages to the administrators of colonial towns advising them to organize their own defence. Within a few decades urban life as it had been known in Exeter was probably no longer possible. The Dark Ages had begun.

The age of the sea hawks

Given the cultural advancement of Spain and Portugal during the fifteenth century and their geographical position at Europe's western extremity it was almost inevitable that they would extend their horizons westward. The south-west peninsula of England, dominated by Devon, has a similar relationship to the British Isles as a whole as has Spain to the continent of Europe. Following the Reformation England began to question the wealth and might of the Hispanic peoples.

In the first three decades of the sixteenth century, though Devon was in the front line and no doubt aware of some international tension, diplomatic peace reigned. To support this a marriage between Catherine, the daughter of Ferdinand of Aragon and Isabella of Castile, and Arthur the eldest son of Henry VII of England, was proposed. This allowed the balance of power to be maintained in spite of increasing French influence in the English Channel and the Breton ports.

The Infanta disembarked at Plymouth on 2 October 1501, and was received enthusiastically. She made one of her first public appearances when she went to St Andrew's church in fine style to offer thanks for her safety following a stormy voyage. After a short stay in Plymouth she continued her journey to London, stopping en route at Exeter where she was warmly welcomed by the Cathedral clergy and the local men of substance; she was accommodated for the night at the Cathedral deanery.

Within three months of marriage Arthur died. Catherine's second marriage, to Henry VIII, paved the way for an alliance with Spain and in 1509 four royal ships and an imposing array of knights assembled at Plymouth to sail to Cadiz to assist the Spaniards in their struggle with the Moors. Murmurings of religious disapproval in Devon came when Henry VIII married his second wife Anne Boleyn. These were highlighted when some Plymouth priests suffered imprisonment in Launceston Castle for expressing opposition to the marriage.

The religious bias was reversed when Mary with her strong Catholic leanings ascended the throne. Protestantism was for the time being overthrown; relations with Spain established a more friendly basis and Mary had visions of wedding the heir to the Spanish crown. To facilitate these proceedings a group of Spanish nobles disembarked at Plymouth in 1554, the year of the marriage, with suitable presents. They were treated with great hospitality. This was dimmed somewhat when the impact of religious change became more resented by the seamen of the country and the county. This resentment increased rapidly and by 1557 Philip on one of his visits to his wife suffered the indignity of having to sail into Plymouth Sound unattended by the traditional naval escort.

Calais fell to the French in 1558 and England lost her one remaining foothold on the Continent; and feeling more secure, at least for the time being, the English were free to turn their attention westwards as the Spaniards and Portugese had been doing for nearly a century. The idea that England might become an empire builder began to grow in the imaginations of a few Devonians. Even before this time, whilst the marriages of Henry VIII were distracting the attention of the nation, William Hawkins, the principal Plymouth sea captain, had armed the *Paule of Plimmouth* and made his way to the coast of Brazil. He traded in ivory and other commodities and won the confidence of the natives sufficiently to persuade a chieftain to accompany him to England where he was introduced to members of the Court at London. During the following decades a number of native Americans were brought to Devon. Uprooted from their tribal cultures, it is probably that they led miserable lives.

It was not until Elizabeth came to the throne that Devonshire seamen, who combined hardy courage with an ardent Protestant faith, followed in the wake of the Spanish sea captains and the Conquistadores. Whilst the Queen was still young the mariners of Devon were ploughing through the waters of the Caribbean hoping to claim the untold treasures believed to lie beyond its shores. Some of these pioneers had passed through the religious disturbances and had seen their parents suffer persecution. Individuals such as the school teacher, Thomas Benet, put to death at Exeter in 1531 by being burnt, because he expressed anti-Catholic views, had not been forgotten. There was a determination to challenge and subdue both the Catholic claim to universal empire and the iniquity of the Inquisition. The enterprises which ensued were to lead to England's maritime supremacy. From the beginning the Spaniards regarded them as piratical. Against this labyrinthine backcloth of intrigue, counter intrigue, religious upheaval, and empire-building aspiration the now-famous sea-dogs of Devon emerged from the wings to play their parts.

In the valley of the river Dart lived three families which were to become prominent in the history of discovery. Humphrey Gilbert and his two brothers Adrian and John were born at Greenway, a house in private ownership, on the hill opposite the village of Dittisham a little way up the river. Otho Gilbert, the father of the boys died when Humphrey was only eight. His wife, Katherine Champernowne of Modbury, whom it is usually assumed must have been a remarkable person, then married Walter Raleigh who was the occupant of a large, thatched farm-house called Hayes Barton situated a kilometre west of East Budleigh, near Exmouth. At this home, which is sometimes open for members of the public to view it, a son named Walter was born in 1552. As he grew up he would almost certainly have spent much time with his half-brothers on and beside the Dart and at another seat of the Gilberts, Compton Castle, near Torquay. Not far from Greenway, at a farm named Sandridge, the boys had a younger friend called John Davis.

About two years after Humphrey's birth in 1539 a child who was to be christened Francis Drake was born at Crowndale a kilometre south of Tavistock. Though it appears that the original house has been replaced it is still a working farm in private ownership. The Drakes were related to the Hawkins family, two brothers of which, William and John, were contemporaries of Francis Drake. As merchant seamen based at Plymouth they contributed to the early evolution of England's sea-power. Among three generations of the Hawkins family, whose predecessors came from Tavistock, there were two by the name of John and three called William. Two Williams, father and son, were mayors of Plymouth.

John Hawkins, the son of the older William, led the San Juan de Ulua escapade and then became treasurer to the navy in the critical years before the sailing of the Armada. Though young Drake was introduced to ships on the Medway, William Hawkins watched over his first voyages in distant waters. A second generation of adventurers with Drake as its natural leader came of age. Like their forerunners they sometimes engaged in slave-trading, which carried no stigma.

The most-renowned of the north Devon buccaneers was Sir Richard Grenville—'Grenville of the Revenge'. He was Cornish, but having married Mary St Leger of Annery near Bideford was always associated with the northern port. Born in 1542 he was a cousin of Walter Raleigh. The two famous sailors William and Stephen Borough, who were born at Northam, were slightly older than Grenville. Stephen is remembered for his exploration of northern seas. He named the North Cape and commanded the first English ship to sail to Russia. William accompanied his brother on these voyages and in 1583 became comptroller of the Royal Navy.

The achievements of Sir Francis Drake, Sir John Hawkins, Sir Richard Grenville and Sir Walter Raleigh, which combined commercial profit and glory, stand out in an age of daring individual initiative that has no counterpart in the changed conditions of today. Success was gained not only through their personal energy but because of the support of Queen Elizabeth and her ministers, hesitant though it was. The Spanish Ambassador heard that plots were being concocted and in his dispatches to his homeland he recommended caution. It is not the purpose of this part of the chapter to follow all these machinations and the actions which followed them in any detail but simply to take note of a few events as they affected Devonians and their county.

Drake had made his first voyage to the Spanish-held coasts of the Caribbean — The Spanish Main — in 1565. A year or two later news reached Philip II that John Hawkins was preparing to make a suspicious voyage with some ships belonging to the queen and, furthermore, 'Arms and ammunition were being drawn from the store of the Tower of London.' Thus Hawkins was tricked and nearly captured at San Juan de Ulua, the modern Veracruz, in 1568. It looked very different from the Spanish viewpoint — 'Hawkins, the pirate, in an audacious attack, seized the port of San Juan de Ulua and as was his custom, asked for permission to trade under the threat of setting fire to the whole town. The Spanish Viceroy thought that to come to terms with a pirate would be dishonourable.' Francis Drake, who was the captain of one of the Plymouth ships, just managed to get away when the Spaniards broke their word of honour and attacked the English flotilla whilst it was at anchor. The experience coloured his thoughts about the Spaniards for the remainder of his life. Spanish sources describe how Hawkins, too, made his escape and leaving behind many sailors set sail for England where 'almost dying of hunger and thirst', he arrived in 1569. From this date Spain gradually became more aggressive towards England.

Hawkins was called upon to reorganize the Royal Navy and his natural successor as the leading Devon sea-captain was Drake who, in the Nombre de Dios incident of 1572, took some revenge and captured numerous Spanish ships. In the meantime, on 4 July 1569 Drake married his first wife, Mary Newman, in the parish church of St Budeaux overlooking the river Tamar. Mary was separated from her husband for long periods whilst he was at sea; they had no children.

Drake embarked at Plymouth on 13 December 1577 to start his voyage of circumnavigation. It was an expedition on a greater scale than any previous voyage of discovery or trade. His flagship was the *Pelican*, four other vessels accompanied him and a number of small pinnaces were stowed away on board until required for inshore surveys. Not least among the many highlights of the journey was the landing on the coast of California, which was claimed for the queen. In his renamed ship the *Golden Hinde*, and after many adventures, he returned, cautiously, to Plymouth on 26 September 1580.

The voyage had made him very rich and he became a national hero. He bought Buckland Abbey, which had been in the ownership of Sir Richard Grenville. The first floor and various partition walls had been installed by Grenville in what had been a monastic church belonging to the Cistercian order. It was to be Drake's home for the rest of his life and of Mary Drake for her remaining two years. Today, housing the Drake memorabilia, the mansion brings alive the spirit of Elizabethan Devon.

Drake's voyage of circumnavigation was followed by Humphrey Gilbert's founding of the Newfoundland colony in 1583. The exploration of the coast of north Carolina by two of Drake's captains took place in 1584 and the discovery of the north-west Passage was made by John Davis in 1585. In the latter year Sir Richard Grenville commanded a fleet of seven ships which took West-Country people to America. It was through his colonization of Carolina and Virginia that a flourishing trade in tobacco was gradually built up. In this process of exploration and the seeking of personal wealth through somewhat haphazard enterprises strung out along 2400 kilometres (1500 miles) of the American seaboard, Catholic Spain was challenged and, ultimately, the survival of England as a Protestant state was ensured. As a result, it may be of interest to note that England's relationship with north America is at present 400 years old, being almost equally divided by the American Declaration of Independence of 1776.

Drake carried out a brilliant attack on Cartegena on the coast of south America, and in the following year, 1587, the daring raid on Cadiz was as important in giving England an interval in which to prepare her defences against invasion as was the Munich Agreement prior to World War II. In the hazardous years between 1586 and 1608 a journal was kept by the Brauntonian, Philip Wyot, who was then town clerk of Barnstaple. The original document has unfortunately, been lost, but one or two copies of it were in existence when Lysons visited north Devon in 1810. Some of the substance of the commentary appears to have been preserved in a series of papers read by John Robert Chanter in 1866. They help to make evident the mood prevailing in Elizabethan Devon.

Orders were given for fire beacons to be made ready and attended by night and day in the Barnstaple area during 1586. The ground floor chambers of the sturdy church-towers served as convenient strongholds where arms and armour were stored. Every man was asked to have his armour in readiness. An inspection of the able men of the hundreds of Braunton,

Fremington and Shirwell by the magistrates led by Lord Bath, Sir Richard Grenville, Mr Hugh Ackland and Mr George Wyot took place on 24 February 1586. Later in the same week a similar muster of the men of the town was held. Whilst these events were taking place a Barnstaple sea captain, known as James Wilson in north Devon but referred to as John Wilson in State Papers, was one of many Englishmen held in confinement in Spain. He was being offered freedom if he would put his knowledge of English coastal waters at the disposal of his captors who wanted him to pilot the Armada through the Channel. He was fortunate to be released unharmed and was questioned by the English authorities about his experiences. Until the 1960s an inscription in the Queen Anne's Walk at Barnstaple drew attention to his courage in resisting the demands and threats made by the Spaniards.

In 1588 Wyot recorded that there was another review on the Castle Green at Barnstaple and that five ships sailed across the 'Bar'; they were on their way to join Drake's ships riding at anchor at Plymouth. How many of these vessels were Barnstaple-owned and how many were supplied by the Grenvilles of Bideford? This question has been the cause of prolonged local discussion. Wyot gave the impression that the likelihood of an invasion was causing widespread anxiety.

Preparations to deal with the threat were being made throughout the county. The Lord Lieutenant, William Bouchier, Earl of Bath, took up his post at Plymouth. John Gilbert of Greenway, one of his deputies, lived a mere three kilometres from Galmpton Warborough, a mustering point for the Brixham district. Another deputy Lieutenant, Sir George Cary of Cockington, controlling somewhat inadequate forces, was in charge of the defence of the Torre Bay area.

To Spanish observers the galleons setting out from Corunna appeared to be in splendid array and kept perfect formation. They were first noticed by the English off the Lizard, according to the calendar which we use today, on 29 July 1588. Thomas Fleming of Barnstaple, commanding a barque, the *Golden Hinde*, one of the ships detailed to keep watch in that area, returned to Plymouth under full sail to give the alarm. From the Hoe a signal was made to the fire beacons situated at St Budeaux, Weston and Hardwick. By means of the co-ordinated beacons on the hilltops the whole county could be warned within an hour.

Drake, who was Vice-Admiral under Admiral of the Fleet, Lord Howard of Effingham, and his fellow captains are said to have been playing bowls when the news was received. Without doubt they were taken by surprise. It is possible, however, that the game was being played at a place closer to the Barbican than the modern green situated alongside the Hoe, and the open sea beyond the Sound was under constant surveillance. Events unfolded slowly in the age of windpower. There was a lengthy interval whilst the ships were warped out of Sutton harbour against both tide and wind and in this time a leisurely game of bowls could be finished. But the Spaniards' report that they had created 'panic at Plymouth' may not be entirely rhetorical.

The Duke of Medina Sidonia commanding the Armada allowed the opportunity to attack and perhaps annihilate the English fleet, there and then, to pass. He had been ordered, so he alleged, to give battle only when joined by the ships under the control of Alessandro Farnese, Duke of Parma, the Spanish regent for the Netherlands. On the other hand Medina Sidonia did not know exactly how the English forces were disposed. English and Spanish ships first met at sea on 31 July. The Armada, harassed by the English, had passed beyond Plymouth when an incident that was to have repercussions in Devon took place. The *Nostra Señora del Rosario*, one of the finest galleons, being the flagship of the Andalusian squadron was apparently in collision with another Spanish ship. There are differing descriptions of what happened, but it seems likely that her foremast was wrecked. She was allowed to fall astern of the Armada in order not to put the whole fleet at risk. The crew may have been struggling to reset the sails when she was challenged by Drake and surrendered without resistance. The episode is surrounded by mystery but possibly the Spaniards were so convinced of their ultimate victory that they regarded their plight as temporary. The admiral and 40 officers were taken off and arrested before the prize was turned over to the captain of the privateer *Roebuck* who towed her back to Torre Bay. Having confiscated ten of her fine brass cannon and other useful equipment the English captain set off to rejoin his fleet, leaving the magistrates ashore with the tricky problem of deciding what to do with approximately 400 Spanish soldiers and sailors who were still on board.

Cary of Cockington and Gilbert of Compton sent for advice—'We desire to know your lordships' resolution, what shall become of these people, our vowed enemies?' In the preceding years numerous English seamen, including many Devonians, had been taken captive by the Spaniards. At San Juan de Ulua alone 400 men took part, but only 70 returned to Plymouth. Many received sickening treatment at the hands of the Inquisition.

To return to south Devon. The situation was no doubt extremely tense when Cary decided to act. Summoning troops from St Marychurch he had the Spaniards imprisoned in the tithe barn which still stands beside Torre Abbey. A magnificent building of early date, it has ever since been known as the Spanish Barn. After a week, 211 of the prisoners were taken to the greater security of the Bridewell for Devon situated in the parish of St Thomas just outside Exeter. Some prisoners died in the barn and the tradition is that they were buried between the building and the sea. Cary felt that he had certain responsibilities to the Spaniards and he made a personal contribution to supplement the government allowance in order to provide them with adequate food. Other magistrates were reluctant to incur any expense and there is a suggestion that Gilbert appropriated part of the subsistence allowance. The ship was towed to the Dart and then to Chatham where she was dismantled.

Little is known of the prisoners who survived, but stories which have been passed from one generation of Devonians to the next may throw some light on the matter. Gilbert is reputed to have employed 160 of the captives on the improvement of his grounds at Compton Castle. A somewhat similar tale is told of Holcombe Court, where above the great hall and running the full length of the front of the building is the gallery built in 1560. Some Armada prisoners are reputed to have been kept in ten small rooms to which access is gained from the gallery and, in one of the ground floor rooms, a plaster frieze is thought to be of Spanish workmanship.

Following the damage inflicted on the Armada the remaining seaworthy ships rounded the north of Scotland but, on the voyage south, many of these came to grief and English officials reported that numerous survivors were massacred in Ireland.

A legend would have us believe that one galleon was wrecked on or near the north coast of Devon. Bideford has some 'Armada Guns' which, whilst certainly of foreign origin, have not been proved to be Spanish. Some of the survivors of the wreck are said to have become integrated with the inhabitants of the small hamlet of Bucks Mills—a remote spot until the nineteenth century. The physical characteristics of certain of the villagers were regarded as supporting evidence. It is a fact that one Spanish ship, under the impression that she was heading for Spain, went aground—revealing an astonishing degree of disorientation—near Bolt Tail on the south Devon coast. Some of her crew were saved.

The defeat of the Armada did not eliminate the possibility that there would be another attempt to conquer England. Though history shows that Spain had been much weakened, rumours of invasion were rife in Devon for several years and the general situation was far from being static. In the year after the Armada's defeat the English expedition to Portugal, under Drake and Sir John Norris, fell short of what was hoped of it. There was a similar disappointment in 1591. Sir Richard Grenville was second in command of a squadron which it was planned should intercept the Spanish treasure fleet on its way home from South America. His ship the *Revenge*, manned by 'Men of Bideford in Devon', was cornered by the Spaniards, but his defiant bravery, in the face of overwhelming odds, has been an inspiration to generations of his fellow countrymen. In the immortal words of Lord Tennyson's 'Ballard of the Fleet':

> *The Stately Spanish men to their*
> *flagship bore him then,*
> *Where they laid him by the mast, old*
> *Sir Richard caught at last,*
> *And they praised him to his face with*
> *their courtly foreign grace;*
> *But he rose upon their decks, and he cried;*
> *'I have fought for Queen and faith like*
> *a valiant man and true;*
> *I have only done my duty as a man is*
> *bound to do:*
> *With joyful spirit I Sir Richard Grenville die!'*
> *And he fell upon their decks, and he died.*

In 1592 John Davis discovered the Falkland Islands and in 1595 Raleigh sailed for the northern coasts of south America. Drake and Hawkins set out again for the West Indies in 1596 with the intention of continuing the fight against Spain, but during the voyage both men died from natural causes and were buried at sea. At the beginning of the seventeenth century the Plymouth Company was given the right to colonize the north American coast between Virginia and Newfoundland.

Raleigh became ensnared by the policies which were evolving in Anglo-

Spanish diplomatic circles and one of the most infamous acts to which the English government and monarchy has ever stooped took place. He was beheaded in 1618. Only two years later the Pilgrim Fathers, inspired by his descriptions of the New World, sailed from Plymouth. There could be no memorial more appropriate to this gallant many-sided patriot, with his desire to interest English people in colonization, than the fact that the vast daughterland of north America is inhabited by English-speaking stock. With his fellow Elizabethan-Devonians, Sir Walter Raleigh had helped to ensure a British foothold in world history and prepared the way for the host of emigrants—the merchant adventurers, the discoverers, the colonists, the educators—of whom the nation may be justly proud.

Devon and North America

The Pilgrim Fathers—the first true Anglo-Americans—came from the south-east of England and were strangers to Devon. Having repaired and refitted their ships, the *Speedwell* and *Mayflower*, at Dartmouth they resumed their voyage, but after further buffeting were obliged to seek the safety of Plymouth. Island House at the Barbican is reputed to be the place where many of them lodged. Plymouthians had long sympathized with the demand for freedom of worship and there was keen interest in the emigrée community which had already been to Holland in search of a suitable home. Disappointed with Leyden where they had spent ten years, the Pilgrim Fathers became attracted by Raleigh's account of the natural resources of America and in their own words 'were already well weaned from the milk of the mother country'. The ships were thoroughly overhauled and the *Speedwell* being considered unfit for a long voyage, was sent back to London. Before leaving Plymouth the travellers assembled at St Andrew's church, where the vicar was evidently in sympathy with Puritan ideals. When, after their trans-Atlantic voyage of nine weeks duration Cape Cod was sighted the community who had found hospitality at Plymouth, Devon, landed at a place which had already been named Plymouth by John Smith.

Devon sailors had already had much contact with the New World by 1620, the year of these events and, often with good financial support from London, much effort had been put into Virginia and other parts of America; the port books of Barnstaple and her sister port of Bideford show that in the same year seven of their ships sailed for America. Merchants in Plymouth and other ports were steadily exploiting the new continent. In 1622 the

Abraham of Plymouth was fitted out and loaded with stores useful to both natives and colonists; bear skins, fish and pipe-staves were eventually received in exchange. At Richmond Island, close to the south-eastern, Port Elizabeth, names no longer used, the nucleus of a trading station was established and in 1631 a contract was completed between the President of the Council on the one part and Robert Trelawney and Moses Goodyear, a pioneering Plymouth merchant and son-in-law of Samuel Jennings, the owner of the *Abraham* on the other, to develop the natural resources of New England 'from the sea to the Main Land'. Somerset-born Ferdinando Gorges, *c.* 1566-1647, for many years governor of the forts and island of Plymouth, accepted the administration of the area where he enforced his own laws until Charles I required him to return to England to apply his military expertise to the defence of the crown. In 1623 the king had urged his Lord Lieutenants of Devon and Cornwall to encourage people to go to America. Between 1630 and 1640 a large number of Devonians are thought to have settled in Massachusetts and Virginia.

In a letter written to a relative soon after his arrival, as Deputy Governor of the province of Maine in 1640 Thomas Gorges, a young cousin of Ferdinando, following his description of the voyage had this to say: 'The country here is plentiful yieldinge all sorts of Inglish graine and fruite, the rivers pleasant well stored with variety of fish the woods well treed with statly cedar, lofty pines, sturdy oaks and walnut trees with Raspberry and Gooseberry trees and vines in abundance'. The seaboard colonists enjoyed a bountiful supply of sustaining natural resources upon which they established quite a high standard of material comfort. The identification of considerable quantities of north Devon pottery of seventeenth-century manufacture at Jamestown, Virginia and Plymouth, Massachusetts, in the 1950s has led to the fact that the ports of Barnstaple and Bideford continued to be much involved in trade with the colonies.

Bideford had been the home of Sir Richard Grenville who, with Sir Walter Raleigh, was one of the first explorers of Virginia. The principle commerce in which the town engaged was the import of tobacco, the total annual value of which was second only to that of London. American independence and then, at the turn of the century, the Napoleonic Wars caused the decline and eventual collapse of Bideford's activity, the peak of which had occurred at the Restoration of the English monarchy and lasted until the early eighteenth century.

In 1666 the *Samuel* of Bideford and the *Philip* of Barnstaple sailed for Virginia fully aware of the danger of encountering hostile Dutch ships. Later, in 1705, it was recorded that of 63 ships from various English ports anchored at Hampton Roads, off Kecoughton, seven were from the Taw estuary ports. The extent to which north Devon trade with the colonies was organized is indicated by the fact that there were several instances of members of a family living on opposite sides of the ocean for the purpose of facilitating transactions for each other. The exchange of American raw materials for pottery has been proved and noted; it is reasonable to assume that other manufactured goods such as textiles, furniture and metalwork were also exported from Devon.

The poorer outlook for colonizing from England in the latter part of the seventeenth century is illustrated in the founding of North and South Carolina. When the proprietors began to settle their lands they discovered that it was difficult to attract the right type of emigrant. By the last decade of the century convicts, paupers and debtors were being sent out by English judges and magistrates. After the Restoration emigration was regarded as harmful to the state and the Act of Toleration of 1689 made it less likely that highly-motivated people, with independent views on worship, would feel the need to leave England. Even in 1740, John Kenrich, a burglar who had been sentenced to death at Exeter Quarter Sessions, was granted a Royal Pardon on condition that he should be transported to America for a term of seven years; in 1764, a Royal Pardon was similarly granted to Thomasine Hall condemned for the same offence in the same court. The death sentence was commuted to one of transportation to America for 14 years.

By the early eighteenth century there were 13 British colonies along the seaboard of America. Although each colony managed its own affairs all were subject to laws made by the British Parliament, which regulated trade and international relations. This system, by which Americans were governed partly by governments of their own choice and partly by Parliament, worked well until 1765. The question of the power of Parliament and the rights of the colonists arose when the home country tried to raise taxes to provide for the military defence of the settlers. Americans objected to the new laws, firstly, because they felt that they could defend themselves and, secondly, because they were not represented in Parliament. France had ceased to be a threat since she had lost all her possessions on the north American mainland to Britain and Spain. The quarrel came to a head after the famous 'Boston Tea Party' which induced Britain to take repressive measures. Fighting broke out between some British soldiers and Massachusetts militia-men on 18 April 1775, at the Battle of Lexington. The first news of the hostilities reached Plymouth in an unpleasant form; the *Charming Nancy* and other transports disembarked hundreds of wounded soldiers and many worried and miserable widows and orphans.

It was Lord Shelburne, the first Marquess of Lansdowne, who as Prime Minister, finally conceded independence to the colonies. One of a few portraits of him painted by Sir Joshua Reynolds hangs in Saltram House, Plympton, the seat of John Parker, a friend of the Marquess; it is interesting to speculate what the outcome might have been had the conciliatory policies which Shelburne originally advocated been adopted by the British government as a whole.

At the outbreak of the war a British army captain, John Greaves Simcoe, born in Northamptonshire but educated in Exeter, arrived in north America. He took part in many actions before he was wounded at the Battle of Brandywine River. Subsequently he was given command of the Queen's Rangers, a corps of loyalists recruited within the American colonies. He returned to England in 1782 and in 1785 bought an estate at Wolford five kilometres (three miles) north of Honiton. Simcoe had become a Member of Parliament when, in 1792, he was appointed first Lieutenant-Governor of Upper Canada. In the following summer, accompanied by his young wife, he returned to Canada and established the country's first capital at Niagara, which he renamed Newark, an arrival point for United Empire Loyalists. In escaping from the intolerance then being shown, to their political opponents, by the victorious Republicans of the United States the English loyalists fled north and settled in Upper Canada, a vast region bounded by the Great Lakes to the south and the Albany River in the north; partly represented today by the province of Ontario. Simcoe remained governor until 1794. His name is still remembered in Canada where many buildings such as Simcoe Hall of the University of Toronto and the Simcoe Museum, are named after him; he himself named Lake Simcoe after his father. Simcoe was responsible for the decision to move the site of the capital from Newark to a more secure position, now known as Toronto. He returned to Devon in 1800 and built Wolford church as a private chapel on his estate.

For political reasons the British government halted emigration altogether in 1775, but it was allowed to recommence after the end of hostilities; the real lull came during the Napoleonic Wars and the War of 1812. Napoleon's decrees forbade neutrals and allies of France from trading with England or her colonies. Britain with her formidable sea-power replied with a series of measures which had the effect of blockading Europe. The American ship *Sally*, for instance, was captured by H.M.S. *Indefatigable*. Nearly new, well found in stores, fit for general purposes and capable of putting to sea at a trifling expense she was auctioned at Plymouth in 1808 and sold for a derisory sum. Though the British barred American ships from European ports Napoleon was not in a position to prevent their trading with England. The British merchant community refused to submit to Napoleon, but strongly urged the government to avoid hostilities with our largest remaining customer, the United States; American mercantile interests were also opposed to the war. These warnings were heeded too late and war broke out, causing great hardship to both countries by reducing their commerce. The United States were opposed to the right to search as exercised by the British captains and the impressment of a large number of Americans to serve in British ships; the consequences were serious. A large number of British ships were captured on the high seas by the Americans.

In 1813 H.M.S. *Pelican* and the U.S.N. brig *Argus* fought an action in the Channel in the course of which the Commander of the American vessel received mortal wounds and one of his midshipmen was killed outright. They were buried in St Andrew's churchyard, Plymouth, and a tombstone was set up on which was incised 'Here Sleep the Brave'. As a result of engagements such as these the British took American prisoners. The prison on Dartmoor, at Princetown, had originally been built to accommodate prisoners of War of French nationality, but on 3 April 1813, a draft of 250 Americans was housed in the already-crowded French quarters; a further 250 were marched up from Plymouth on 18 May 1813, and others followed at later dates. They settled in fairly peacefully but, before long, on American Independence Day, were defiant enough to fly two United States flags from the rooftops. Following the abdication of Napoleon the French prisoners were released and by June 1814 the prison housed only Americans. They had by this date adopted the routines and activities established by the French. Many were occupied in furnishing the prison, others worked as smiths, carpenters, craftsmen and nurses. The prison church, St Michael and All Angels, which had been built by the Frenchmen was completed and furnished by the Americans. The first service was held there on 2 January 1814.

In August 1814 there was an attempt to break out of the prison; some progress had been made on two shafts and an escape tunnel before they were discovered by the guards. Hostilities between Britain and America ceased on 14 December 1814, and the prisoners were naturally eager for repatriation to take place; this had not commenced by April 1815 and, aggravated by a food shortage, a state approaching mutiny developed. A mass-escape appeared to be imminent and the extremist element among the prisoners made the situation appear worse than it was, scuffles broke out, stones were thrown at the guards and when they opened fire nine prisoners died. Five other prisoners had to undergo amputations and 50 others received hospital treatment. An international inquiry was later to find, somewhat equivocally, that the Prison Captain was correct in his assessment of the situation but that the firing was inexcusable. The release of the prisoners was, however, drawing near. On 19 April 1815, 249 were returned to Plymouth, followed, a week later, by 350 more, and by this time prison restrictions had been considerably relaxed.

Recent generations of English people have forgotten the War of 1812 as an unnecessary and unpleasant episode of the greater Napoleonic epic, but patriotic Americans remember it as a landmark in their early national growth. It was indeed unfortunate that the first foreign war of the young republic was fought against the homeland, but the terms of the peace treaty left the way open for the development of Anglo-American friendship.

During the years between 1832-53 there was again substantial emigration from Britain to North America. Local ships registered in north Devon transported some 10,000 people across the Atlantic without loss of a single vessel or a significant number of passengers from illness. One ship, the *Lord Ramsay* launched at Quebec in 1832 is known to have sailed back and forth on the Atlantic run for 21 years. The arrival of the ships in Canada was arranged to coincide with the spring thaw and the melting of the ice on the great rivers. The object of these voyages was to take out emigrants for as little as £3 per head and to bring back much-needed timber. Another ship engaged on these long, dangerous journeys was the *Margaret*, owned by a Torquay timber merchant.

One of the people who took part in what amounted to a mass-movement across the ocean was a young civil engineer named Edgar Dewdney, a native of Budleigh Salterton. He emigrated to Canada at the age of 24 in 1859 and worked on exploration and road construction in British Columbia. One of his undertakings was a trail through the mountains just north of the frontier with the United States. It was a difficult task because the vallyes lie mainly against the direction of travel. The trail ran from Hope to Wild Horse Camp, near Cranbrook, and today, with a few variations of route and much enlarged and improved, it is known as Highway Number Three, but it started as the Dewdney Trail. In 1881 Dewdney was appointed Lieutenant-Governor of the North-West Province.

Simcoe, who had been so active in Canada in the eighteenth century, died at Exeter in 1806 and a few years later John Flaxman, the famous neo-classic sculptor, was engaged in the designing and execution of a memorial to him. This may be seen on the south wall of the south aisle of Exeter Cathedral chancel. Part of the monument consists of a high-relief carving of an Indian brave; damage sustained during an air raid in World War II has been repaired. Simcoe is buried in the grounds of his family chapel at Wolford. In 1966 the deeds of this building were handed over to the Prime Minister of Ontario in a ceremony on the site; a part of Ontario in the heart of Devon. In Canada, a memorial to the Simcoes stands near their former home at Niagara-on-the-Lake.

At Princetown on Dartmoor the construction of St Michael's and All Angels, it may be recalled, was completed by American prisoners of war. The interior of the church having been remodelled in 1908 the east window was unveiled in 1910 as a memorial to the 218 who had died in captivity. A century during which there had been a gradual reappraisal of the Anglo-American relationship had passed when, just before World War I, the restoration of the Prysten House at Plymouth was put in hand. At the same time the tombstone, originally set up in 1813 to honour Captain William Allen of the *Argus* and his midshipman Richard Relphey, was discovered. American citizens then resident in Plymouth began the custom of holding a service at the graveside on 30 May, American Memorial Day. When, after the war, work on the Prysten House was continued the American Society of the Daughters of 1812 arranged for the mounting of the tombstone in a granite panel for the restoration of the doorway of the house which faces St Andrew's church. To symbolize the harmony which had been achieved by the English speaking peoples on both sides of the Atlantic the doorway was named 'The Door of Unity'. A short Anglo-American service is now established as a regular event and takes place beside the door and the adjacent tombstone on Memorial Day.

Because of the strong feeling of kinship which, in spite of differences, has been sustained in the present century the American presence in Devon during the Second World War can be discussed in the next section of this chapter. It will ever be the cause of pride among patriots of Devon that in the latter years of the war they were called upon to be the hosts of a large number of American servicemen and women; the forces which so successfully stormed the Normandy beaches on the 6 June 1944, trained in their midst and sailed from their ports. Since the 1950s the county has been visited by many Americans; ex-servicemen have returned to revisit places which they knew in the 1940s and in addition since the 1960s many ordinary Americans have come as tourists. Throughout Devon they are aware of place-names which they have known in the New World. Apart from its unfamiliar hedges and lack of large forests the county is a reminder of the rolling, green farming country of New England.

Two World Wars

Britain had not been involved in a major international conflict since the Napoleonic Wars to which there had been a reassuring finale—the spectacle of the dictator Napoleon, held prisoner by the Royal Navy in Plymouth Sound. The Crimean War had taken place from 1854 to 1856 and the Boer War started in 1899 and was over in 1902. Devonians were involved in both hostilities, especially the latter under the command of General Sir Redvers Buller VC—a popular man in his own county in spite of his military errors—but these were not major wars and they took place far away from the British seas.

It is not surprising that following Britain's Declaration of War on Germny, because of her violation of Belgian territory, on the 4 August 1914, the mood of Devonians was optimistic. The photographs of the period show smiling young volunteers, massed on the platforms of the railway stations. It was a fine summer, with luck the 'away season' would be rounded-off during the autumn and Christmas in Devon could be anticipated with customary warmth. Some holiday events were cancelled but others continued as if nothing had changed. In the meantime the first battalion of the Devonshire Regiment arrived in France and by the 15 September was in action on the river Aisne; its duty was to help stem the German advance on Paris. Before the end of the year the war of attrition became sadly evident and millions faced each other in expectation of deadly conflict.

As early as October 1914 Plymouth Sound framed an amazing sight. Thirty-three liners, in line-ahead formation, steamed in; they carried the Canadian Volunteer Army and units of the Newfoundland Army. The ships were originally due to dock at Portsmouth, but two enemy submarines were reported, one in the vicinity of the Isle of Wight and another in a position off Cherbourg, so the 25,000 men were unexpectedly disembarked at Devonport. It took 92 trains to transport them to Salisbury Plain.

With no fewer than 25 Regular, Territorial and Service Battalions taking part, the Devonshire Regiment fought in all the main areas of conflict and earned an impressive number of battle honours including those of Ypres, Loos, the Somme and the Bois des Buttes. It also saw action in the Italian campaign, and was engaged in operations in Egypt, India, Macedonia, Mesopotamia, Palestine and Russia. The county not only recruited men for its own battalions, but was continually called on to make good the general wastage in manpower. Towards the end of the war the regiment gained renown in its fight at the Bois des Buttes—one of the most heroic resistances of the war.

The battle took place near the village of Roucy, which was situated in the French sector of the river Aisne and started on the 26 May 1918. Preceded by a barrage from about 2,000 field guns, the Germans attacked the section held by the second battalion of the regiment under its commanding officer, Colonel Anderson-Morshead, who calmly wrote orders that there would be no retirement. The battalion suffered very heavy casualties; the majority of them came from Crediton and surrounding parishes. A roughly-hewn memorial cross of Devon stone was erected at Bois des Buttes in 1921. C. T. Atkinson, in his official regimental history wrote: 'It commemorates what must always be one of the special features of the long-drawn-out struggle of 1914-18, the way in which the road to victory lay through disappointments and often apparent failure.' During the war the Devonshire Regiment sustained a total loss of 5,787 lives.

As became an historic maritime county, the men of Devon rendered efficient service in the Royal Navy and also played a part in the auxiliary sea services such as mine-sweeping. Others helped to supply food by tenaciously carrying on their traditional fishing despite the threat of enemy attack. Devonport, as one of the three Home Ports which were Manning Ports of the navy, had a big contribution to make. Much new shipbuilding was undertaken; the battleship *Royal Oak*, a cruiser the *Cleopatra* and a number of submarines together with the three 'Q Ships' of Commander Gordon Campbell were constructed and fitted-out beside the Hamoaze.

The only large-scale naval contact during the war occurred at Jutland. The battle has been compared as far as numbers are concerned with Trafalgar. Victory at Trafalgar was complete, but the result at Jutland was relatively indecisive. Losses on both sides were considerable and as the news filtered through it cast a shadow of grief over Plymouth. A large proportion of the 6,787 British casualties came from the West Country. Three major ships, H.M.S. *Defence*, *Indefatigable* and *Warrior*, all manned from Devonport, were total losses. The helm of H.M.S. *Warspite*, another ship based on Devonport, was jammed at a critical moment but fortunately she survived to serve in World War II. The Devonport built and manned flagship of Admiral Beatty, H.M.S. *Lion*, managed to survive. To save the ship as a whole a mortally-wounded marine officer in charge of 'Q' turret, which had received a direct hit, order the flooding of the magazine. Events similar to this and including those of World War II are commemorated by the Naval Memorial situated on Plymouth Hoe (described in more detail in the Plymouth section of chapter seven).

During the early days of the war Devonshire women were called upon to help receive and care for the man Belgian refugees who fled to Britain and it was not long before the county became a reception area for the wounded. The Exeter hospitals did notable work and at Torquay the Town Hall was requisitioned for use as a Red Cross Hospital; several similar hospitals were set up in the larger houses in the Torbay area and also in other parts of the county. Sphagnum moss, which is highly-absorbent, was collected in large quantities on Dartmoor and dried and used in the dressing of wounds.

Food production was vitally important and the wives and daughters of farmers together with the Women's Land Army made considerable contributions to the war effort. In spite of being a food-producing area Devon itself experienced shortages and by June 1917 the *Western Times* was complaining that whilst the men abroad were engaged in immortal deeds of sacrifice 'Their wives and children have been allowed to be victimised on all hands by profiteers. No one has a right to make a profit out of war. He who does is beneath contempt'. The article then went on to ask why it was that a 4lb loaf of bread cost 10d in Ashburton, 11d in Honiton and 12d in Holsworthy?

Meanwhile the burden of war on the United States of America was slight compared with that which European nations endured. America insisted that she was an 'associated power' rather than an ally. Nevertheless her contribution, in the form of the expeditionary force, was decisive in tipping the balance. Unlike their descendants of World War II, the two million Americans who were involved went direct to France.

News of the Armistice was first received in Devon by the naval wireless stations at Plymouth and Torbay. Rejoicing began by ships in the harbours sounding their sirens, and ashore the people expressed their relief by flocking to the churches to give thanks. The impact of the war on the people of Devon was impressively shown after its close by the monuments to the fallen which appeared in almost every town and village throughout the county. In the centre of the province, Exeter, the simple County War Memorial erected in the Cathedral Close is a refined design by Sir Edwin Lutyens. In the Cathedral itself the sacrifices of the Devonshire Regiment are recalled in a bronze high-relief, the work of J. A. Stevenson, whose idea was to suggest the stoic qualities of the Devon fighting-man. Another memorial of more symbolic character, erected in the Northernhay Gardens, Exeter, was designed by John Angel, a native of the city.

The outbreak of World War II was immediately felt by the people of Devon because, following the Munich Crisis of 1938, the authorities had decided that, in the event of war, the county would become a reception area for evacuees. Even in January 1939, eight months before the war began, the Mayor of Exeter, appealing to his citizens to be ready to receive evacuees, expressed the hope that the geographical situation of the city would afford a greater measure of protection than the more vulnerable areas. The need for increased food production was also understood at once. In many quarters there was a feeling, following the experience of World War I, that this was to be 'total war' from the very beginning. The Devonshire Regiment was in the process of preparing for action. Devonport was fully committed to maintaining its historic role as Home Port of the Royal Navy. Many Devon men were already serving in ships of both the navy and the mercantile marine when war was declared. Two weeks after the opening of hostilities the aircraft carrier H.M.S. *Courageous* was torpedoed and sunk with a lost of 514 lives off the south-west coast.

The Dunkirk Evacuation took place at the beginning of June 1940 and with the fall of France the German Air Force could easily attack the south-west. This was contrary to the British assumption that the threat from the Luftwaffe would come from across the North Sea and in distinct contrast to the experience of the first world war when Devon was not within range of enemy aircraft. As the war progressed many evacuees wondered why they had not stayed at home.

When the aerial bombardments of Plymouth and Exeter took place and the air raid sirens wailed throughout the county, people as far away as the north Devon hills could see the tell-tale glows on the distant horizon and hear the faint thunder of destruction, but at the time could only speculate on the magnitude of the events which were taking place.

Devonport with its extensive dockyard and associated heavy industry, its harbours and military installations, often situated close to residential areas, was an obvious target. Obsolete 'Gloster Gladiator' fighter aircraft were brought to Plymouth's grass airfield and 'Spitfires' were moved to Hampshire to help cover the area and yet not leave south-eastern counties vulnerable. Attacks were sustained in the autumn of 1940, but the 'Blitz' which obliterated the city centre of Plymouth and that of Devonport came in January, March and, in an increased intensity, between 21-24 April 1941. The official estimates are that by then 1,000 high explosive bombs and land-mines and 27,000 incendiaries had been dropped on the area. Although the people of Plymouth responded splendidly to the ordeal it was revealed, 30 years later, that the question of sustaining morale was raised at a meeting of the Civil Defence Committee of the War Cabinet on the 23 April 1941. There were 1,172 deaths and in addition large, undisclosed service casualties; 40,000 people were left homeless and severe destruction was caused in the dockyard.

The first bombs fell on Exeter on the 9 August 1940, but the notorious 'Baedeker' raids took place in 1942. To put events in perspective—and if the World Wars have not resulted in a wish for a wider consciousness then the sacrifices which were entailed were made in vain—we have to start, as has been pointed out with detachment in *The Bombing of Exeter* published by the Institute of Education of Exeter University in 1973, at the strategically unimportant German Baltic town of Lübeck. It was a place to which the heritage of medieval architecture gave a civilized character. In the German way it was well cared for. On 28 March 1942 Lübeck was bombed by 234 aircraft of the Royal Air Force, which reduced it to a smouldering ruin. The bombing was the deliberate policy of Sir Arthur Harris, chief of Bomber Command, as part of his bold campaign to demonstrate to Britons and Americans how effective bomber aircraft might prove to be in bringing victory. If one keeps Lübeck in mind one can perhaps better understand the secret communiqué which went out from Hitler's headquarters on the 14 April 1942: 'Besides raids on ports and industry terror attacks of a reprisal nature are to be carried out against towns other than London.'

The worst of the Baedeker raids, so termed after the famous German publisher of guide-books, as far as Exeter was concerned took place on 24-25 April and 3-4 May 1942. In the latter of these unwarrantable attacks the Junker fighter-bombers flew up the easily identified Exe estuary and arrived over a city, which had already been damaged, at about 1.30 a.m. Flares and incendiary bombs were dropped as markers for the main force which followed. From the viewpoint of civilians the fires appeared to threaten the whole city. Fire tenders from as far away as Reading were rushed to the scene, but their task was made difficult as some of the water mains had been fractured by the high-explosive bombs. Many buildings were left to burn out. The German pilots descended to as low as 175 metres (about 570 feet) in order to achieve maximum accuracy; their rear gunners discharged their machine guns on the areas around the conflagrations. It was reported in the *Express and Echo* a few days later that an enemy pilot, interviewed on the German radio, had said: 'People were running everywhere and firemen were frantically trying to deal with the fires. It was a fantastic, fascinating sight'. Nine nights later, on the 12 May 1942, the first 1,000-bomber raid was directed against the industrial and Cathedral city of Cologne.

Among the Exeter buildings which were hit was the City Hospital, one of the oldest municipal hospitals in the country; it housed 200 patients. The building was struck by an overwhelming number of incendiaries and patients had to be evacuated by nursing staff. The Telephone Exchange was also hit; work continued until its staff were forced to fight their way out of the blazing building. Bedford Circus, a near-perfect example of Georgian architecture of national importance was destroyed. The German bomb-aimers carried out their orders with skill; neither of the two strategically important railway stations was hit nor, apart from a stray bomb which fortunately destroyed only two flying buttresses and the vault which they supported, was the Cathedral. It was bad enough, but compared to what might have happended it can be described as slight. Destruction was concentrated on the shopping, commercial and residential heart of the city. Fortunately, Queen Street with its Victorian buildings and half of the historic High Street survived. Thus was the tragedy of war enacted at Plymouth, Lübeck, Exeter and Cologne in the nineteen-forties.

Exeter and Plymouth were by no means the only Devon towns to suffer air attacks. Even Torbay was the scene of 44 raids; 313 bombs fell on the area in 'Tip and Run' incidents. Over 160 civilians were killed and 154 suffered from injuries requiring hospital treatment quite apart from 311 slightly injured. Excluding the centres of population, that is to say Exeter, Plymouth and Torbay, high explosive bombs fell on Devon on 210 days during the war and there were many enemy sorties with incendiaries and other missiles. The total number of civilians killed in these raids on smaller centres of population was 306, in addition six were reported missing and 284 were seriously injured.

The activity which took place in Devon skies was not, however, confined to enemy aircraft. Although the hilly nature of the county does not lend itself to their construction, there had for many years been aerodromes near Exeter, Plymouth and at Dunkerswell and there was another on the flat land beside the estuary of the river Taw at Chivenor; all these bases saw action during the war. Others were built at Bolt Head, Yelverton and Winkleigh. From an indifferent site at Chivenor far-reaching forays were carried out and the aerodrome's main runway was eventually strengthened so that it could receive the 'Flying Fortresses' of the Americans. Originally designed as an 'advance landing ground', the airfield at Bolt Head entered RAF history at the end of 1941 and in life-saving operations alone it more than justified its existence. During the latter part of the war, when air-power came into its own and it was vital to have more airfields, farmland at Winkleigh in central north Devon was requisitioned and the air base was constructed. The first aeroplane landed there in April 1943. The United States Air Force used this airfield for pre-invasion activities; the 406 Canadian Squadron equipped with 'Mosquitos' used it from February 1944 to patrol the Brest peninsula where enemy land and sea targets were attacked.

During the early months of the war many gun emplacements and other fortifications were built on or near Devon's coasts in case the threat of invasion became a reality. The Local Defence Volunteers, who were later to be renamed the Home Guard, developed from a partially-armed service into a force to be reckoned with, prepared, as it was throughout the kingdom, to adapt itself to guerrilla warfare should it become necessary. Little was it realised as such precautions were taken that Devon was featuring, in August 1940, in German invasion plans. It seemed most unlikely that Torbay and Woolacombe would be the sites at which German tank-landing craft would unload their cargoes, but that is that is implied by maps, photographs and coastal profiles then being issued to German officers. Plymouth and Exmouth, together with similarly-equipped Cornish ports, were being considered as disembarkation points for large transports. The life story of every civilian residing in these areas would have been radically altered if these plans had been put into effect, though whether or not the Germans were properly equipped to carry out operations of this type successfully is debatable. The disadvantages of south-west England as a bridgehead were better understood by the Germans in 1941. The *Detailed Geographical Survey of England for Military Purposes* (*Militärgeographische Einzelangaben über England*), published in Berlin, stated: 'The assembling of large bodies of troops, their deployment and movement will run into difficulties in respect of accommodation and supplies and on account of the broken landscape.'

The battle-training areas which were established in various parts of the county were the scene of much activity. Part of Dartmoor had served this purpose since 1875, but the ranges were extended in the 1940s. Braunton Burrows and its surrounding beaches became the site of assault courses, both British and American; and the adjacent Taw-Torridge estuary could offer everything that was required for the practising of amphibious manoeuvres under varied tidal conditions. In south Devon one of the most fertile stretches of agricultural land in the county was given up in preparation for the invasion of Europe. Three thousand people, their possessions, farm stock and equipment were moved out of an area of 121 square kilometres, including parts of six parishes. The period concerned was the last six weeks of 1943 and the first six months of 1944. The purpose of the evacuation was to allow American forces to practise assault-landings in an area which included Slapton Sands, the topography of which closely resembled the localities in Normandy where it was planned the liberation of Europe should begin.

American service personnel were present in Devon in a large number in the latter years of the war; the south-west was to a considerable extent their training area and place of assembly and the base from which they launched their attack. American ships, sailors and troops became a common sight at Devonport dockyard and the speed and efficiency with which they erected their living quarters on the bombed-sites was watched with much interest. In 1943 the Britainnia Royal Naval College at Dartmouth became the Amphibious Force Training Centre for the United States Navy and, just before 'D-Day', so.ne 4,000 American sailors were quartered in that area.

The men from the prairies and the Confederate South, from the shores of the Pacific and those of New England, were not all to endear themselves to their cousins of Old England, who, to the Americans, appeared to be 25 years behind the times. But many friendships were made and in off-duty hours and in various ways the Americans supported local community activities. The 'Stars and Stripes' still displayed in Cullompton parish church was one among many similar testimonials through which mutual respect was expressed. Some Americans were able to reestablish contact with Devonian relations after generations of separation. Above all this was clear—had there ever been any doubt in Devonian hearts that Britain would remain free—when, after the events of Pearl Harbour, American involvement at the side of the Allies became visible in the form of mechanized troops within the county and aerial Armadas above it, native confidence was turned into certainty of victory.

Devonians watched the build-up of armed might through the summer and winter of 1943 and there was much discussion as to when and where Hitler's defences would be breached. High-ranking British and American officers assembled at the historic Royal Hotel, Bideford, within sight of the quay 'where once a Grenville trod and Raleigh wrought' to confer in secret in order to formulate their strategy.

Plymouth Sound contained a collection of strange-looking ships which made their final preparations in safety, for the last incursion by the Luftwaffe occurred on 30 April 1944. Along the waterfront special concrete embarkation-hards and slipways were being cast. Even people who lived in the area had to have special identification papers because it became strictly out-of-bounds to the general public. In addition, as the great day approached, flotillas of naval craft which had been congesting the Torridge estuary in the north were seen to pass across the 'Bar'; they were on there way to join those riding at anchor in the south Devon harbours. A big convoy of larger ships from other western ports steered past Lundy. The river Dart saw the embarkation of 485 American landing and beaching craft. This epic event is commemorated by a modest memorial which is to be found on the quayside at Dartmouth.

The United States fourth infantry division which formed part of the

American First Army successfully stormed the 'Utah Beach' in Normandy on the 6 June 1944; it had trained in Devon and sailed from the south Devon ports. Whilst their American cousins were fighting on the western beaches, the second battalion of the Devonshire Regiment, part of the British and Canadian Second Army, moved through a cleared section of 'Gold Beach' to capture a village several miles inland; it was an assignment which was vital to the success of subsequent landings. At the same time detachments of the twelfth battalion of the Devonshire Regiment alighted behind enemy lines as part of the activities of the Air Landing Brigade, of the British Sixth Airborne Division, beyond the flank of the bridgeheads.

It was to be many years before the scars of war healed, but with the sailing of the invasion fleet and the successful establishment of the Normandy bridgeheads Devon was no longer in the front line. Two tragic wars which are possibly destined to change human attitudes more than any other events for thousands of years, were drawing to a close.

Some dates and events

Kent's Cavern occupied by early man *c*40,000 B.C.
Arrival of Neolithic people from France *c*3,000 B.C.
Megalithic period *c*2,000 B.C.
Bronze Age *c*1,500 B.C.
Iron Age *c*500 B.C.
Trading post active at the site of modern Exeter *c*150 B.C.

A.D.

*c*48 Arrival of the Romans in Devon.
*c*410 Britain severed from the Roman Empire.
*c*500 Migrations to Brittany begin. Partial depopulation.
*c*500 Celtic missionaries first active in Devon.
*c*600 Saxon conquest and settlement of the West begins.
*c*680 Winfrith, St Boniface, born at Crediton.
 900 Saxon *burhs* founded at Exeter, Halwell, Lydford and Pilton.
 909 The see of Crediton with Eadulf as first bishop.
 997 Tavistock and Lydford sacked by the Danes.
1003 Exeter sacked by King Sweyn of Denmark.
1005 Exeter made a bishopric.
1068 Exeter retaken by the Normans after an uprising.
1133 Norman Cathedral consecrated at Exeter.

1147 Second Crusade sails from Dartmouth.
1190 Third Crusade sails from Dartmouth.
c1200 Rise of the tin and textile industries commences.
c1300 Growth of Plymouth and Dartmouth.
1349 The Black Death first reported in Devon.
1356 Fleet of the Black Prince at Plymouth en route for Potiers.
1369 Gothic Cathedral completed at Exeter.
1373 Chaucer at Dartmouth.
1403 Plymouth burnt by Bretons.
1404 Breton attack on Dartmouth foiled.
1439 Plymouth; first English town incorporated by Act of Parliament.
1497 Perkin Warbeck attacks Exeter without success.
1539 Humphrey Gilbert born at Greenway on the Dart.
c1541 Francis Drake born at Crowndale Farm, Tavistock.
1549 Prayer Book Rebellion commences at Sampford Courtenay.
1552 Walter Raleigh born at Hayes Barton near East Budleigh.
1564 Construction of Exeter Ship Canal commenced.
1577 Drake sails from Plymouth to circumnavigate the globe.
1578 John Hawkins of Plymouth becomes Treasurer of the Navy.
1583 Humphrey Gilbert founds the colony of Newfoundland.
1584 Drake's captains explore the coast of North Carolina.
1585 John Davis sails from Dartmouth to discover the NorthWest Passage.
1588 Spanish Armada sighted off Plymouth.
1592 John Davis discovers the Falkland Islands.
1595 Raleigh's expedition to South America.
c1600 Expansion of the Devon ports.
1606 Plymouth Company given right to colonize American coast.
1609 Sir Thomas Rowe sails from Dartmouth to explore Amazon.
1618 Execution for political reasons of Walter Raleigh.
1620 The *Mayflower* departs from Plymouth for New England.
1622 F. Gorges, governor of Plymouth, granted territory in New England.
1639 F. Gorges becomes the first Governor of the colony of Maine.
1642 Civil War skirmishes at Exeter, Modbury and Torrington.
1643 Plymouth; three-year siege by Royalists commences.
1643 Barnstaple, Bideford, Dartmouth and Exeter fall to Royalists.
1644 Barnstaple reverts to Parliament then surrenders to Royalists.
1645 Tiverton Castle captured and Exeter surrounded by Parliamentarians.

1646 Dartmouth, Exeter and Torrington fall to Parliament.

1666 Construction of Plymouth Citadel commenced.

1685 Devonians support the Monmouth cause.

1688 William of Orange lands at Brixham and proceeds unhindered.

c1700 Development of Plymouth Dock.

c1720 Bideford and Barnstaple become large tobacco importers.

1723 Joshua Reynolds born at Plympton St Maurice.

c1800 Decline of the Devon textile and mining industries.

1801 Nelson visits Plymouth.

1815 Napoleon held prisoner on board ship in Plymouth Sound.

1824 Plymouth Dock renamed Devonport, commemorative column erected.

c1832 Twenty-year surge of emigration to north America commences.

1844 Bristol and Exeter Railway, later the G. W. R., reaches Exeter.

1846 the Duke of Wellington visits the Citadel, Plymouth.

1848 The South Devon Railway reaches Plymouth and Torquay.

1854 The North Devon Railway reaches Barnstaple.

1859 Brunel's Tamar Rail Bridge opened at Plymouth.

1860 London and South Western Railway opened to Exeter.

1904 The German Fleet visits Plymouth Sound.

1914 Devonport, Stonehouse and Plymouth united under one authority.

1918 Devonshire Regiment awarded 63 battle honours.

1922 University College of the South West incorporated at Exeter.

1940 Aerial bombardments of Plymouth and Exeter commence.

1944 Part of Allied Invasion Fleet sails from south Devon ports.

1951 Dartmoor designated as a National Park.

1955 University College becomes Exeter University.

1961 Tamar Road Bridge opened at Plymouth.

1977 The M5 Motorway reaches Exeter.

CHAPTER FOUR

Architecture in Devon

The county of Devon is richly endowed with parish churches, a splendid cathedral, manor houses and many examples of vernacular architecture. Though the quality of individual buildings may not be of the highest order the large number of good, modest buildings is not in doubt. There are perhaps 500 parish churches, approximately 1400 manor houses and traditional farm-houses and several thousand cottages. The church furnishings are particularly interesting; quite apart from the renowned rood-screens and bench-ends, Devon claims a sixth of the stone pulpits and a fifth of the medieval pulpits in wood remaining in England (ecclesiastical wood-carving is described in Chapter Five). The best architectural examples tend to be concentrated in the more prosperous towns, especially those in the southern half of the county; but one of the pleasures of visiting the buildings of Devon is that unexpected interesting details are widely distributed and may be found even in the more remote parishes.

A question frequently asked by visitors arriving at the Devon tourist offices is: Are there any castles that we may visit? In particular castles which are 'lived-in' are sought. Travellers who have visited the intact castles of France, Germany and Spain are likely to feel that those of Devon are fragmentary and so will those who know our own Berkeley and Bodiam. Apart from the notable exceptions of Dartmouth and Plymouth, the true fortifications of Devon survive only as ruins and they hardly reach double figures. Furthermore, the large stately-homes of the age when the English country house no longer needed to be fortified and which are a feature of some English counties are represented in Devon by Bicton, Castle Hill, Saltram and Ubrooke and on a smaller scale by Arlington Court, Clovelly

Court and Killerton—each in its own way a house of character set in parkland, yet each small and homely compared with the palatial mansions of the Midlands and Home Counties. It is to the castles of Devon that attention is first given in this chapter; thereafter the examples are dealt with in chronological order according to the recognized styles from the Roman occupation to the nineteenth century.

Castles and fortifications

When considering the military architecture of the eleventh to the thirteenth centuries Devon has four castles in a ruinous condition: the Rougemont at Exeter, Gidleigh, Lydford and Okehampton. In later days the large-scale fortifications constructed at Plymouth were designed to repulse seaborne attacks. Castles situated in inland Devon are generally on a small scale.

The Rougemont Castle, built or rebuilt by William the Conqueror in 1068, survives only in the form of a much-restored Norman gate-tower. Lydford belongs to the twelfth century; the keep stands on a mound or motte and there are visible remains of former bailey enclosing a rectangular compound to the west. The rectangular stone keep of three storeys, the main surviving part of the castle, was erected in 1195 for use as a prison. The castle as a whole had lost its military importance by medieval times, but it became the seat of the Stannary Court where offenders against the tin laws were kept prisoner. Around the castle the land surface dips steeply towards the gorge of the Lyd. Gidleigh castle, a small structure, probably originated in the last decade of the thirteenth century and is considered to be contemporary with Okehampton; it now consists merely of a keep.

Situated on a large rocky spur, on the outskirts of the present town, Okehampton castle commands the valley of the Okement. In the Norman period this was the strategic pivot from which the way in and out of Cornwall could be barred. The Department of the Environment, in whose care it is, has done good conservation work in recent years. The keep, standing at the highest point of a considerable site, is assumed to be Norman, but the details of the chapel and living quarters suggest the Gothic period. The castle in its original state must have been one of the most impressive in Devon. It is not surprising that it is now considered as a most romantic ruin. It was owned by the Courtenays for three and a half centuries; the family had come from France and were always a prominent force in English affairs.

The well-preserved shell-keep of Totnes castle stands on the hill not far from the town centre. Like many of the early thirteenth-century castles it was built on the site of an earlier castle, by Baron Judhael, in the time of William I. Judhael of Totnes founded the Priory and Castle at Barnstaple. The remaining castle mound suggests that here also was a circular keep on a smaller scale. Excavations carried out by B. W. Oliver in 1927 established that the foundations of the keep, consisting of two concentric walls, do indeed indicate a similarity to Totnes. A radial trench dug at the base of the mound revealed the existence, 4.3 metres (14 feet) below the surface, of the bottom of a moat 15.3 metres (50 feet) in width. Similar in size to Barnstaple is Plympton mound at the top of which some substantial remains of a circular keep still survive; adjacent to the mound the clearly defined shape of a large rectangular bailey may be seen.

Berry Pomeroy, Bickleigh, Compton, Powderham and Tiverton castles were built later than the above-mentioned. In each there are parts from different periods and the stylistic picture is sometimes slightly confusing. All eventually served domestic rather than military needs and with the exception of Berry Pomeroy continue as homes today. Tiverton castle is not very imposing, but it stands in a good position at the top of a cliff overlooking the river Exe. Two towers of the original structure, one round in plan and the other square remain; it seems apparent that a Great Hall was positioned between the two. On the east side there is a solidly-built gatehouse possessing in common with other parts of the building, some Tudor windows.

One of the more impressive of these castles is Berry Pomeroy. It is situated on the edge of a rocky escarpment amidst woodlands and some distance from the village and church. An 'L-shaped' range of living quarters backs onto the escarpment and defensive walls enclose the other two sides of the four-sided courtyard. At the angle of these walls there is a massive gatehouse with flanking towers. The most southerly of the two walls and the gatehouse are the only parts of the early fourteenth century which survive; they were erected by the De la Pomerois. The substantial ruins of the living quarters, with their range of mullioned windows, are all that remain of the house which the Seymour family built at the end of the sixteenth century.

Compton Castle is associated with the Gilberts, the south Devon family whose most famous son, Humphrey, founded the first English colony— Newfoundland. The building is situated north-west of Torquay and was obviously not sited with defence in mind. It appears that defensive works, in the form of curtain walls with towers, were first carried out about 1440-50 when the French were raiding the Devon coast. Today its towers and battlements present a varied and picturesque skyline. Within the building several pleasant rooms including the hall have been restored after a long period of neglect between 1800-1930 and made habitable again. Though the Gilbert family cannot claim an unbroken tenancy of their ancestral home it is now back in their possession.

Bickleigh, owned by the Courtenays along with Tiverton and Powderham, consists of fragments of an earlier range of buildings. The large gatehouse with its vaulted entrance suggests earlier eras, but the dominant influence is the Tudor period. Throughout the castle the rooms, with their cool, white walls and period furnishings, convey a charm which dispels some of its violent associations.

The significance of Powderham Castle is not immediately obvious today. It had no natural defences but was built in a strategic position for the protection of the Exe estuary at the end of the fourteenth century. Since then, the river bank has been reconstructed farther away from the castle. At first Powderham appears to have been little more than a fortified manor strengthened by four angle-towers; it was the chief Coutenay castle in Devon. It has often been altered and it cannot be simply classified.

Perhaps the best-known of Devon castles is Dartmouth. Today, with its sister castle at Kingswear on the opposite side of the mouth of the river it proves a picturesque subject on a calendar or postcard; it is, nevertheless, an example of the purely functional architecture of the period when it was first recognized that the requirements of domestic and military buildings could safely be separated. When it was begun in 1481 it was the first English castle planned with the idea of mounting artillery in such a way that there was an operational flexibility in the field of fire. Like all true castles this pair, guarding the entrance to the river Dart from whose banks the hills rise steeply, was planned to take full advantage of the terrain. Dartmouth Castle consists of two adjacent towers, one circular in plan and the other square; they stand on bedrock. The guns were mounted in the basement rooms near the waterline with the living-quarters for the garrison on the two floors above. The gunports were unusual at the time in that they were specifically designed to allow a degree of traverse for the cannon without increasing the size of the 'ports' themselves; in order to achieve this freer movement the openings were splayed internally. The armaments of Dartmouth castle were intended to be used in conjunction with an iron chain which was suspended, or perhaps floated across the river mouth on pontoons, in times of danger. Should the two castles fail to prevent the entry of enemy ships, a small blochouse, built a mile upstream near the quays themselves, at Baynards Cove, could engage them. This latter emplacement is but a short walk from the centre of Dartmouth.

Devon has a major example of seventeenth century military architecture in the form of Plymouth Citadel. It stands on the site of an earlier fort, a common feature in the history of fortresses, on an irregular rock-bound bluff. In medieval days a castle with four angle-towers existed at Lambhay, on the hillside near the Mayflower Steps; it was from these towers that the city coat of arms originated. The successor to that building, a small fragment of which still survives, was probably the fort built by Sir Francis Drake after the defeat of the Armada and this was eventually replaced by the Citadel.

The plan of the structure as it exists today can best be visualized as an irregular star consisting of a massive defensive wall within which, in addition to several buildings, there is much open ground. Many outer-works of the Citadel were removed in the latter part of the nineteenth century; until then it was possible for it to be suppled from the sea. In the language of military architecture the fortification was originally an irregular bastioned pentagon, complete in itself and consisting of three regular and two irregular bastions strengthened by two ravelins and horn works; they are surrounded by a deep moat on the north and west. The ramparts are 1.2 kilometres (about thee quarters of a mile) in circumference and in places 18 metres (60 feet) high and 6.1 (20 feet) wide. The chief military engineer to Charles II, Bernard de Gomme, commenced work in 1667 and construction was completed in 1675. The walls are built of limestone with granite dressings, but the main entrance and the west sally port are of Portland stone, so also are the three remaining, large ornamental-corbels at the upper angle of the north, south and east bastions. These corbels are thought to have been designed to support stone sentry-boxes.

Out of the original inner buildings only four survive: the present guard-room, the Governor's House, the storehouse—converted in 1844 to a barracks—and the Chapel of St Katherine-upon-the-Hoe. The chapel was enclosed by Sir Francis Drake's fort about 1590 and served as the garrison church which is still in use today. However, the original chapel was demolished in 1666 and was replaced by the present building. The frescoes

1   Hound Tor, Dartmoor: the core of a once much larger mass of granite.
Traces of a medieval village lie nearby

2 *Top* In contrast to the rest of the county the extreme south-east consists of chalk seen here at Beer Head

3 Hartland Quay: folded sedimentary rocks exposed to the Atlantic storms which have destroyed the quay

4 *Top* Sika deer on the granite tableland of Lundy. Many species of mammals may be found in Devon

5 Devon's hedgerows still form an extensive wildlife habitat: this lane, with its trimmed banks and mature oaks, is in the South Hams

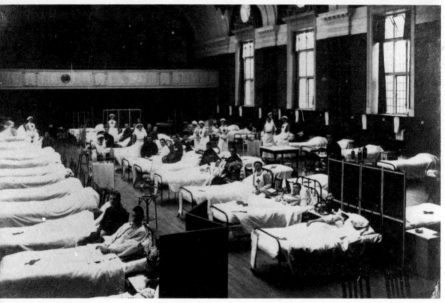

6   *Top* Ottery St Mary railway station, 1 September 1914: recruits leave to join the army

7   Torquay town hall used as a Red Cross hospital, in about 1917

8 The new city centre of Plymouth, looking towards the Hoe with Smeaton's Tower and the Naval Memorial

9   *Top* Torquay: the Tithe Barn of Torre Abbey, also known as the Spanish Barn and reputed to be the place where Armada prisoners were kept

10   The Almshouses, Moretonhampstead, with their arcade of distinctly rural proportioning and workmanship

11 Lake Farm, Poundsgate, near Ashburton, which was built in 1661

12 *Top* Dartmouth Castle, with St Petrock's church. Kingswear appears on
the opposite bank of the river Dart
13 Okehampton castle, depicted by the Buck brothers in 1734 before
romantic landscape was fully appreciated

14 *Top* Arts and Science buildings at the North Devon College, Barnstaple:
    since the 1950s the modern styles of architecture have affected Devon
    significantly
15 Castle Hill, Filleigh: an engraving from a study by T. Allom showing the
    mansion as it was until the fire of 1934

16 Queen Anne's walk, Barnstaple: no other north Devon building reflects Renaissance sensibility so truthfully

17 Exeter cathedral, the choir: an example of decorated vaulting. On the right is the bishop's throne, dated 1316

18   St Andrew's, Cullompton, showing how the rood-screens divided the 'hall churches' of the fifteenth century

19 An example of medieval panel painting on the parclose screen at Ashton

20, 21, 22 *Top Right and Below* Bench-ends, East Budleigh. The examples on the left and right, showing sheep shears and scissors, may be associated with wool merchants

23 The Norman font at St Mary Steps church, Exeter, one of the many such
fonts which survive in Devon

24 Devon lace: a late nineteenth-century specimen of a quality which collectors may still acquire

25 Brunel's Royal Albert Bridge, 1859, and the modern road bridge, viewed from the Cornish side of the river Tamar

on its east wall were painted by a non-commissioned officer of the Royal Engineers during the first World War; he was killed in action in France and no record was kept of his name. The Citadel's famous gateway is described in the section on Baroque architecture. It was originally provided with a drawbridge over the moat; the two slots in the stonework through which the chains passed are still to be seen above the springing line of the arch.

The Citadel, guarding Sutton Pool and the expanding town surrounding it, did not long remain the only fort in the area because of the possibility of invasion from the European mainland. The Dutch with their formidable sea-power were a threat to Britain in the early seventeenth century and in the eighteenth century the aspiring French were the chief forces that had to be reckoned with. The authorities in London were aware of the development of Cherbourg as a naval base and chose Plymouth as an English equivalent. A line of fortifications was begun beyond the limits of the town and dockyard in the mid-eighteenth century and further work was carried out on them until the mid-nineteenth century. In 1860 Lord Palmerston was instrumental in establishing a much more substantial series of forts in a wide arc around the city region. Two of these forts blocked the strategically important Maker peninsula in Cornwall; and a further related line of forts and permanent batteries were built into the ground roughly five kilometres (three miles) north of the Citadel. They formed a defensive line between the natural barriers of the rivers Plym and Tamar and, together with the forts that ring the Sound, had the effect of turning Plymouth into one of the most heavily defended cities in Europe. In their final form these forts were the forerunner of such defensive systems as the Maginot Line and Hitler's Atlantic Wall. Today, half buried in the ground, they are either overgrown with vegetation or put to peaceful purposes.

Except for Dartmouth Castle and the Citadel there are no castles of national repute in Devon, but there are in addition to the castle ruins, several fortified houses most of which are still occupied as homes. The appearance of these country seats has changed with the times, but at a number of places the gatehouses remain in their original form. Among the best of them is one at Bradstone Manor, south of Lifton, near the Cornish border. It is a picturesque three-storied structure with multiple gables surmounted by four large pinnacles and two of smaller size. In the same quarter of Devon at Morwell, south-west of Tavistock, the manor is more commodious than most for it was the country residence of the abbots of Tavistock. The Morwell gatehouse also has pinnacled turrets and there is a rib-vaulted inner gateway; most of this work derives from the fifteenth century.

Shute Barton, overlooking the lower valley of the river Axe, is one of the best and largest examples of a fortified manor house in the whole of Britain. The house as it exists today was built by Sir William Bonville in the 1380s. Extensions built in the latter part of the fifteenth century were later removed. The sixteenth-century gatehouse with its great doors, polygonal turrets and crenellations now stands astride the entrance drive flanked by grass and trees. Dorwich House, situated near Sandford in central Devon, has an embattled single-storied gatehouse probably of sixteenth century date though the house associated with it was rebuilt in Victorian times. At Tawstock, in north Devon, fire destroyed the sixteenth-century house in 1787 and the east front was rebuilt in an eighteenth-century version of Gothic; it has angle-towers and a castellated pediment. The gatehouse of the Tudor mansion with two polygonal turrets remains facing the hillside so that it cannot be seen to the best advantage; it bears the date 1574. By this time domestic architecture in Devon, with the exception of Castle Drogo completed in 1930, was in the process of being divorced from its defensive role. It is indeed significant that Dartington Hall, under construction in the fourteenth century at about the same date as Shute Barton, lacks any semblance of being fortified.

Roman remains

From what has been stated Chapter Three it is apparent that Roman occupation in Devon was centred on Isca Dumnoniorum, Exeter, and the south-east quarter of the present county. The actual remains of buildings which have been preserved have led historians to conclude that Isca was very much a frontier city: a bulwark strong enough to withstand armed threats to the Roman flank from the Dumnonii who occupied the remainder of Devon. Until the 1950s there were known to be two sites of villas: one at Holcombe near Uplyme, which is near the Dorset boundary; the other not far from the centre of Seaton. The visible remains are of minor importance even though, during 1978, the ground plan of the Seaton site has been discovered to be more extensive than was formerly thought to be the case. Small sections of Roman Road had been discovered in the Haldons and near North Tawton. They seemed to be sections of roadways formerly radiating from Exeter. In other parts of Devon there were various stretches of road known locally as 'Roman' whose actual origins were far from clear. The new knowledge which has been brought to light in recent years has been the result of careful excavation and research. Some investigations, the unearthing of the observation posts on the north Devon coast, for instance, comes more properly under the heading of archaeology and the structures discovered were intended to be of a temporary nature. But the remains of the buildings which have been revealed by the excavations in the Cathedral Close at Exeter confirm that the modern city lies across the site of a Roman colonial town adjacent to which there was a fort of the Claudian period.

Saxon

The centuries which followed the Roman withdrawal from Exeter must have seen a gradual deterioration in standards and, even within sight of the city gates, saw a return to building methods associated with a rural economy. It is doubtful whether or not Roman methods had ever been adopted by the native population. The excavations at Holcombe on the Devon side of the boundary with Dorset, which have been described by P. J. Fowler in *The Roman West Country*, appear, however, to show a development over three centuries; from an Iron Age farm, into a large corridor-type villa with an octagonal bath house of Roman type. But it is more characteristic of Wessex than Devon.

The Saxon conquest of Devon was complete; there is a noticeable scarcity of Celtic place names and yet there is not much visible evidence of their architectural work. The only known Saxon structure is the crypt of St Giles, Sidbury. It is a simple cell-like space underneath the chancel of the present church and is approached through a trap-door and a flight of steps. There are only a few such crypts in the country as a whole.

Parts of Saxon crosses decorated with typical linear interlacing have survived as, for instance, at Colyton where a piece is on display in St Andrew's; at St Brannock's at Braunton, where a section forms a window lintel and at St James', King's Nympton, where another forms a step; there are undamaged examples at Copplestone and within the Priory of St Nicholas, Exeter. At St Edmund's, Dolton, the font consists of parts of two separate Celtic crosses. The uppermost was inverted in order to make a larger bowl, thus the design is upside down. It is decorated with a human head from the mouth of which issues two animal forms suggesting the heads and necks of giraffes. Both pieces have considerable interlacing including five parallel lines of figure-of-eight work. Several examples of the reuse of cross shafts exist in other counties. St Andrew's church at Buckland Monachorum contains an extremely simple granite font of large bulbous form which is thought to be of Saxon origin.

The buildings of town and village in one period are sometimes superimposed on the street plan of an earlier one. The commodious village squares of Bradworthy, Northlew and North Molton have often been the cause of comment; it does seem that they are instances of the survival of Saxon ground plans.

Norman

The transeptal towers of Exeter Cathedral are major examples of Norman work. The church existing at Exeter at the time of the arrival of the construction-minded Normans was obviously one which they would wish to surpass. Bishop William Wavelwast commenced the building of a larger church which was consecrated in 1133 and it must have been magnificent; its nave probably ended in the usual style of Romanesque churches as a semicircular apse; and it had two sturdy towers standing north and south of the nave. They remain a unique feature among English cathedrals and are only represented in Europe at the cathedrals of Geneva, Lyons and Barcelona. The lower parts of the towers, up to the height of the nave, present impregnable surfaces suggestive of fortress walls. Above these levels there are superimposed bands of blank arcading and a frieze of intersecting arches on the north, and circular windows on the south. The battlements and rectangular pinnacles with their pennants, though similar to those of the Norman, White Tower of London, do in fact derive from the fifteenth century. Some Norman masonry remains in the lower walls of the cathedral as it does within the walls of countless parish churches throughout Devon. The Normans built so substantially that, rather than remove their work, it was easier to incorporate it in the new. The buttresses outside the north wall of the nave are also Norman; and the 1.8 metre (6 foot) thick walls of the chapel of St Edmund, at the north-west corner of the building, have suggested to some observers that the original Norman Cathedral embodied additional towers at its west end.

During the Norman period parish church plans were cruciform and they often had a tower above the crossing. Axminster, Crediton, Colyton and Tawstock churches still retain this feature though their towers have been reconstructed. St Mary's, Honeychurch near North Tawton, is a small church the plan of which has not changed since Norman times; though its history reveals that it was improved in the fifteenth century, it has been altered very little since.

Sidbury church tower, though not placed above the crossing, certainly appears to be basically Norman work. Its south and north facing elevations both have two-light Norman openings though there is also work of several other periods. Within the tower, on the ground floor, there is a room which is covered by the earliest rib-vault in Devon and its four corbels are unique. Two of these are carved with different lion masks, one has an Atlas figure and the fourth is carved in the form of a mythical beast; judging by their workmanship they appear to be Norman but they could be earlier. Another interesting Norman feature at Sidbury is the exterior of the east chancel wall which is decorated with a characteristic diaper pattern, cut in low relief.

A thatched chapel, situated just outside the walls of Bickleigh Castle, was used as a cattle byre for many years and the windows and door arch suggest Norman origin. The belief that it is second only to the Sidbury crypt in age is probably correct.

Far more numerous than complete structures are fragments such as Norman door surrounds, tympana and fonts which, for reasons that have never been satisfactorily explained, survive in quite a large number of churches; if they were ever brought together in a gallery they would make an impressive display of Norman architectural sculpture. Norman door arches are to be found at some 40 places in various parts of the county. Richly decorated examples may be seen at Bishopsteignton, Buckland Brewer, Shebbear and Woolfardisworthy near Clovelly; the last named has beaked heads and werewolves combined with the usual chevron mouldings. The tympanum at Bishopsteignton is remarkable for its primitive treatment; at Bondleigh, near Winkleigh, a semicircular tympanum in the porch depicts a lamb with a halo between two eagles. Within this church two Norman capitals with simple volutes are let into a wall.

At Down St Mary, near Copplestone, the red sandstone tympanum in the south porch portrays either St George and the dragon or it could refer to the local legend of a ghostly black dog said to amble through the village at night. In common with almost all these Norman-period carvings it has a crude simplicity more akin to African carving than to the fully-evolved sculpture of the Christian church in later centuries; it is tempting to regard them as Anglo-Saxon.

More than 100 Norman fonts survive in Devon. Many of these are of elementary form, like an egg cup. Simple undecorated examples may be seen at Clovelly and Instow, in north Devon, and those with decoration of the four semicircular surfaces at, for instance, High Bickington, north Devon. This decoration frequently consists of typical Norman chevron or cablework mouldings as found at Bideford; there are several in which rosettes are incorporated. The font at St Michael's, Alphington, near Exeter, is usually described as Norman but could, perhaps, be even earlier. The lower two-thirds are filled with a series of intersecting semicircular arches. The upper part is occupied by a border in inter-spiralling scroll-work within which there are various field-sport motifs: an archer, a figure with a spear, and another carrying a hare on an axe, and various birds and beasts complete the design. The suggestion that it was influenced by late eleventh-century calligraphy has been made by Professor Talbot Rice in his book on English Art of this period. Although its exact age is debatable this is certainly the best decorated font of its type in the county. At Marystow church, near Lifton, similar semicircular arches are to be seen between corner heads. The font at Ashwater, near Holsworthy, incorporating long-limbed beasts is more characteristic of Cornwall than Devon. Another primitive but animated carved Norman font is at Luppit, near Honiton. Without exception, and surprisingly, these fonts are older than the churches in which they stand.

Monastic houses were an important addition to the architectural scene in the wake of the Normans. Houses of the Cluniac and Cistercian Orders were founded in Devon. There is a considerable number of sites but very little of architectural importance remains. For instance, the church of Buckland Abbey, founded in 1278 for the Cistercians, only survives as the framework in which the Grenvilles and Francis Drake inserted an Elizabethan mansion.

Gothic: Early English

A new method of building based on the use of the pointed arch was introduced into Britain from France, where it had originated during the construction of the monasteries in the middle years of the twelfth century. Surviving examples of the thirteenth-century variation of the style, the Early English, are by no means plentiful and it was not until 1275 and the rebuilding of the main body of Exeter Cathedral in the fourteenth century, and in the second phase of English Gothic, that Devon produced an example which can be considered important at a national level. However, the period is not entirely unrepresented.

The Chapter House of Exeter Cathedral was built in the Early English style and the lower half of the building constructed during the period of office of Bishop Brewer, about 1225, retains its original form. Consisting of a rectangular hall situated beside the south tower, adjacent to the former cloisters, the thirteenth-century work consists of that part of the walls below window level. Groups of three Purbeck marble shafts, originally intended to carry a stone vault, are attached to the walls. The upper stage of this lower part of the wall is enriched by two blank arcades with grouped shafts. The capitals throughout are of the distinctive Early English style known as 'stiff leafed'. The windows of the upper walls and the fine low-pitched roof are of fifteenth-century date; there is evidence to support the theory that during the thirteenth or fourteenth century the upper part of the hall was damaged by fire and was replaced for that reason.

St Andrew's church at Aveton Giffard is the county's best example of a parish church of this period; although it was partially destroyed by enemy action in World War II it has, thankfully, been carefully restored. The tower over the crossing has not been rebuilt as high as it was originally but it is still contrasted with a smaller adjacent tower, of circular plan, by means of which access is gained to the belfry. Apart from St Andrew's, lancet windows and other Early English details are to be seen in various churches. Three of the best lancets are in the ruins of Frithlestock Priory near Great Torrington.

Though Buckfast Abbey exhibits some of the characteristics of this style and the nave walls appear to be Norman the building as we see it today was constructed by Benedictine monks between the years 1907-32. However, the Early English period is not the phase of Gothic architecture in which Devon is most rich.

Gothic: Decorated

The name given to the fourteenth-century development of Gothic architecture in Britain is 'Decorated' and Devon has a major example in the form of the nave and chancel of Exeter Cathedral. The whole of this great edifice survives in the single style—the longest unbroken stretch of medieval vaulting in the world. It is an excellent example of the aesthetic balancing of structure and style, a structural balance in that all Gothic architecture calls for the balancing of physical forces, a stylistic balance between the austerity of Early English vaulting, and the luxuriance of fifteenth-century fan-vaulting. The clustered columns of the nave have the same almost classic qualities that have been the subject of comment with regard to Chartres Cathedral; the vault ribs spread like palm fronds and yet are absolutely functional, the structure is decorative in the best sense. Ornamentation, where it occurs, in the corbels immediately above the nave piers and in the vault bosses for instance, enhances the structure. The whole building, with its outward thrust, is more securely contained than most cathedrals because the Norman transeptal towers serve as outsize buttresses.

Precise dating of the building is possible due to the survival of contemporary records. Building operations occupied three generations. It was begun in 1275 and by 1309 it was finished as far west as the crossing; the first bay of the nave was completed in 1317. The nave was completed by Bishop Grandisson, who had become bishop at the early age of 35, in 1327; he was able to write to Pope John XXII that the Cathedral 'is marvellous in beauty and when finished will surpass every church of its kind in England'. John Grandisson remained in office until 1369, by which time the cathedral, very much as it stands today, was completed. Most visitors to the edifice are unaware that his remains lie in a small mortuary chapel built within the west façade near its main entrance. The chapel was desecrated during the Civil War but is still structurally intact and retains a sanctified, monastic atmosphere. It was the decision to build the sculpture screen beyond the functional, load-bearing wall that enabled this chapel to be formed. The sculpture screen is somewhat surprising at first sight for it seems to slice through the design lines of the façade. However, there are in the screen sufficient echoes of the upper part of the true façade to unify the two. What a wonderful symbol this massed display of kings and demi-figures makes; and how much easier it has been to appreciate the sculptures since the removal of a layer of grime from them in the 1950s; in 1978 restoration of some of the damaged forms commenced. The cathedral contains much excellent ornament and sculpture of the 1275-1350 period quite apart from the screen.

In spite of the scale and richness of Exeter Cathedral it appears, with the exception of Ottery St Mary, to have had little direct influence on the design of other Devon churches. Bere Ferrers, Haccombe and Tawstock are among the few places whose churches retain much fourteenth-century work. Windows of the Decorated period occur here and there. The five-light east window which includes a star-like motif within a circle at Plympton St Mary, where there is also other fourteenth-century work, is said to be modelled on Exeter. On the whole the Decorated style was not popular in Devon though Slader has been able to compile an impressive list of examples.

The church at Ottery St Mary is second only to Crediton in importance among the parish churches of Devon. Bishop Grandisson, who had originally come from Avignon, bought the manor of Ottery from the Chapter of Rouen which had held it since the Norman conquest. In 1335 he converted the church into a collegiate foundation and decided to rebuild it. There are many interesting features in this church of which its three distinct types of vaulting are notable. The continental style known as 'flamboyant' did not affect England very much, so the chancel vault, consisting of a solid tunnel-vault of masonry superimposed with a curvilinear rib system presents a swirling pattern unusual in English design of this period.

The domestic architecture of the age is represented by a major example in the form of Dartington Hall. The builders are grouped around a quadrangle measuring 73 by 48 metres (245 by 157 feet) and the first impression that they create, due to the absence of any pretence at fortification, is monastic. This was, however, essentially a private mansion the origins of which go back to the twelfth century; but evidence still remains of slight alterations during later periods. It was mainly built in the 1380s by John Holland, Duke of Exeter and half-brother of Richard I. He was a tempestuous character whose pleasant home appears to have had little influence on him. The quadrangle is entered through a gatehouse made in a range of buildings which includes a good example of a fourteenth-century roof. The hall, with its well restored, hammer-beam roof is on the opposite side of the quadrangle; under the same roof were the Duke's living quarters and the kitchen. The two sides of the peaceful courtyard are now almost completely enclosed by ranges of domestic buildings; those on the north are the more interesting being almost entirely original and consisting of servants' dwellings. The upper floors are still reached by the type of outside stone stairways which were a feature of cottages in parts of Devon. Dartington had fallen into disrepair when in 1925 it was bought by Dorothy and Leonard Elmhirst; they turned it into the centre of a wide-ranging and enlightened organization embracing commerce, education and the arts.

The buttressed tithe barn at Buckland Abbey, built in the early fourteenth century and second largest in England, has changed very little in the intervening years. In writing about this period the famous long-bridges of Barnstaple and Bideford should also be remembered.

Gothic: Perpendicular

Fifteenth-century church architecture is the most common in Devon. According to Pevsner 95% of the work visible in the pre-Victorian churches dates from 1360-1530, which he aptly describes as the 'Golden Age' of Devon church architecture. This reflects in some measure the growing wealth of the county deriving from wool production and the other basic industries. Churches were enlarged and the work paid for by prospering merchants. Much earlier building appears to have been replaced by what was in fact a style that was more materialistic in its aspirations—a style that was to lead to the domestic charm of Elizabethan architecture. After this period, when almost every parish had expended its resources on its church, Devon turned its attention to wider horizons. The disenchantment with the Catholic faith and the ensuing relgious strife are reflected in a lack of attention to churches in general. Though there is so much fifteenth and early sixteenth-century work, it has several times been pointed out that the designs were standardized to a remarkable degree and, away from the centres of population, reconstruction was not on an extensive scale.

This great period of building produced a characteristic church plan consisting of a continuous nave and chancel of five or six bays, with north and south aisles running the full length of the building. The aisles are usually the same height as the nave. There is no structural division between the nave and the chancel in the form of a chancel arch, but the functional division of the space is marked by the rood-screen spanning the width of the church. To the east of the screen the parts of the aisles enclosed are used as side chapels and are divided from the chancel by parclose screens. These chapels are usually reserved by prominent families in the parish and contain their pews and ancestral monuments. A western tower and a south porch usually form a part of the scheme which is common in most of Devon.

The majority of towers were put up with the intention of making a strong visual impression and are of the type that have buttresses at right angles to the walls and set back a little so that the true corners are visible. In north Devon good examples are to be found at Chittlehampton, Chulmleigh, Combe

Martin, Holsworthy and South Molton; and in south Devon at St Andrew's, Plymouth and St Eustace, Tavistock. The most elaborate towers of all have polygonal stair turrets placed centrally against their main façade as at Ashburton, Harberton, Ipplepen, Kingsteignton and Totnes in south Devon. The down-to-earth Devonians had it seems little time for 'Dreaming Spires' pointing the way to heaven, but some do exist in the Barnstaple and Kingsbridge districts. Some have been lost through fire at, for instance, South Molton; it was, perhaps, similar to the broach spires still existing at Barnstaple, Braunton and Swimbridge, all near South Molton; they bear a marked resemblance to each other.

The culminating form of the Perpendicular style is its fan-vaulting of which Devon has a few examples. The best of these are to be seen above the Greenway aisle at Tiverton, the Lane aisle at Cullompton and the Dorset aisle at Ottery St Mary. The north-west porch of Exeter Cathedral has an attractive fan-vault; it is the only one in the building. The parish churches at Holcombe Rogus, near Sampford Peverell, and Torbryan, near Newton Abbot have smaller examples in their south porches; that a Torbryan, though slightly damaged, incorporates four carved demi-angels. However, the almost standard covering of the Devon churches is the timber roof known as the wagon roof—distinguished by having a curved brace to each rafter. Most of these have carved bosses which conceal the joints of the main intersections and the timbers are sometimes elaborately carved, especially the wall plates. Among the more notable roofs of the Perpendicular period are those of Cullompton, Chulmleigh, Harberton, Hartland, Hatherleigh, Sampford Courtenay, Stoodleigh, Tavistock, North Bovey, North and South Tawton and Widecombe-in-the-Moor. At St Mary Magdalene, Chulmleigh, for instance, there are wagon roofs over the nave and two aisles all having the same height. At each point where the nave and chancel rafters meet their wall plates, angels with outspread wings wearing crowns and carrying scrolls have been carved. Each intersection of a roof rafter and a beam has a carved boss. In this church, too, the plastered ceiling between the rafters is painted pale blue, the rafters are green, and the bosses and angels in red, blue and gold, stand out. Buckland Monachorum, has a roof in which much of the structure is hidden by the plaster ceiling, 16 large carved angels, each carrying a musical instrument, project from the concealed hammer-beams. The church of St James at Swimbridge has varied and richly decorated roofs including ceilures; carvings of angels are placed along the wall plate of the nave roof. To return to Exeter for a moment, the ten columns supporting the fine fifteenth-century roof of the Cathedral Chapter House each incorporate a graceful niche of the same period.

Comment on the famous rood-screens and carved bench-ends of the Devon churches will be found in the woodcarving section of Chapter Five. As far as the stone-carving is concerned the pulpits, fonts and monuments of the Perpendicular period are widely distributed in the churches of the county. On the whole, and with the exception of Exeter Cathedral, their standard of craftsmanship and state of preservation is not of a high quality. Stone pulpits are usually polygonal and in the six or eight sides there are often figures of the saints in the niches under flush or projecting canopies. A group of churches in south Devon has distinctive pulpits in which sturdy frames between the panels take the form of near-luxuriant polychrome carving of foliage and fruit; they hint that Devon was becoming involved with exploration of the sub-tropics. Wooden pulpits of the same form are described in Chapter Five. Most of the stone fonts of the period have a similar octagonal form. The figure carving that sometimes forms a part of these fittings is often of the most primitive type as if little progress had been made since Norman times; the font of All Saints, North Molton, bears this out.

Many of the Perpendicular chantry chapels and recessed monuments are noteworthy as ornamentation. This is very often due to the relative scale of the relief carving rather than to true appreciation of finely-carved forms. The overall design of the Kirkham Chantry at St John's church, Paignton, arrests the eye of the beholder and examination of the detail reveals some fine workmanship. Unfortunately, deliberate damage and neglect have taken their toll of this type of work. Typical examples of architectural ornament in conjunction with figure sculpture are to be seen at Ashwater, Bideford, Bondleigh, Colyton, Heanton Punchardon, Shirwell and Woodleigh. St Peter in Chains, Ashwater, has two somewhat damaged effigies representing members of the Courtenay family under a canopy dated 1442. St James the Great, Bondleigh, near North Tawton, has a battered figure probably representing the first rector of the church; the effigy lies in a tomb recess surrounded by quatrefoil decoration. The churches of Saints Nicholas and Ciriacus, South Pool, and St Mary, Woodleigh, both situated in the Kingsbridge area have Easter Sepulchres, with resurrection carvings, recessed in the north walls of their chancels. Of the two, Woodleigh is the more ambitious, having in addition carvings of the 'Deposition' and the 'Angels

Appearing to Women.' Unfortunately, both of these examples are in an imperfect state of preservation. In north Devon, St George's Georgeham, has a carving of the 'Crucifixion' in a similar state of preservation. The church dedicated to St John the Baptist, Holcombe Burnell, near Exeter, has a 'Christ Rising from the Tomb.' The church of the Holy Cross, Crediton possesses a combined triple-sedilia and recessed tomb of this period. The quality of the carving is among the finest, but again, regretfully, the work has been deliberately damaged. The exterior of the Greenway aisle of St Peter's, Tiverton, has an elaborately carved façade and south porch; built at the beginning of the sixteenth century it is unique in Devon.

Elizabethan

On first acquaintance the county may not appear to be an area in which half-timbered building construction was as important as it was in the south-east, the Midlands and Yorkshire; but sufficient examples survive to indicate that the method was often used in the towns from the early sixteenth century. The Elizabethan style of 'E' and 'H' house plans, together with the half-timbered town houses in which the upper storeys jut out over the streets, was popular in Devon about 1560-70 and continued to be an influence for many years after the death, in 1603, of Elizabeth. The window tracery of the Perpendicular was reduced to simple mullions, subdivided by transoms where size demanded it. The prosperity of many Devon towns of this period was reflected by the domestic architecture. Only comparatively few examples have survived, but even so they probably count as second only to those of Yorkshire and Cheshire in importance. The oldest of such town buildings is, in fact, of pre-Reformation date, the Prysten House of St Andrew's, Plymouth. It was built by the Plympton Priory and though much restored still has ogee-headed windows. The central courtyard has an open timber balcony on three sides, an unusual and attractive feature which is not original however, having been restored in the early 1960s. Close to the Prysten House, at 33, St Andrew's Street, there is a fine sample of the domestic architecture of the later sixteenth- and early seventeenth-century. Its three floors are supported by stone party-walls, of massive scale, on a foundation of bedrock. The main east façade is entirely timber-framed with mullioned and transomed windows, richly moulded, extending the full width of the building and the side party-walls are carried forward so that they are visible from the street. Inside the house there is a spiral stairway similar to the one in the equally interesting 'Elizabethan House' which is to be found in New Street in the Barbican, it is mentioned in Chapter Seven; the poles to which the stairs are joined could be ships' masts.

In Exeter High Street there still stand some good examples of buildings dating from the 1560s. One pair, numbers 223 and 225, on the north side, is five storeys high. The ground floors have always been used as shops and the shop-front style has changed with the times since they were first used by wealthy Elizabethan merchants. The upper floors give us a clear picture of the character of timber-framed building favoured in Devon. The projecting bay windows of the first and second floors have elaborately carved wooden sills and cornices. Above these the two uppermost floors overhang them. The merchants' own rooms were usually on the first and second floor and the attics were reserved for the servants or apprentices. It is to be borne in mind that this was originally a pair of houses each of necessity extremely narrow because original medieval plot widths were themselves narrow. At the rear of the front building there usually lies a small courtyard beyond which were further buildings. Examples of similar houses with back-blocks exist in Plymouth, Topsham and Totnes and formerly existed in Barnstaple; they are almost unknown in other counties.

Somewhat different from the town houses, on their valuable but narrow sites, are the country houses where Elizabethan work can still be found more or less intact. One of the best examples of an early Tudor house in Devon is Holcombe Court near the central section of the Devon-Somerset boundary. It originated about 1560 when Sir Roger Bluett reconstructed a typical one-storied manor house. In 1850 Holcombe was sold to William Rayer, who carried out a sympathetic restoration. The oldest part of the house, dated about 1530, is the south front which is dominated by a three-storied entrance porch and tower. To the right of the tower lies the great hall, over which is the long gallery with its fine plaster cornice and ceiling.

Until the Parker family moved into Saltram House in the middle of the eighteenth century they lived at Boringdon, where the ruins of their once splendid mansion remain in a commanding position near Plympton. Saltram itself still possesses at its centre a Tudor courtyard around which the work of later centuries has been developed. At Bowringsleigh, near West Alvington in the Kingsbridge area, a fifteenth-century manor was converted into an Elizabethan house by the Gilberts. Victorian work now obscures much of the original. However, a fine wooden Renaissance screen with fluted

Corinthian columns survives in the hall. Only a kilometre from Willand stands Bradfield, one of the largest country seats of the Tudor period. But although the hall has a fine hammer-beam roof and carved dates of 1592 and 1605 can be seen, much has changed since 1860. Near the picturesque village of Cockington, at Torquay, there stands in original 'E' plan house which was converted into one of the Georgian period. Nearby, at Newton Abbot, and on the Torquay road, lies Ford House built in 1610. It is a symmetric 'E' plan building which presents semicircular instead of triangular gable-ends. Farther inland in the valley of the Teign, and near the village of Dunsford, sits the Tudor mansion of Great Fulford with its square courtyard surrounded by mullioned and transomed windows of the period. The house possesses some of the earliest single-rib plasterwork in the county; since recorded in the Domesday Book in 1085 it has never changed hands. The 'E' plan was adopted by Sir Thomas Wise when he built Sydenham, his home near Lifton. Time, however, brought changes and although it still has a drawing room with Elizabethan panelling the general characteristics are predominantly Jacobean. It is pleasant to reflect that with the exception of Cockington the homes mentioned are privately owned.

In north Devon, the manor of Weare Giffard in the Torridge valley near Bideford was originally surrounded by both inner and outer defensive walls in which the present, oddly isolated, gatehouse could play a military role in turbulent times. The house now standing was built in 1450 in the 'H' plan manner with the great hall in the centre and two long, projecting wings on either side. Although the manor has changed owners many times the atmosphere of centuries lingers. Here are still the minstrel gallery, the wide open hearth, Renaissance low-relief work above the Tudor linenfold carving and secret panels, all under a superb hammer-beam roof. It is not surprising that ghostly legends persist.

Some people would consider that at Cadhay, near Ottery St Mary, is preserved the finest of Elizabethan architecture in Devon. Its history goes back to the thirteenth century, but John Haydon rebuilt it in the mid-sixteenth century from the materials of the nearby ecclesiastical college which was demolished in 1545. The building still retains many of the essentials of his structure. The south gallery, a common late-fifteenth century requirement, is 18 metres (60 feet) long and when it was constructed in 1587 had the effect of creating the attractive inner courtyard the walls of which have a chequer work of sandstone and flint.

Two groups of almshouses, one situated at Barnstaple and dated 1627, and the other at Moretonhampstead and dated 1637, have similar granite colonnades. However, the Barnstaple design (the Penrose Alms Houses), incorporating an 'E' plan block and having a charming inner courtyard, is the more ambitious of the two.

Renaissance and Baroque

It is suggested by the foregoing and from subsequent sections of the book that the Renaissance influence was gradually introduced into Devon buildings in the form of wood and stone carving in fortified manor houses and mansions and in the details of rood-screens, bench-ends and monuments of the parish churches, during the first half of the sixteenth century. Renaissance and Baroque architecture in their purest form are not well represented in the ecclesiastical architecture of Devon and little church building took place during these periods.

It is significant that Charles church, Plymouth, built in 1657 and named after Charles I, is pointed out as the only completely new church built in Devon during the seventeenth century, for it is Gothic in style though it had some classic interior features. The church was burnt out in an air raid and its shell, isolated on a traffic island beyond the east end of the Royal Parade, is retained as a memorial to the civilians who died in Plymouth as a result of the second World War. St George's, Tiverton, completed in 1731 is one of the best in the county of Devon in the manner established by Wren in his early churches. Rectangular in plan and constructed of yellow sandstone it has a pedimented façade and a clock turret from which the timepiece has been removed. Internally, the galleries are supported by pillars of a square section which in their turn, bear Ionic columns and the three shallow barrel-vaults still in their original colours.

The Exeter Guildhall demonstrates how buildings were adapted to meet the requirements of advancing time and how the architectural forms were superseded by later fashions. The interior planning and detail indicates the Perpendicular era, but the projection over the High Street pavement, supported by hefty columns, was added in 1592. It is a rugged provincial interpretation of the Renaissance which was understood more fully in later centuries. In the sixteenth century entirely new buildings were few, but monuments and furnishings in the new fashion were inserted into the churches of the earlier periods. There are large Renaissance memorials in the churches at Colyton, Dunsford, Tawstock and smaller ones at many others. They usually have columns or pilasters and brackets supporting a cornice or vault below which are polychrome sculptures often enriched by a background of heraldry, low-relief work and gilded inscriptions. These memorial monuments were often installed with little regard to the space available. The huge monument to Sir Thomas Wise at Marystow is, for instance, not in proportion with the interior as a whole. Few people nowadays are sympathetic to these memorials of death. On the other hand there are some delicate, gracefully proportioned tombs among them; there is a good example commemorating Frances Lady Fitzwarren, at Tawstock.

The Baroque was nowhere as popular in Britain as it was on the Continent and, compared to Italian models, English examples have an air of faintheartedness about them. Devon's best example is the gateway to the Citadel at Plymouth. It has two superimposed orders in which the columns are used in a purely decorative way. The lower storey has paired Ionic pilasters; on the upper storey a pair of detached Ionic columns flank a large niche situated immediately above the archway. The two stages are crowned by a narrower segmental pediment supporting a globe and flanked by single obelisks with crown finials. The gateway bears the Royal Arms and Cipher and in addition the arms of John Grenville, Earl of Bath. Above the Grenville arms is the niche already mentioned which houses four cannon balls. It is thought that it once held a statue of King Charles II and an inscription above tends to confirm this. However, it is known that it had been removed before the Earl of Bath surrendered the Citadel to William of Orange. Like much of the Devonian work of the period the gateway is really a composite structure having Elizabethan, Jacobean and Baroque elements. The design is now considered to be the work of Sir Thomas Fitch (1637-88); he was prominent in the building world of London and there is evidence that he acted on occasion as an architect and surveyor, but the gateway was formerly likened to the work of Wren.

Unlike most English architects Sir John Vanbrugh, who was born in London though his father was Flemish, worked confidently in the Baroque style and was the designer of Castle Howard and Blenhiem. The Gun Wharf at Morice Yard, Devonport, built in 1718—a curious symmetric composition in a castellated style, much of which still stands—has been attributed to him; he was indeed Architect to the Ordnance between 1718-25 and designed somewhat similar buildings at Portsmouth and Chatham.

The so-called Queen Anne's Walk at Barnstaple forms one side of what was probably intended to be a three-sided cloister colonnade and it functioned as a commercial exchange, the statue of Queen Anne being added later. It was designed to give semi-enclosure to the busy quay, one part of which lay in front of the colonnade. Built in 1708, in the Tuscan order, its entablature incorporates the coats of arms of local families in high-relief. It forms, as a whole, a free interpretation of the order, but even so no other north Devon building represents Renaissance sensibility so truthfully. Unfortunately, it became isolated from the river when the Ilfracome branch of the London and South Western Railway was constructed in 1874, the track being laid along the quay. The branch line is no longer used, which means that an opportunity now arises to restore to the structure some of the original intentions.

During the eighteenth century Georgian and Palladian influences dominated the design of the country seats such as Castle Hill near South Molton, Clovelly Court in its beautiful surroundings, Saltram House near Plympton and Ugbrooke near Newton Abbot; they are well-preserved reminders of a graceful way of living. With the coming of the nineteenth century the style didn't change much but continued in such places as Arlington Court near Barnstaple, and in Foulston's Regency legacies at Plymouth referred to in the following section. One of the most famous architects of the period, Robert Adam, was responsible for some fine rooms at Saltram and Ugbrooke. His noted rival James Wyatt designed the music room at Powderham. The eighteenth-century country home of Castle Hill, mainly the work of William Blore, was destroyed by fire in 1934, but was rebuilt and it remains Devon's most sophisticated example of the linking of a house and its surrounding landscape by means of a central axis, in the formal style of William Kent.

Nineteenth century

Long before the machine age, industrial buildings which utilized water power existed in all parts of Devon. Mill leats diverted stream and river water to the waterwheels, which turned grist mills in nearly every parish. The textile industry flourished from the fifteenth to the eighteenth centuries and tucking mills were situated at Ashburton, Barnstaple, Buckfastleigh, Sticklepath, Tiverton and North Tawton. When cloth ceased to be produced some of the mills were converted to the manufacture of paper. Comparatively few of these early industrial buildings survive. The mining of metals had been carried on from early times, but of the former large number of mine buildings, only the Wheal Betsy engine house near Mary Tavy survives more or less intact. It housed the beam engine by means of which the underground workings were kept free of water.

But, in general, Devon was bypassed by the Industrial Revolution and consequently was spared some of the soul-destroying and repetitive appendages which marred the development of towns and countryside elsewhere. The county gradually retired to the wings of the national stage, but this did not mean that it was cut off from the cultural and fashionable influences enjoyed by the rest of the nation. Georgian and classical architecture were well represented and this was reinforced when John Foulston came to live and work in Plymouth. Although only one nationally-recognized Gothic revivalist, G. E. Street, was actually a Devon man, several well-known practioners of the style are represented by buildings in the county. In addition Devon architects such as John Hayward (*fl.* 1840-70), designer of the Royal Albert Memorial Museum, St Luke's College and Exeter Prison, and his son Pearson Barry Hayward (1838-88) were responsible for many churches, though it cannot be claimed that these are as interesting as the works of the visiting architects. Much more is known about the lives and work of the personalities concerned in this period and it is convenient to describe them in more or less chronological order.

One Devonian architect, Andrew Patey (1783-1834) used new materials imaginatively in conjunction with traditional forms. He introduced cast-iron shafts to support an octagonal lantern above the circular roof of the chancel of St James, West Teignmouth, in 1820 and by reason of this it is unique among Devon churches of the period. A fourteenth century tower was incorporated in the scheme. Patey also designed St Michael's, East Teignmouth, built in 1822 in the Norman style, and he was responsible for the central feature of Den Crescent, the Public Rooms whose function has since changed.

John Nash (1752-1835) employed an even greater range of styles; he is of course best known as the architect of London's Regent Street and Brighton Pavilion. The year 1800 saw the completion of Luscombe Castle, near Dawlish, which he designed for Charles Hoare, the banker. It is an example of a freely-grouped castellated mansion in the Gothic style, having an octagonal tower and giant porch; it is situated in a pleasant wooded valley.

Nash also designed the nearby villa known as Stonelands; completed in 1817, it was for a time the home of Sir John Rennie, mentioned in this section.

Similar experiments with style, in combination with a growing use of cast iron as a structural reinforcement, marked many undertakings in Devon during this century. John Rennie the elder (1761-1821) can be described as an inventive civil engineer. His first work in Devon was Plymouth breakwater which was commenced in 1812 and completed, together with the lighthouse at one end, in 1844. This construction was a major undertaking involving the dumping of three and a half million tons of limestone between marker buoys. Finally, when the mass of material had been compounded by the action of the waves it was encased with dressed granite and, with its carefully designed cross-section, it has successfully withstood the assaults of the sea to this day. Though the inter-relationship of land and water had always provided many good anchorages in the Plymouth area, the ever-increasing tonnage of naval ships meant that they had to lie up in the Sound itself if they were to be avilable to sail on immediate orders. Being open to the south the Sound was never completely safe in a southerly gale until the construction of this shield.

Sir John Rennie (1794-1874), son of the above-mentioned John Rennie, designed the Royal William Victualling Yard at Stonehouse. This was built to house the supply departments of an expanding navy. Extending over 14 acres, nearly half of which were reclaimed for the sea, it soon became a landmark, and though neo-classic in its outward appearance it embodied a degree of functional planning unusual for the period; its roofs for instance were made of iron. The main façade consists of three parallel buildings and the massive gateway carries a large statue of William IV standing proudly. The yard was equipped with machinery designed by George Rennie, brother of Sir John.

Dartmoor Prison at Princetown was commenced in 1806 under the direction of Daniel Alexander (1768-1846) and the material used in the construction was granite. From an architectural point of view the overall plan of the original prison deserves more attention than it has so far received. Though few readers of these pages are likely to have the opportunity of studying it from the inside, the circular site, surrounded by its high wall, and the radial plan, by which the main buildings were laid out like the spokes of a wheel, was certainly in advance of most planning in England at the time; so too were the cast-iron piers used as structural units and also providing the means by which the prisoners' hammocks were suspended. The radial plan survives though the building themselves have been much changed. Alexander was also the designer of the Old Lighthouse, on Lundy, an original and well-proportioned example of building in granite.

A minor but interesting example of the early use of prefabricated cast iron units to create a structural framework occurs in the form of the palm-house of Bicton Gardens near East Budleigh. The upper part of these very early greenhouses, *c*1820, takes the form of three graceful semi-domes. Of the same period, and equally purpose-orientated, are the stone warehouses on the east quay at Exeter; they were erected by local building firms. At the same time, 1834, cast iron was being used to bridge the Longbrook Valley to make the northern exit from Exeter easier. The bridge has six arches each with a 12.2. metre (40 foot) span. Together with the masonry approaches, the overall length is 244 metres (800 feet) and it is one of the earliest instances of the application of the new industrial techniques to civil engineering in Devon. The arch spandrels contain tracery derived from Gothic architecture—a good example of the difficulty often experienced at the time in thinking of new materials and techniques except in terms of the older forms.

John Foulston (1772-1824) was not Devon-born, but came to Plymouth where he spent much of his working life. He also carried out work at Torquay and influenced the development of the town. He was a skilful architect in the classic Greek idiom and an imaginative town planner. It was Foulston who, by designing Union Street in 1815, gave material expression to a wish to link the 'Three Towns'—Plymouth Dock, Stonehouse and the town that had grown up around Sutton Pool—as the entity, Plymouth; actual administration unification did not take place until 1914. Unfortunately, many of Foulston's classical buildings were destroyed and some of his designs were never carried out. Nevertheless, those plans that did come to fruition gave a classic character to Plymouth that, lasting more than a century, made it one of the most distinctive of provincial cities.

Apart from Union Street, which was articulated about halfway by a circus and was considered, at the time, to be of extravagent width, the best examples of his public buildings are to be seen at Devonport. The finely-proportioned former Town Hall forms the focal building of Ker Street. The terraces which lined the street have not survived, but Foulston's Civil and Military

Library, 1823, originally intended as a Classical and Mathematical School and now the Oddfellows Hall, is an interesting exercise in the Egyptian style which became fashionable in the early nineteenth century when it first attracted the serious attention of north-European designers. Beside the Town Hall, on an outcrop of rock, stands the Doric column designed by Foulston and erected in 1824 to commemorate the establishment of Devonport in its own right. The column, 38 metres (125 feet) high, is not on the axis of Ker Street though it is aligned with Union Street, from which it may be seen in the distance. For the space between the Town Hall and the column and the Egyptian building, Foulston designed Mount Zion Chapel which was erected by subscription as a centre 'for Calvinistic Worship'—curiously enough it was conceived in an oriental style. Foulston explained that he thought a happy result might be obtained if in a series of edifices, grouped in close proximity, he exhibited the best characteristics of Greek, Egyptian and Oriental architecture. Unfortunately the chapel has been demolished.

Within a mile of these buildings stand other examples of Foulston's work. They are Albermarle Villas consisting of eight varying units disposed along a rising site which has distant views of the Sound and Penlee Gardens, Stoke Damerel, consisting of 13 residences grouped along the north side of a drive. In the centre of Plymouth, St Catherines, Lockyer Street, was constructed of Dartmoor granite in 1823. Several Greek motifs were used in its decoration; unfortunately it no longer exists, but on the east side of the same street, Windsor Villas, six identical units, typical of his domestic architecture, may still be seen. At Saltram House to the east of the river Plym, there is a good example of Foulston's interior work in the form of the library. It was in fact a conversion of two former rooms. The Plymouth Room at the City Museum and Art Gallery has some of the original perspectives by Foulston which show work such as the Public Baths and an Armada Arcade which were not actually carried out. One of Foulston's last public buildings, St Paul's church, may be seen in Durnford Street, Devonport and close to it is another house designed by him. The church is not one of his most inspired works.

Charles Fowler (1800-67), another architect who worked in the classic style, designed both the Lower and Higher Markets in Exeter, the town of his birth. The Doric portico of the Higher Market survives in Queen Street and is a reminder that, in London, Fowler's work may be seen in the form of Covent Garden Market. The façade of the Higher Market at Exeter has been retained in its original form together with the central ambulatory and rear portico, though the market itself, and much besides, gave place to the Guildhall Shopping Centre, a comprehensive development of which it became a part, in the 1970s. Fowler was also the designer of St Paul's church, Honiton, being a free interpretation of the Norman style.

Like most other English counties Devon has a number of buildings whose style was determined by the revival of interest in Gothic architecture. In addition to local architects such as John Hayward some of the more important nationally-recognized Gothic Revival architects are represented by buildings within the county. Unfortunately, but possibly of necessity, much genuine medieval work was swept away during the nineteenth century in the name of 'restoration' and was replaced by soundly constructed but generally uninspired work.

Sir George Gilbert Scott (1811-78) was active in Devon and carried out restoration work at some important Devon churches including St Andrew's, Plymouth, and Exeter Cathedral. He was also involved in the design of new buildings including the workhouses at Bideford, Tavistock and Tiverton and the chapel at Luscombe Castle. However, the visiting architects mentioned below were all responsible for complete buildings of much interest.

A. W. N. Pugin (1812-52) was passionately fond of the late thirteenth- and early fourteenth-century Gothic which he saw as essentially Catholic; he was however, rarely allowed to fulfil his dreams in a lavish manner. Lady Rolle of Bicton House commissioned him to design a mortuary chapel, situated beside the church associated with the house, to commemorate the death of her husband. The mausoleum has been described by Pevsner as 'amongst the most convincing buildings that he designed.' The monument, with its figures, heraldic leopard, greyhound and intertwined foliage in high-relief is supported by the design of the floor consisting of heraldic inlay tiles in blue, orange and brown, whilst above there is a small but beautifully coloured ceiling. Pugin also designed the glass for the church of St James, Alfington, near Ottery St Mary.

William Butterfield (1814-1900) was known as an uncompromising High Church architect who used stone and multicoloured brick to create stripes and geometric pattern in his original interpretations of the Gothic style. A conspicuous feature of his interior decoration was the use of low-relief diapers which do not always seem to be in sympathy with the structure as a whole. Several buildings were designed by him in south Devon. The church of All Saints at Babbacombe near Torquay, built during 1868-74, is characteristic of his work. It is basically simple, but even the columns made up of drums of different coloured marbles, the darker tones being at the top, reveal to some extent his thinking. The main sub-divisions of the interior walls are marked by raised stonework; within the shapes defined in this way there are alternate courses of red and grey sandstone. This decorative scheme has aroused mixed feelings but can be best appreciated as heraldic patterning. Local marbles from Petit Tor are used in the church, which also possesses a font, pulpit and lectern designed by Butterfield. Additional work by him may be seen at St Bartholomew's, Yealmpton and at St James', Alfington; they are both early works, being completed in the 1850s. Alfington, in the Early English style, is extremely basic and not characteristic; the interior of Yealmpton, in the Decorated style, has examples of his inlay patterning and painted roundels. This church has also a low chancel-screen made of local Kitley marble. At Exeter he designed the Cathedral Choir School and, in Victoria Park Road, Exeter School built in red brick with grey brick diapers and freestone mouldings. He was engaged to take charge of the restoration of the church at Ottery St Mary. Here he designed the font, which is one example among many of the craftsmanship that he encouraged in his churches. Other work by him includes the memorial cross commemorating Bishop Patteson who was vicar of St James', Alfington, for two years and was murdered as a missionary in the Melanesian Islands of the South Pacific ocean. The cross stands some 2.5 kilometres north of Ottery St Mary on the A30 road.

John Loughborough Pearson (1817-97) was an outstanding Gothic church architect who worked in an Anglo-French variation of the style. He is represented by several buildings in Devon, the earliest being St Matthew's, Landscove, near Buckfastleigh; another is St Mary's, Dartington, which Slader describes as outstanding. He restored Atherington in north Devon in 1884 and was responsible for the east window at Broadhempston church near Newton Abbot. His best known work in Devon is All Saints, Bamfylde Road, Torquay, 1884-90; here he introduced a wide polygonal apse and, repeating the style of his London churches, hoped to rib-vault both nave and aisles in stone. Unfortunately, for financial reasons, this was carried out only over the aisles, the nave roof being finished off in open woodwork; the church, including the vaulting panels, is of red sandstone. Among Pearson's better-known works outside Devon is Truro Cathedral

George Edmund Street (1824-81) was a pupil of George Gilbert Scott. He travelled extensively and started his practice at Oxford where Webb and Morris were among his first assistants. He liked to work out the designs of the smaller details of his buildings, including their furnishings, himself; St John's, overlooking the harbour at Torquay, is a most notable example. The interior of the church is full of surprises. There are two large paintings by Burne-Jones, who also designed the west window which in turn was made by the famous William Morris company. The arcade columns, the chancel-rail and steps are formed from local marble which was quarried at Ashburton and also at Petit Tor only eight kilometres along the coast. The mosaic panels were created by an Italian from Murano. The fabric of the church is composed in the main of limestone from the cliff against which it is built and which had to be cut back in order to create the site. The tower of St John's was designed by A. E. Street, brother of G. E. Street, and was not erected until 1884. G. E. Street also designed the church of St James at Huish, near Dolton in 1833, but it is not among his best work. He is of course most famous as the designer of the Law Courts, adjacent to the Strand, in London.

William Burges (1827-81) planned Knightshayes Court near Tiverton for John Heathcote-Amory. It is a rare survival of his work, but little of his elaborate interior decorative scheme was completed. The house has an almost symmetric front elevation, more Tudor than Gothic, in which freestone window tracery is seen to advantage against the red sandstone walls. Various Gothic features such as turrets and lancet windows, all marked by the deliberate robust details favoured by Burges, are seen to better effect in the rear and side elevations. The interiors, some of which have survived, were designed both by Burges and J. C. Crace, they are good examples of the influence that William Morris and the Arts and Crafts Movement exerted in that period.

Whilst Victorian church designers were seeking inspiration by looking back in time, engineers were using industrial techniques and materials to create new forms that were eventually to lead to the architecture of the twentieth century.

Isambard Kingdom Brunel (1806-59) made no compromise when he designed the Royal Albert Bridge to carry the Great Western Railway across the formidable river barrier between Devon and Cornwall. The railway track had to be elevated sufficiently above water-level to take advantage of the lie of the land and allow the tall-masted ships of the period to pass underneath. The solution that he devised was an ingenious one: it combined the arch and suspension principles. The two arches consist of eliptical tubes 5 metres (16 feet 9 inches) wide, having a curved length of 140.5 metres (461 feet). The outward thrust of these arched-tubes on their abutments counteracts the inward pull of the suspension chains. The tubes were constructed on the Devon side of the Tamar near Ferry Passage; and were tested on the site with a load of 1,190 tons. They were floated out, with the help of the Admiralty, and positioned above the supporting piers on which the ends rested when the tide went down. The problem was then to raise these immense structures to a height of 30.5 metres (100 feet) above water-level at high spring tide and keep them there on the stone abutments. Under each end, three hydraulic jacks were placed; the one in the centre alone, or the two others together being sufficient to lift the end of the span. Lifting was done three feet at a time and occupied the last quarter of 1857 and most of 1858. The masonry towers were built up and allowed to set under the spans as they were jacked up. On the 3 May 1859 Brunel's greatest undertaking and one of the world's most ingenious bridges was officially opened; in the same year Brunel died and to his memory his name was set up on the cappings of the bridge.

Two architects who represent the transition period in the domestic field between the nineteenth-century styles and the architecture of the twentieth century were Shaw and Lutyens. The buildings of Richard Norman Shaw (1831-1912) are representative of later Victorian tendencies. He had formerly designed brick houses under Dutch influence, but he is best remembered for his work at Bedford Park, Middlesex, the earliest Garden Suburb. He also came under the influence of the Gothic revival and, in some of his large country houses he reintroduced the Elizabethan style; Flete, situated on a hill-side overlooking the valley of the Erme in south Devon, is one such building. Shaw incorporated the moderately-sized Elizabethan house, which stood there, in the much larger mansion with its varied elevations which he planned around it. The prominent tower housing the main doorway is not dissimilar to that at Holcombe Court and it is a reminder too, of Castle Drogo. Flete is indeed more suggestive of Lutyens than typical of Shaw.

Sir Edwin Lutyens (1869-1944) was greatly influenced by the Arts and Crafts movement and he clearly experiments with the basic forms of his buildings and sometimes achieves genuine monumentality. Castle Drogo,

Drewsteignton, is a complex structure, though when Lutyens commenced it in 1910 most of his work had been domestic in scale. The visual pleasure of Castle Drogo rests both on its proportions and on the treatment of wall planes which are set off, one against the other, by the non-alignment of the two main parts of the building and by the use of recessed sections of façade. It is also a good example of the correct and fine use of local material in this case Dartmoor granite. Lutyens was involved with other buildings in Devon, among them Littlecourt, Tiverton, in 1914; Saunton Court in 1932; and the Drum Inn at Cockington in 1934.

The buildings mentioned in the above paragraphs are decidedly picturesque when compared with the new architecture, based on the use of the steel frame and reinforced concrete, which was being developed by the leading architects of the period. It was not until the rebuilding following the end of the second World War that these modern influences spread widely in Devon. Genuine examples of 'modern architecture' built during the first half of the twentieth century are uncommon. The only group, consisting of schools and related buildings, was constructed in the 1930s to the designs of William Lescaze, among others, in the vicinity of Dartington Hall. Born in Geneva, Lescaze, (1896-1969) practised in New York, where he helped to introduce the international style in domestic buildings, and it is pleasing that Devon has some examples of his work. Unfortunately, much of the domestic building of the day consisted of monotonous ribbon-development on a large scale and is to be seen in most of the town and city suburbs. Today, new community buildings such as schools and hospitals are a reminder that since 1950 the county has been involved in a great surge of activity in which the influence of 'functionalism' and the widespread use of mass-produced structural materials and cladding is clearly evident.

Though there are many books on the subject of the buildings of Devon no single work attempts to treat the subject exhaustively. Since 1952, however, students have been greatly assisted by being able to refer to Professor Nikolaus Pevsner's two volumes in the Buildings of England series: *North Devon* and *South Devon*. The provide a lively and usually reliable commentary on almost every building of note at that date. In 1968 a detailed study *The Churches of Devon* by J. M. Slader was published and with its careful analysis of the Gothic periods and architectural features and furnishings in the form of appendices, it is essential reading for anyone interested in the subject; so too is the relevant section of the regional guide of the former Ministry of Public Buildings and Works and much information about Devon buildings is given in *Regional Architecture of the West of England* by A. E. Richardson and C. L. Gill, published in 1924. There are many detailed articles on individual buildings and themes in the *Transactions of the Devonshire Association* and in the case of ecclesiastical buildings leaflets may be purchased at many of the churches. The Devon County Council have recently published *Devon's Traditional Buildings* in which the work of ten experts on the subject is brought together.

Building materials and methods

In the following paragraphs, which should be related to the relevant parts of chapter one, attention is drawn to materials. The wide variety of rock types found in Devon has had a profound influence on building construction. The areas where sedimentary rocks occur, those consisting of granite and those where the red sandstone is found have each produced distinctive architectural form and colour. Though not always of the best quality, stone is available everywhere in Devon and its presence accounts for the relatively late use of bricks.

Large areas of central, north and south Devon did not have access to building stone of the best quality, but local quarries extracted the sedimentary rock and sandstones which could be used for building coursed stone walls and sometimes produced serviceable roofing slates. These rocks were the material used in the construction of farm buildings throughout much of Devon and in some instances stone and cob were used side by side. Though the stone is sometimes of a texture that does not enable it to be 'dressed'; farms and bartons made of it have been mellowed by the effects of climate and the growth of lichens. With their protective trees, such buildings become focal points in the landscape of which they seem to be a part; this is not surprising for the small quarries from which the stone was hewn will, as often as not, be situated close to the buildings themselves.

GRANITE: On Dartmoor and around the moorland fringe granite is almost universal as a building material. Evidently boulders, large and small, were originally scattered over the surface of extensive areas of the moor. These formed a readily-available material for the building of field walls; indeed the making of an enclosure was the obvious way of using the stone cleared from the land. This same 'moor-stone', as it was called, formed the rubble masonry of medieval Dartmoor farms. Though granite is an extremely hard stone to work and its use for window tracery and arch mouldings results in the loss of crisp detail so that very little is attempted, it is sometimes produced as dressed stone with even faces. There are several good examples of this 'ashlar' work on and around Dartmoor; for instance, the churches at Chagford, Drewsteignton, Mary Tavy and Widecombe-in-the-Moor and the prison at Princetown. Castle Drogo, overlooking the Teign valley, is a twentieth-century example. In north Devon the granite which appears in churches such as those at Alwington, Clovelly and Woolfardisworthy was brought from Lundy where there are several granite buildings including one splendid example, the Old Lighthouse.

RED SANDSTONE: As pointed out in Chapter One, the red rocks of the Permian period occur along the south coast from Budleigh Salterton to Paignton and their extension inland covers a considerable area including Exeter and Crediton. The rocks were quarried at an early date at various localities. The stone was used for the Roman wall, the Norman castle and the medieval wall of Exeter; and it was extensively used in the church building of the late fourteenth and fiteenth centuries. Both Romans and Normans quarried the red basaltic rock of the Northernhay and a volcanic outcrop of Heavitree has been identified as the source of the stone used in the medieval churches. The intensity of the red varies from one district to another, but almost everywhere it has the warmth associated with red and it compensates for the absence, until the late seventeenth century, of the varied reds of brick. The colour is often strong, the church of St Mary Steps, for instance, having stone of an almost crimson hue. Red-rock quarries of medieval date are situated at Broadclyst, Poltimore and Whipton in the Exeter district, and at Exminster, Kenn and Ugbrooke south and south-west of the city. As close inspection of the exterior walls of the churches will reveal, the rock is often a breccia, the consolidated fragments of which it is made up being clearly visible.

BEER FREESTONE: The most useful of the Devon rocks from the stone mason's point of view is Beer stone. The underground quarries from which it is extracted are situated about one kilometre from the village; evidence that the stone may have been quarried there during Roman times has come to light among the remains of that period in Exeter. It can be cut easily and its lack of grain allows the monumental mason to produce mouldings and other decoration with the minimum of difficulty, yet it hardens after exposure to air. When quarried it is cream in colour but after a while it turns greyer. The older cottages of Beer and such local churches as Salcombe Regis, Sidmouth, and Ottery St Mary embody it in their structures. Beer stone was also used at other places along the south Devon coast to which it could easily be transported by sea; it was for instance used in the construction of the stone screen at St Mary's, Totnes; but it does occur as far inland as Ashton. The façade of Exeter Guildhall, with the exception of the granite columns, is also an example of its use.

LIMESTONE: The Middle Devonian limestones of south Devon are prominent as a building material at Brixham, Newton Abbot, Plymouth and Torquay. Some of the beds are almost entirely organic in origin and consist of accumulations of coral debris; they are quarried near Ideford in an almost white form, but more common are those that are of cool grey pigmentation. The bulk of Plymouth breakwater was constructed of limestone which was quarried conveniently close at Oreston and transported to the site in barges; the embankment formed in this way was faced with Dartmoor granite.

MARBLES: Many of the Devon limestones are sufficiently hard to take a high polish and rank as marbles. They are quarried at Ashburton, Ipplepen near Newton Abbot, Plymouth and Torquay. In the last century they were widely used for the interior decoration of churches. A good example of the use to which they were put is the Victorian font of St Mary's church at Ottery. It was designed by William Butterfield in 1850, the bowl is cut from Ipplepen marble and the base derives from a Plymouth quarry; another Butterfield font in a local marble is to be seen at All Saints, Babbacombe. St John's overlooking the harbour at Torquay has Devon marbles in the form of clustered shafts with bands of contrasting colour.

LAVA: Found in isolated patches to the north and west of Exeter and was quarried at Silverton, at Budlake near Killerton, at Raddon west of Thorverton and at various other places. The grey-green volcanic rock of Hurdwick, a quarry within a kilometre of the centre of Tavistock, is much in evidence in the buildings of the town.

FLINT: One of the less common building materials as far as this county is concerned is flint, but in east Devon where it occurs in association with the chalk, it was used in the construction of the church at Axminster and a few other buildings in and around the town.

BRICK: Apart from its use by the Romans, brick was not in common use as a building material in the county until the middle of the nineteenth century. Records tell use that Stevenstone House was rebuilt in brick by the 1540s, but the Custom House dated 1681 is one of the earlier examples in Exeter, and it appears that it was the beginning of the eighteenth century before brick was more widely used, although clay suitable for its production was available within Devon. In the rural buildings chimneys were frequently extended or reconstructed in brick as it became available.

COB: The 'cob' of the cottages and farms is typical of the rural buildings of Devon; it was seldom used in the urban areas. Made from a compound of clay and straw, sometimes with the addition of river pebbles, it could easily be produced and its survival in almost every part of Devon testifies to its load-bearing and insulating properties when properly maintained. Cob walls have to be made a metre or more thick and they need to be built on a plinth of stone, or preferably slate, to protect them from rising damp. The material was cheap and widely used; any industrious man could partake in the work of raising the mixture onto the wall and treading or pounding the plastic material into form in layers, each of which was left to dry out before building the next. The rough surfaces were trimmed when dry and the final finish to the wall surface was a thin coat of limewash probably of biscuit colour in earlier times, white during the nineteenth century; it is no longer true to say that cob is whitewashed in the north and buff-washed in the south of Devon. As soon as it became easily available, pitch was applied to render the first foot or so of the outside wall more impervious. Carried on its rough-hewn timbers, the thatch roof required a pitch in excess of 45 degrees and had to overhang the walls; it probably required patching about every 25 years and renewing every 25-40 years. This then is the ethnic architecture of Devon. The style was highly functional; far from being dainty it would border on austerity were it not for the flowers of climbing plants often cultivated beside the front porch. Unfortunately, there is a failure on the part of those who move into the area to appreciate the true nature of the style—the comment applies equally to some of the local inhabitants. Modern mass-produced sun porches, large deliberately 'crafty' windows and vivid paintwork have no place in the genuine Devon cottage. It is not easy today to discover an unadulterated example, but they do still exist, even in groups in some villages.

CHAPTER FIVE

Some Devonian Crafts

Whether the four basic occupations of agriculture, mining, fishing and the production of textiles, or the smaller-scale trades and crafts are concerned, Devon is a place where industrious men and women have been able to work to the advantage of themselves and their communities; this is as true today as it was when Drake set his sails to circumnavigate the earth. The importance of the county in relation to England as a whole and the Devon industries in relation to each other has, however, varied considerably over the centuries. Crafts are associated with industries. With fishing, for example, went ship-building, which in essence involved working with wood. It comes as no surprise, therefore, that woodcarving has flourished in Devon—not only to provide the utilitarian necessities of life, but also as an embellishment of church, town hall and manor house. It may be noted that in the fifteenth and sixteenth centuries Devon enjoyed a good standard of living because trade and industry were thriving. In this chapter, four basic materials: thread, metal, wood and clay, each with its own special qualities, underlie the distinctive work produced by Devon craftsmen.

Devon lace

Two different methods are employed in the production of lace, one associated with the needle, the other with the bobbin. In order to understand the characteristics of Devon lace it is first necessary to have some appreciation of these techniques. In 'Needlepoint Lace' the pattern, in the form of a drawing, is sewn down on a strong material. The design lines are then overlaid with thread secured in position by another thread which is taken down through the underlying material. The thread so fixed becomes the framework on which the design in the form of filled-in shapes or openwork motifs is developed, using the buttonhole stitch. Needlepoint has been aptly described as 'self-supporting embroidery' because when the work is finished it is detached from the backing material. In 'Bobbin Lace' the pattern, in the form of a 'pricking' made of paper or thin card, is attached to a pillow and the threads are supplied from a number of bobbins which are of sufficient weight to keep the correct tension as they hang at the side of the pillow. Pins are used as the fixed points between which solid woven areas, lines or joining-bars are made through two basic movements of the bobbins—twisting and crossing; pins are also used to retain the developing work in position on the pillow.

The earliest Devon lace is reputed to have been a needlepoint made by the nuns of Ottery St Mary early in the sixteenth century. Even if this is correct no known examples remain to prove it; however, the manor was held by the Chapter of Rouen in Normandy, a lace-making region, so there may be some truth in the supposition. A further possibility is that the nuns were responsible for the importing of continental lace and it is of course possible, too, that some form of primitive lace or drawn-thread-work was produced in Devon during even earlier centuries.

The lace-producing areas of Europe were widespread: Scandinavia, the Iberian peninsula and Greece were all much involved. The craft reached its greatest refinement in Italy, France and the Low Countries and possibly it was from the latter that bobbin lace production was introduced to Devon, the well-known 'Honiton Lace' being of this type. Among the refugees who were able to escape from the Duke of Alva's reign of terror were some Flemish Protestant lacemakers who are believed to have settled in Devon and also in other lace-making areas of England between 1568 and 1577; it should be noted that the Collegiate Church at Ottery St Mary had been dissolved by Henry VIII in 1545. At this time the Low Countries were far in advance of England in the development of weaving techniques and similar activities. Although the full details of the arrival of the refugees are not known, a continental influence is evident in the lace. South-east Devon eventually benefitted from the transfusion of this new skill; Beer, Branscombe, Ottery St Mary, Sidbury and Upottery became the most active centres. The best work was unaffected and soundly-made and the total effects which were created had much delicacy. Honiton was the point of dispatch for the London market. The use of the term 'Honiton Lace' has led people to believe that lace-making was confined to the town.

Bobbin lace is also known by other terms; 'Pillow Lace' and 'Bone Lace' refer to equipment used in its production. In Devon the pillows were usually made with a diameter of 320mm (just in excess of a foot), though they would sometimes be larger; they had a depth of about 150mm (six inches). They were made of cotton and tightly stuffed with bran or chopped straw. In some regions a stand was used to support the pillow and this may also be true of Devon, though old photographs show Devon lacemakers with the pillows on their laps. A cover cloth, usually blue in colour in the Honiton district, was used to protect the pillow when it was not in use. It has been suggested that fish bones were originally used as pins and that the bobbins were made from the foot bones of pigs and sheep. Spindle wood was considered to be the best material from which to fashion bobbins and the Devon examples are light in weight, having small heads and slim shanks with points at their lower ends. Early Devon bobbins were decorated with coloured spots or stripes, some were engraved with initials or rhymes, but most were extremely simply finished. The method of using this equipment is attributed to the Flemish Huguenots, although Flemish lace, in its turn, appears to have been derived from Italy. The technique as it was practised in Devon involved the production of small separate sections or motifs, usually referred to as 'sprigs', which were then assembled either by sewing on to a net 'ground' or by joining with a series of needle-made bars. Before the introduction of cheap, machine-made net the connecting ground was also made on the pillow.

Other types of lace produced in Devon took the form of continuous strips. 'Trolley Lace' consisted of strips worked round and round a bolster. Braid laces were sometimes produced, using fine pillow-made or machine-made braid or tape as a foundation. A lace of this description was associated with Branscombe and was known as 'Branscombe Point'. The design was drawn on brown paper and the tape was then arranged on it in accordance with the design. Working between the tapes with a needle, in-fillings were developed and elaborated. Other laces were made in deliberate imitation of foreign styles in an attempt to broaden the scope of the local craft and arrest its nineteenth-century decline.

Travellers who passed through Devon during the seventeenth and eighteenth centuries remarked on the production of lace in their journals. They were seeing the cottage industry at its peak—a metre of lace would have cost just over £6 in 1698 and craftswomen, able to maintain a good standard of living, were distributed over a wide area. For much of the eighteenth century Devon lace was said to be the equal in quality and similar style to that of Brussels, but in general English lace could not compete with the fine naturalism of Flemish and French work. By this date Devon had developed its own distinctive, somewhat simplified style; the designs are often based on flowers, especially roses, and leaves, the infilling of which almost always consisted of a network of tiny squares or rectangles sometimes referred to as 'leadworks'.

The hand-made net connecting-ground was time-consuming to produce and when John Heathcote established his lace factory at Tiverton, in 1816, the cheaper machine-made product was soon in demand for this purpose. Machine production began to reduce the market for the hand-made variety and as less work was done so the design standards tended to fall—unless the work happened to be supervised by a skilled designer. Renewed impetus was given to the industry when Queen Victoria placed an order for her wedding dress in 1839; it now forms part of the collection of the London Museum. The work of making it was organized by Miss Jane Bidney of Beer and production was shared by 100 workers. In due course the Queen ordered a christening robe which has been used for royal christenings ever since. The Great Exhibition of 1851 also stimulated interest in Devon lace.

If the 'prickings', by means of which the original drawings were interpreted, passed from one worker to another they were liable to be misunderstood and the design deteriorated. When this was combined with poor workmanship the result was shoddy, uninspired lace. Mrs C. E. Treadwin of Exeter, an influential lace worker and dealer of the third quarter of the nineteenth century, helped to maintain standards when they were generally in decline. She produced sample sprigs and expected her workers to keep to the high standards which they set. A sumptuous wedding veil which she made is now on display in the Honiton Musuem. A fine lace flounce of this period probably made by the Tucker family of Branscombe may be seen at the Royal Albert Memorial Museum, Exeter; it measures 3.6 metres by 0.76 of a metre (12 feet by 30 inches) and was originally exhibited at the South Kensington Exhibition of 1862. Apart from major works such as these, frills, cuffs, collars, bonnets and handkerchiefs form the bulk of Devon output.

Classes, originally set up in the eighteenth century, were still operating in the third quarter of the nineteenth. Both boys and girls started between the ages of five and seven and were 'apprenticed' to the teacher; in addition to instruction in the craft they were taught to read and write. The accommodation and conditions left much to be desired, but the classes prevented the total collapse of the craft. Even in the first half of the present century the local tradition was being quietly encouraged in south-east Devon. During the 1970s demonstrations of pillow-lace making were given at the Arts Centre at Budleigh Salterton, and in 1979 the English Lace School was opened at Tiverton with the aim of promoting the craft and the appreciation of its history. Opportunities to learn the traditional technique of making Devon and other laces are now provided at the school.

The standard work on the subject is the *History of Lace*, by Mrs Bury Palliser, which was first published in 1865; it contains a chapter on Devon lace. A report on the 'Honiton Lace Industry' was produced by Alan S. Cole for the House of Commons in 1888. The *Honiton Lace Book* by 'Devonia', of unknown publication date, was in effect an instruction manual through which the stitches could be learnt. In 1908, *Devon Pillow Lace*, by A. Penderel Moody, appeared. Though couched in the style of the period it nevertheless contains much historical and technical information on the subject. Nineteenth-century Devon lace is among other types described in *Victorian Lace*, by Patricia Wardle, published in 1968. Examples of Devon lace may be seen at the Allhallows Museum, Honiton, and the Victoria and Albert Museum, in addition to the Exeter Museum. Though on the whole Devon lace may not always reach the delicacy of the best, it is highly regarded. At the present time it is enjoying a vogue and old examples which have been 'moth-balled' for generations are once again being brought into use as articles of personal adornment.

Fine metalwork

Not only was the output of the Devon goldsmiths between the sixteenth and eighteenth centuries of considerable volume and aesthetic interest, but in addition the county had the distinction of being a silver-producing area. Silver-lead ores were mined in south-west Devon at Bere Alston and Bere Ferrers on the river Tamar and at Combe Martin on the Bristol Channel coast. There is a suggestion that the Tamar mines may have been worked by the Romans; both sources were of considerable importance by the end of the thirteenth century. Combe Martin silver, for instance, helped to pay for the Hundred Years War, 300 Derbyshire and Welsh miners being brought in to help extract it. During that period the mines were part of the country's main sources of supply and they came under the direct control and supervision of the crown. Gold is occasionally found in association with silver. When Henry V sold the manor and borough of Combe Martin to Richard Pollard in 1537 he retained 'the gold and silver mines'. If gold was worked at Combe Martin insufficient was left to be detected by modern geologists, although the metal has been recorded, in the present century, not far away at the Bamfylde Mine near North Molton. There has been intermittent mining activity in both south-west and north Devon throughout the intervening years—until 1875 at Combe Martin.

The Combe Martin lodes did not always produce ores from which the silver could easily be extracted and in 1587 Adrian Gilbert, of the south Devon seafaring family, brought in Bevis Bulmer, the North Country mining adventurer who was then at work in the Mendips; he introduced a successful process and both men made a fortune. Two commemorative cups were made from the last silver mined at that date, 1593. One of them was presented to the Earl of Bath, whose seat was at Tawstock near Barnstaple, and the Lord Mayor of London received the other. Both cups were engraved with inscriptions indicating that Bulmer had been responsible for smelting and refining the Combe Martin silver of which they were made. The London cup was melted down in 1643, but the silver was used again and still survives in the form of three tankards. In the nineteenth century silver from Combe Martin was used by Henry Ellis, the Exeter goldsmith and his son in a variety of brooches such as shawl clasps; they incorporated a recess in which the point of the pin could be safely housed—a device which he patented. Some of these brooches were manufactured in Birmingham, but both the Exeter and Birmingham examples have 'Combmartin Silver' inscribed on their backs.

In all probability there was a tradition of fine metal craft in the larger centres of population in Devon during the medieval period. The first record of a goldsmith mentioned in the Royal Albert Memorial Museum catalogue refers to an Exeter craftsman named Hamelin who was active in 1218. There is a Plymouth record for 1281, and, in 1370, Hugh Holbrook and his wife were recorded at Barnstaple which, apart from Exeter, was the main Devon centre of the craft. It has been suggested that the production of fine metalwork in both towns goes back to the establishment of their mints. The Exeter mint was situated in the medieval street of the same name on the north side of Fore Street and was thought to have been the site where, in later centuries, the assaying of gold and silver took place; but recent research casts doubt on the idea that permanent premises were ever acquired for the Exeter assay office. It appears that certainly from 1816, if not before, the assay masters carried out assaying at their own premises. Exeter received metalwork from individual smiths established in Barnstaple, Dartmouth, Torrington, Totnes, Plymouth and places in Cornwall and other parts of the south-west. At certain dates, however, all Devon goldsmiths were obliged to send their work to the London Company of Goldsmiths for assay purposes; or, they had to sell it unassayed although it may have been illegal to do so.

Very little Devon domestic silver has survived from before 1660. Most of the pieces, whether secular or ecclesiastical, differ little from those made in other parts of the country, but there are some slight regional variations and preferences. A considerable boost was given to the Exeter and Barnstaple craftsmen in the early 1570s by the necessity of modifying church plate as a result of the increasing Protestant influence in the Church of England. There was a need to replace the old Pre-Reformation chalices, one of which still exists among the plate owned by St Michael's church at West Hill near Ottery St Mary, with the larger, more utilitarian communion cups. A considerable number of these cups, of a very pleasing proportion and design, were raised and seven of them are housed in the Exeter Museum. Each has the form of an inverted, truncated cone splayed slightly just below their vertical or concave rims; the profile of the rims distinguishes these cups from those made elsewhere. Another recurring feature is the band of engraved Arabesque and strapwork ornament with which the cup is often encircled.

The church of St James the Apostle at King's Nympton possesses a typical example with a paten cover which, when turned over, stands on its flat knop; the cup has a neatly cast and turned foot and the outward splay under the rim referred to above. It was made of thick gauge silver about 1574 after the visit to Exeter of the wardens of the London Goldsmiths' Company and is now on loan to the Victoria and Albert Museum. Over 130 similar cups are attributed to the same maker, John Jones; they are distributed throughout the south-west. Two of them are included in the collection of Exeter Museum; one of these presents an engraving of a view of Exeter together with the city arms and those of the Fortescue family.

Perhaps the best known and most beautifully proportioned cup of this type is the one made by Richard Hilliard at about the same time for St

Sidwell's, Exeter. The cup itself is undecorated apart from a narrow band of decoration around the rim and can be seen, together with a smaller cup which he made for St Peter's at Brampford Speke, at Exeter Museum. A Hilliard 'tazza', a wide saucer-shaped bowl, which formerly belonged to the church of St John the Baptist, Colaton Raleigh, where it was used as a font cup, is now on loan to the Birmingham City Museum and Art Gallery. A strong supporter of the Reformed church, Hilliard was an eminent citizen of Exeter, attaining the offices of Bailiff and Sheriff. When he died in 1594 his second son Jeremy carried on with the craft of the goldsmith. His first son, Nicholas, is better known than either of them, being the Elizabethan miniature painter. The portrait which he painted of his father, at the age of 58, may be seen in the Victoria and Albert Museum.

Other communion cups of fine design and workmanship, usually having the out-curved rims, were produced by the highly-rated Barnstaple goldsmith Thomas Mathew. One of these cups forms part of the plate of Barnstaple's parish church, St Peter and St Mary Magdalene; others belong to the parish churches at nearby Braunton, Landkey and Swimbridge. Unlike Hilliard's cup mentioned above, the Swimbridge cup has a more substantial knop, and engraved bands of strap-work decoration and foliage enhance its appearance. There is similar decoration on the cover together with the date 1576. St Michael's church at Marwood and St Werburgh's at Wembury also possess chalices made by Mathew. As befitting the area, the plate owned by the churches in the vicinity of Plymouth is above average both in quality and quantity. Including the Wembury cup there are 12 chalices of the Elizabethan period in the deaneries of Plympton and Plymouth, all but one being of Devon craftsmanship; no less than eight of them were created by John Jones of Exeter. St Andrew's, Plymouth, has a magnificent collection of plate, most of it being silver-gilt dating from 1590 to 1861, which has few equals in England. In contrast, neither Exeter Cathedral nor the important parish churches of Crediton and Ottery St Mary possess goldsmiths' work of outstanding interest.

Fine secular cups made in London during the Elizabethan era are possessed by both St Mary's of Plympton and St Budoc's of the St Budeaux suburb of Plymouth. Of the two the latter, though made entirely of silver, appears to be influenced in its design by the coconut cups of the period in which the natural nut shell was enclosed in silver bands. During Elizabethan times, too, Exeter goldsmiths contributed to the current practice of mounting pottery jugs in silver; they served as wine jugs and, in rural parishes, as communion flagons. In the collection of Exeter Museum are a number of examples of brown-mottled Rhenish ware, probably from Cologne, embellished with repoussé work in the Germanic style. Others, made in Exeter, may be seen at the Victoria and Albert Museum. Two are in the collection of the Metropolitan Museum, New York.

Silver spoons were originally made for individual use. The usual pattern of the early period was comprised of a shallow bowl of distinctive shape attached to a straight stem which ended in a cast figure of an apostle, a saint, or a seal-top. Many were made with an eye to their value as investments and variety of design was no doubt considered. In Barnstaple an interesting variation was produced between the years 1590-1630, when instead of the above-named motifs a three-quarter-length oriental figure wearing an elaborate head-dress was evidently in demand. These have been variously described as Buddha, Khrishna or Vishnu spoons, and though they have suggested the influence of sailors returning to the port from the east they remain a mystery. Were they travel status-symbols? Do they indicate a deeper involvement with eastern religion? The answer may be simply that they represent a recurring interest in strange imagery such as produced the gargoyles of the medieval churches. A few Buddha spoons carrying the Plymouth mark have been noted and one bears the date 1660; apart from these exceptions, Barnstaple origin, between the dates given, seems to be the general rule. Continental design patterns have been suggested as the origin of another variation produced at Barnstaple in which the silver-gilt terminal consists of a half-length female nude similar in type to a caryatid. The bodies are more clearly defined than in the Buddha knops with the arms being almost separated from the torsos. A few of these spoons are included in the collection of the North Devon Athenaeum.

In the eighteenth century a certain linear simplicity combined with good craftsmanship can be said to have been the distinguishing characteristic of Devonian domestic silver. This was particularly true of the Queen Anne period, 1702-14, when the work of the Exeter smiths was well abreast of the time. The tendency in London from 1720 was towards complexity of form and ornamentation, calling for the development of new techniques; Rococo influences took over from 1730-40 and wealthy Devonian families requiring such elaborate objects would have placed orders in the capital. Judging from the work produced at this time it is evident that the Exeter, and other provincial smiths, lagged behind the London fashion. The pieces which they produced retained the simplicity and workmanship of earlier years. These qualities were acceptable to the eighteenth-century merchants and squires and today pieces of this period are collected for the same reason.

Except for flatware, there was a gradual decline in the quantity of Exeter-marked silver in the late Georgian period. Spoons of varied types were assayed at Exeter; the fiddle-pattern in particular seems to have been very popular. Later, during the Victorian era, the testing of larger numbers of such smaller objects tends to give a false impression of the status of the craft in Devon. Much of the business of the Exeter assay office was coming from Bristol, but, after 1860, it gradually decreased. The mass-production methods employed in the Birmingham and Sheffield workshops were beginning to have an adverse effect on the livelihood of the individual craftsmen to such an extent that the Exeter assay office died a natural death just over two decades later.

In medieval times the guild system led to the acceptance of approved standards of purity in the precious metals and eventually to the testing of standards through the assay offices. The marks stamped on the objects provide a framework of precise information. The more important dates, together with a synopsis of the Exeter marks, are given in tabulated form at the end of this section of the chapter.

The original Exeter mark for a Roman 'X' crowned, between two 'mullets' and encircled by pellets; it was, however, subject to a number of variations, and generlizations made about the subject can be misleading. During the last quarter of the seventeenth century the 'EXON' and castle mark appears to have been adopted by some of the city goldsmiths—Exon was sometimes abbreviated to 'XON'. When the Britannia standard was first introduced in 1697 it was stipulated that all provincial work should be sent, for the purpose of having it assayed, to London. The obvious difficulties which this imposed on the provincial goldsmiths in general led them to petition parliament to reopen offices outside London. Approval was obtained in 1701 and from this date the Exeter mark was changed to a triple-towered castle, and a more rational use of the cycle of date letters than had hitherto been the case was introduced. The letters and their enclosing shields were changed at the end of each 23- or 24-year cycle and another was started in a slightly different style; but it is worth noting that date letters were not in regular use in Exeter even after 1701.

The earliest Barnstaple mark consists of a bird within a circle, which is derived from a motif incorporated in the borough seal and is thought to have been in use between 1272 and 1624. From 1625 until the end of the century the mark was altered to a castellated arch between two towers — somewhat similar to Exeter's triple-towered castle punch mark. In the latter examples the letters 'BAR' appear above the castle and 'VM' below it. Some Barnstaple goldsmiths used this mark, but some also registered in Exeter so that they could use the 'X' crown stamp on their work as added proof of quality. The 'X' punch mark, however, did not mean that they could trade in Exeter. This privilege was confined to those who had served an apprenticeship there and who had been elected freemen of the city.

In a similar way, Plymouth goldsmiths sometimes entered their names at the Exeter assay office, though Plymouth too had a town mark based on the arms of the borough — a saltire, or St Andrew's cross, between four castles. Goldsmiths at Plymouth Dock benefitted from the general upsurge of activity experienced in the area during the period leading up to the Napoleonic wars.

Among the best examples of fine metalwork which may be seen in Devon are three steeple cups belonging to the town of Barnstaple. Though not made locally, they merit a few remarks. A steeple cup resembles a chalice, but the cover, its most characteristic feature, is surmounted by a steeple or pinnacle supported by scroll brackets. Each of the Barnstaple cups is approximately 530mm (21 inches) high, about 200mm (8 inches) of this being taken up by the covers. A mayor's name and a date is engraved on each of them. They were made in London. One bearing the date 1625 is by F. Terry. The other two, forming a pair, carry the 1620 date mark and bear the initials 'LS' with a rose below. Not far away a steeple cup of slightly smaller size belongs to the church of St John the Baptist, Instow. This, too, was produced by F. Terry, it bears the London date 1611. The intricate standing salt in the form of Winstanley's lighthouse, in Britannia silver, should be noted. Jackson suggests that it was probably the last salt of this type to be made; it was produced by Peter Rowe of Plymouth in 1698 and it may be seen in Plymouth Museum. As a general rule major works such as these were seldom made in the provinces.

The famous 'Drake Cup' was the creation of a continental goldsmith, Abraham Gessner, of Zurich. It was given to Sir Francis Drake by a grateful Queen Elizabeth I as a new year's gift in 1582, when it is recorded that she presented him with 'a piece of plate of allegorical design a sault of gold like a globe.' The National Art Collections Fund donated the cup to Plymouth Museum in 1942; it consists of a cup and cover in the form of a terrestial globe according to Mercator's projection—a masterpiece which is evocative both of its recipient and the age in which he lived.

The standard reference book on English goldsmiths, which includes detailed accounts of the Exeter, Barnstaple and Plymouth smiths is *English Goldsmiths and Their Marks* by Sir Charles Jackson, first published in 1905. Some of the details of this pioneering study have been modified by more recent research such as forms part of the books of Charles Oman. Once again the *Transactions of the Devonshire Association* provide much information and *Old Country Silver* by Margaret Holland, published in 1971, contains a chapter on Exeter and the West Country.

Dates and details relevant to Exeter hall-marking

1300 Provincial goldsmiths compelled by statute to use 'Sterling' silver i.e. 92.5% pure silver with copper.

1363 A statute compelled the use of makers' marks in the form of initials.

1571 Wardens of the London Company of Goldsmiths visited Exeter in their capacity as supervisors of provincial smiths. There was in all probability a Goldsmiths' Guild at Exeter before this time but there are at present no known references to it.

1575 An Exeter town mark and letters of doubtful significance begin to appear.

1697 Provincial offices were abolished. An act compelled the use of 'Britannia' silver i.e. 95.8% pure silver with copper. It was given distinguishing marks consisting of the figure of Britannia and a lion's head erased—the latter being a heraldic term.

1701 Exeter goldsmiths were incorporated as a company and an assay office was established.

1720 Sterling silver was reintroduced and marked by the leopard's head and lion passant.

1784 A tax was imposed on wrought silver and gold and the sovereign's head duty mark was introduced.

1883 The Exeter assay office was closed.

After the statutory establishment of the Exeter assay office in 1701 Exeter silver marking became more rational than it had been. The Exeter marks between 1701 and 1883 are the most common and are well known to collectors. They can be summarized as follows:

(i) The maker's mark consisting of the first two letters of the surname during the Britannia period or, on the reversion to the Sterling standard in 1720, the maker's initials.

(ii) The Exeter assay mark of the triple-towered castle.

(iii) The variable Exeter date mark usually changed about 7 August.

(iv) The Britannia mark, which was changed in 1720 to the leopard's head crowned and as such continued until 1784 when its place was taken by the sovereign's head duty mark.

(v) The lion's head erased was changed in 1720 to the lion passant.

Mention must be made of the fact that plate of the higher standard metal is still occasionally made and bears the legal mark of the Britannia and lion's head erased.

Wood-carving

Devon is famous for the carved wooden rood-screens, bench-ends and other wood carving of its parish churches. These should be considered as the natural development of the carpentry and joinery skills of the builders and ship-wrights which were also fostered by the monastic establishments. The prosperity created by the basic occupations found a natural outlet in the embellishment of the churches, and both rood-screens and bench-ends survive in greater number than in other counties of England. Devon, with more than 50 outstanding vaulted screens and many more of lesser quality, is particularly well-endowed when compared with other areas. East Anglia, another prosperous region, has very graceful rood-screens which are, however, noticeably different in character, and other regions such as Cornwall and the western part of Somerset possess fine examples.

Even in the churches which retained the cruciform plan there was a need to separate chancel from nave; but when the open-plan churches of the sixteenth century were developed—and a large number of this type was built in Devon—the screen assumed a greater significance. These wide churches often have aisles and nave of equal height so that screens could easily be accommodated. The wagon roofs, though rarely as rich as the roofs of East Anglia, have nevertheless certain regional characteristics and also deserve notice—they are mentioned in Chapter Four. The roof-screen was the architectural element which afforded semi-enclosure to the priest in the sanctuary and yet gave the congregation no reason to feel excluded from the ritual. In the changing emphasis of the present day many clergymen have felt the need to place a nave-altar in front of the screen. The best of the surviving rood-screens still span their churches from wall to wall and on being seen for the first time usually make a great impression. Their construction is based on a robust plate resting on the floor; from this, at intervals of 900mm (about three feet) the moulded vertical shafts are erected, and at a height above 1800mm (about six feet) they curve out in the form of a coving; this supports the cornice which is, by this means, projected outwards on both sides, enabling a platform, usually at least 900mm and sometimes as much as 1800mm wide, to be supported above. This floor originally carried the rood and often served as a minstrel's gallery and was known as the rood-loft. Of interest here is the fact that horizontal jointing, more typical of stone masonry, is frequently encountered at the point where the shafts are connected to the floor plate.

The bays produced between the floor plate and the cornice by the regularly-spaced shafts are further subdivided by a transom at about waist level. The wainscot formed in this way between the plate and the transom is usually subdivided into four, sometimes three, vertical panels with traceried heads. The flat surfaces within these lower units are the ones often used as supports for paintings of the saints (more fully described in Chapter Six). The open space in each bay above the transom is likewise subdivided into four, or three, by vertical sub-shafts and the arcaded heads are filled with tracery.

The coving usually takes the form of Perpendicular fan-vaulting of polygonal section with moulded ribs. The cornice, the crowning glory of the screens, has a strong horizontal emphasis with as many as five bands of carved decoration in the richest examples. These bands are made up of low-relief carving often pierced and undercut, so that a considerable contrast of light and shade is produced; these somewhat fragile embellishments are attached to a strong beam which they totally conceal. The motifs, repeated as a frieze in each band, consist of representations of the fruit and foliage of the vine and oak, but naturalism is often combined with imaginary growths, scrolls and other linear rhythms. Frequently one of the bands is dominated by a strong wavy element in the form of a continuous branch of tendril.

The basic structure of the screens is simple, but the combined effect of the mouldings, the tracery and the richly-carved cornices entitle them to be regarded as the art objects most characteristic of Devonshire. They share certain functional and aesthetic qualities with the main exterior façades of the temples of the Ancient World. The Christian congregation gathers inside the church before the screen as, in a similar manner, the Pagan worshippers assembled outside the temple facing its main façade. Only the priests were allowed to enter the inner sanctuary and the chancel of the Christian church was reserved for the clergy and choir. Both the temple façade and the rood-screen consist of a balance of horizontals and verticals. However, the screens are richly loaded with carved ornament compared with the standard classic façade, and the style and subject of the ornament is strongly suggestive of nature worship—a theme which finds direct expression in a number of Devon churches in such symbols as the 'Green Men' and which would have been well understood in the Ancient World.

Emblems of bishops and monarchs or nobles occur in some of the screens and these can be dated mainly between 1470 and 1520. The majority were carved in oak by local craftsmen and, no doubt, in many instances work of this type must have been a once-in-a-lifetime experience. Some screens, such as those at Harberton and Plymtree, either retain their original colour or have been restored in keeping with the old manner. Others, such as Lapford, abound with crisp carving of pale, age-coloured untreated wood. The earliest type of screen was set in a very simple rectangular framing under a horizontal beam, such as may be seen at St Brannock's church, Braunton and St Mary's, Willand, near Cullompton. In the later examples the decoration is influenced by Renaissance motifs and these may be seen, for instance, at St Michael's, Marwood, and at St James', Swimbridge. Altogether there are well over 100 screens, but some of these are mere fragments of the originals. The Puritans desecrated many and it appears that more than 50 were removed during the almost equally destructive but well intentioned clearing-up operations in the nineteenth century.

Some variations of the basic design described above do occur. Perhaps the most unusual is the Hispano-French influence in three churches: St Andrew's, Colebrooke, St Matthew's, Coldridge and St Mary's, Brushford, all situated in the remoter parts of central Devon. At the first two, the parclose screens have flamboyant characteristics, whilst at Brushford the same style dominates the little rood-screen, which has eight bays the two in the centre forming the entrance to the chancel. In each screen the basic rectangular bay is occupied, not by the usual type of tracery in which the shape of the pointed arch is a recurring motif, but by semicircles and other curves arranged in such a way that they are in accord with each other. The openings so formed are further subdivided by delicate reticulation. Presumably these screens, situated not many miles from each other, are the work of the same craftsman. Whether or not he was a Devonian is debatable. Curvilinear design of this sort did not occur again in Devon woodwork until the Art Nouveau period.

The gallery of the rood-screens, to which reference has already been made, originally carried a representation of the crucifixion and, provided with extensions above the cornice on the east and west it became the minstrel's gallery. Many a spiral stair within a massive church wall still emerges level with a now-vanished gallery. Very few rood-lofts have survived in England, but there is one at St Mary's, Atherington and a small part of one at Marwood, both situated in north Devon. Though neither of these lofts is complete, sufficient remains for a picture of their original structure and appearance to be formed. Atherington, it is believed, provided the model from which the rood-loft at All Saints, Kenton, was fully restored early in the present century. The screen and rood-loft of St Peter's, Lew Trenchard, near Lifton, were accurately restored in 1915, utilizing fragments of the original screen which had been dismantled in 1822 and using a painting of the interior by the Devon artist, Nicholas Condy, as an additional source of reference. St Swithin's church at Littleham near Bideford, has a rood-loft constructed in the 1890s which is based on the rood-loft of Partrishow in the county of Powys and is not, therefore, of Devonian character. Another restored rood-loft may be seen at the church dedicated to St Paul de Leon, Staverton in south Devon.

Apart from the screens already mentioned, those remaining at the following places in the north Devon are among the best and can claim their original vaulting: Bampton, Chawleigh, Chulmleigh, Hartland, King's Nympton and Swimbridge. St Mary Magdalene, Chulmleigh, possesses a splendid example having unusually high vaulting; St Nectan's, Hartland has a screen 14.5 metres (48 feet) in width and 3.6 metres (12 feet) high. Swimbridge has an exceptionally beautiful screen with carving on the transom and in the wainscot panels which is unusual. A clerestory window casts light on the central part of this screen and also on the rich ceilures above. The screen of St James, Chawleigh, has stooling of a type which is almost identical to that of the cross-walk screen in the adjacent Old Manor which was formerly the rectory; it lends support to the belief that the craftsmen who worked on the church screens were more normally employed on domestic architecture.

In south Devon rood-screens of high quality are to be seen in the churches of Bovey Tracey, Bradninch, Cullompton, Dartmouth, Dunchideock, Harberton, Ipplepen and Plymtree. In Dartmouth the redolence of the richly-decorated screen of St Saviour's is a fitting reminder of the period when the mariners of the port first sailed to the tropics and rich merchants paid homage to their church. At St Mary's, Uffculme, near Sampford Peverell, there is a screen measuring 20.4 metres (67 feet): no other Devon screen exceeds this width. Of the Dartmoor churches the screen in St Winifred's at Manaton is the most interesting.

The passing of a screen across a stone column obviously poses a design problem and it is interesting to note how it is treated. The solution adopted at St Michael's, Dunchideock, was to enclose the pillar in a special casing, and at Swimbridge the intruding columns were used as an opportunity for providing small altars framed under forward-curving canopies.

Restorations have been essential during the past century on account of neglect in earlier times. The screen at Ipplepen is worth mentioning as having been partly-restored by the well-known Exeter restorer of fine woodwork, Herbert Read. Representations of birds of a pleasing quality are to be found in the uppermost band of the cornice of this particular screen.

For those who would enjoy further information there is a detailed account of Devon screen work in *Roodscreens and Roodlofts*, by Frederick Bond and the Reverend Dom. Bede Camm. It was published in two volumes in 1909 and is the standard work on the subject.

Fixed seating was gradually introduced into churches at about the same time that the screens were being constructed and many Devon churches were in a position to afford these expensive carved fittings for which there was an ample supply of local oak. The increasing emphasis on the sermon in services, even before the Reformation, had stimulated the church authorities to provide pews. Many of the finest remaining examples are to be found in Devon, the north of the county having rather more than the south. The standard of workmanship was usually more basic than that lavished on the rood-screens.

The typical Devon bench-end, or pew-end, consists of a stout rectangular piece of oak which is only rarely carried up as a finial. The deep-relief carving of the surface is not allowed to extend to the basically solid edge, which is usually treated as a wreath of foliage. The decoration is placed on the outside face and is usually contained by lines of tracery in two tiers; within the shapes so created, a wide variety of design motifs were used: shields with coats of arms or symbols of the passion, figures of saints, animals, occupational symbols such as the plough and spade, together with foliation. It is interesting to see how, during the course of the sixteenth century, Renaissance influences gradually appear; the new details were ornate compared with the sometimes crude simplicity of the earlier work and produced more sophisticated overall design. Probably the new style reached Devon through the woodcut illustrations of Flemish prototypes which influenced craftwork generally. Such motifs as heads in roundels, and foliage and vegetation arranged symmetrically, made their appearance. In a few instances the date was carved on the bench-end, most of these came from the first half of the sixteenth century; even so parish records indicate that money was still being paid for timber and labour during the second half of the century.

The churches in which bench-ends may be seen number over a hundred. In north Devon there is a representative collection at St Mary's, High Bickington, containing some of the few with finials; one of these is surmounted by the lion of St Mark and another by the ox of St Luke. There is another large, varied and richly-carved group at All Saints, East Budleigh, in south Devon. One of these, the first in front of the pulpit, bears the Raleigh arms and is associated with the family of Sir Walter Raleigh; it carries the date 1537 and is quite possibly one of the earliest dated pews in England. The designs of a number of the East Budleigh pew-ends are arranged as single large units instead of being sub-divided. A few twentieth-century replacements fill the spaces where earlier bench-ends have not survived; they repeat the proportions of the originals without imitating their style. St Swithin's at Littleham near Bideford has a group of bench-ends entirely Renaissance in its design. Among the most individual in Devon are a few, among a larger total, at Lew Trenchard; one of them shows a fool or jester looking up at a lady carved in the roundel above, both are wearing horned hats. At the other end of the same pew the florid head of a bearded and hatted man is seen in profile in the roundel whilst, below, a city gateway is represented. A third bench-end in this church depicts the archangel Michael in the act of weighing two souls. Another fine collection of bench-ends is housed at St Brannock's, Braunton. There is a rare survival of a carved bench-front at the church dedicated to St Mary and St Gregory at Frithlestock. It is in company with one of the few bench-ends bearing a representation of a stag.

Because of their special regional characteristics the rood-screens and bench-ends have called for detailed attention; that does not mean that other Devonian ecclesiastical wood-carving should be neglected. The misericords in the choir of Exeter Cathedral are the earliest and among the finest in Britain, and the bishop's throne, a beautifully-cut spire of openwork arches, pinnacles and crockets 18 metres (almost 60 feet) high, is also one of the earliest and best. There are outstanding wooden font covers at Pilton and Swimbridge in north Devon; both consist of a mixture of Gothic and Renaissance elements. Of less aesthetic value is the font cover surmounted by a quaint toy-like dove which is in the Plymtree church, near Cullompton. Seat reservations were of great importance to our forefathers, so it is not unusual to see carved family pews and a few still exist in the Devon churches.

The parish churches as opposed to the Cathedral do not often have work of such excellence, nevertheless the wooden pulpits deserve mention because their survival rate in the country as a whole has not been high. The impressive stone pulpits of St Saviour's, Dartmouth, and St George's, Dittisham, in south Devon, the subject of comment in Chapter Four, set the pattern that is repeated in wood in several pulpits in the district. They have slender stems which spread like vaulting-ribs to support the polygonally-sided pulpit compartments. The uprights, which frame the six or eight sides, are usually richly-carved with a decoration often based on the vine; they combine with projecting canopies to form niches in which there are carvings of the saints. Examples may be seen at Ipplepen and at Torbryan where some pier-casings, formerly belonging to the rood-screen, have been incorporated in the pulpit. Chivelstone, near Kingsbridge, and Kenton, near Dawlish, each have pulpits carved out of a single massive block of wood, Spanish chestnut in the former and oak in the latter church. Because the Chivelstone pulpit retains the basic cylindrical form of the tree trunk, the depth of its carved ornament is rather less than is usual. The Kenton example, which has some striking representations of animals, is one of the most richly-decorated in Devon. Renaissance details occur in the pulpit of the church of St George and St Mary at Cockington, formerly situated in the original parish church of Torquay at Torre Mohun, whilst in St Andrew's church at South Tawton, north of Dartmoor, there is a pleasing eighteenth-century oak pulpit in which the panel decoration consists of the four evangelists in inlay.

In conclusion it can be said that the ecclesiastical wood-carvings constitute a considerable artistic heritage. The majority are situated in country areas away from the main roads and time and effort are needed to find them. A glance at the map will reveal where these memorials to the craftsmen of Devon stand.

Pottery

The making of pottery was a natural development following the discovery of easily workable and relatively pure deposits of clay in several parts of the county. The 'Bovey Basin', which as been mentioned as a geological feature in Chapter One, has yielded clay that has been put to use not only near the point of extraction but to a greater extent in the potteries of Staffordshire, Bristol, London and Swansea.

There are deposits of a clean red clay in the parish of Fremington in north Devon and beds of a similar nature lie beneath nearby Pottington on the outskirts of Barnstaple. These two have supplied the potteries of Barnstaple, Bideford and Fremington for several centuries and from the local quays large quantities were transported to distant areas. Another plentiful source of clay was found at Peter's Marland south of Great Torrington. Because of its qualities it was used as a white slip on decorative ware and, on a large scale, for industrial purposes such as the production of high quality bricks of pale yellow which were popular with local builders in the first decades of the century. South Devon has good red clays in the Torbay area, though they do not seem to have been exploited prior to the development of Torquay. Until the middle of the nineteenth century adequate supplies of wood for the firing of the kilns were locally available, but pottery production in Devon has never really been of a scale that justifies the use of the term 'pottery industry' for it was cheaper to take the clay to the coalfields than to bring the coal to the clay-pits. As a result small potteries near the sources of the clay are characteristic.

Apart from the pottery fragments of Bronze Age date, to be seen in the archaeological displays in the museums, the earliest products of the potters' craft which survive in Devon are the floor tiles to be found in widely-distributed churches of the north and centre of the county. These tiles are usually about 140mm (5½ inches) square and nearly all show considerable signs of long usage. They were made as flat tiles, with the design inlaid in white clay, and also as a low-relief produced by impressing the clay in wooden moulds. The motifs which decorate the surface include a swan, a lion rampant, a fleur-de-lis and a grotesque head, and are finished with yellow or brown glazes. It would appear that the tiles were produced at Barnstaple and perhaps Bideford, from the fifteenth to the seventeenth centuries and they may now be seen in about 20 churches, for instance at Coldridge, Black Torrington, Hatherliegh and Westleigh; some occur in neighbouring Cornwall.

Although the surviving specimens of Devon pottery date from the late seventeenth century onwards it would be strange if there had not been continuous production, from early times, of utilitarian wares to serve the needs of the local population near the sources of good quality clays. Cross Street in Barnstaple was called Crock Street as early as 1345 and at the present time Potter's Lane still exists near the town's Civic Centre; Bideford, too, had a Potters' Lane which is thought to have been situated on or near the site of the present North Road. The more important potteries are given in the form of an appendix to this chapter. Most of the pieces which have survived can be placed in one of three categories: tableware, coarseware and 'Art Pottery', but only a few examples of early Devon tableware remain.

In England as a whole a distinctive type of pottery known as 'slipware' was evolved for use at the table and Devon has the honour of being one of the areas where it was produced. The dull red earthenware was dipped, before firing, in a lighter cream-coloured or white clay reduced to a liquid consistency and known as 'slip'. This lent itself to decoration by scratching through the light-toned layer to reveal the darker body beneath it. This was a means by which simple geometric patterning, such as lines and bands, could be circumscribed on plates and jugs. Freehand plant and floral motifs, more or less stylized, could be used as infilling, or geometric motifs could be used exclusively; more elaborate motifs in the centre of the plates and on the sides of jugs included the human figure, animals, birds and heraldic emblems such as crowns and suns. In the production of slipware there are two firings: one, the biscuit firing before glazing, and the other after. Lead sulphide was the basis of the glaze and it was sifted on as a powder. The outcome of the process is that on red clay the glaze appears as a rich brown; over the slip the colour ranges from lemon yellow to ochre. The technique originated on the Continent and the Italian word *sgraffito* is used to describe it; in the hands of the Devon craftsmen the effect was essentially un-sophisticated.

The north Devon potteries produced cups, beakers, bowls, jugs, plates and dishes. By the middle of the seventeenth century production was of sufficient volume to satisfy the demands of an export trade to the ports of the South-West and Ireland and on a vast scale to the American colonies with which the district had intimate connections. Unfortunately we have only fragments on which to base our knowledge of this tableware. As early as the beginning of the eighteenth century it appears that competition from other parts of the country was starting to have its effect, though local needs were satisfied until the arrival of the railways in the mid-nineteenth century.

It was mainly during the eighteenth and nineteenth centuries that the expressive 'harvest jugs' or pitchers were made in north Devon. Though they had their utilitarian purpose, they were undoubtedly made primarily for the visual pleasure which they gave and for this reason a number have survived. When the Beaford Centre assembled an exhibition of north Devon pottery in 1969 no less than 18 examples dating from 1760-1886 were displayed. underlying the usually extrovert swagger of the all-over decoration and the earthy inscriptions and rhymes is the form, based on a sphere; a broad base, neck and lip were formed and a handle was added. Harvest pitchers are indeed genuine symbols of fertility and fruitfulness and they epitomize a rural culture which has now vanished. The specimen to be seen in the North Devon Atheneaum was made by John Phillips of Bideford for Thomas Fields; it is so hefty that, filled with cider, it would be most difficult to pour from.

In the same archaic style the puzzle jugs, with their multiple pouring places and pierced openings, appealed to the local sense of humour; unless the secret of how to extract the contents successfully could be discovered the would-be imbiber was in danger of recieving a wetting.

Rural potters must of necessity be much concerned with the production of utensils for use in the kitchen, the garden and on the farm. With the decline in the demand for table slipwares at the end of the seventeenth century north Devon potters gave more attention to these 'coarsewares', and *sgraffito* decoration from then onwards was, it seems, confined to harvest pitchers. Fine river sand was obtained at certain selected spots and added to the clay for the production of pans, bowls and pitchers in which food could be prepared or stored. The somewhat crude way in which north Devon coarsewares were finished is one of its notable features. Of particular relevance to the district are the 'cloam ovens'; these hemispherical forms, usually large enough to contain two or three loaves, were installed within the thick walls of the ample fire-recesses of farmhouses and cottages. Their trapezoidal door panels, with which the open side could be sealed when the ovens had been sufficiently heated for the purpose of baking bread, were biscuit-fired. In the contemporary surge of interest in old properties several of these ovens have been discovered beneath layers of plaster, to the delight of the renovators concerned. The ovens are almost unique to north Devon, the nearest counterparts being continental; they were manufactured in sufficient quantity for large numbers to be exported. Cloam ovens were being manufactured as late as 1890 and were used for baking bread as recently as the 1920s, but by this date other events had taken place in both north and south Devon potteries. Fish steins were also being produced in large numbers and were sold to the north Cornish ports where they were used in the salting down of pilchards.

Before describing in detail what is known as 'Art Pottery', which became the dominant product after about 1870, it is worth while to consider certain characteristics of the potteries of the Barnstaple area. The history of one of these, the Fremington Pottery, can be traced back to the late eighteenth century. It was situated immediately south of Muddlebridge, the point at which the main Barnstaple-Instow road crosses Fremington Pill. Old Pottery House is marked on the large-scale Ordnance maps, and beyond Combrew Farm lie the clay pits from which clay is still extracted. The pottery, known as Fremington Pottery, occupied buildings of primitive simplicity situated near the clay pits, some of which have been filled in during recent years, and close to the tidal creek from which both raw clay and the output of the pottery could be shipped to the north Cornish ports for instance. Several generations of the Fishley family in succession ran the pottery and one of them, Edwin B. Fishley, who lived until 1911, was described by Bernard Leach as 'the last English peasant potter'. George Fishley, born in 1771, Edwin's grandfather, founded the pottery and established it as a completely self-supporting concern. Food for the horse, which turned the pug-mill and drew the cart to the markets in the neighbouring towns, was grown by the pottery. Gorse was collected in the locality and used, when dry, in firing the kilns. The clay was dug closer to the pottery than the pits at present in use and was sufficiently clean and fine for the making of small articles without preliminary preparation other than wedging.

Employing about a dozen people, Fremington Pottery turned out anything which was required in connection with cooking or containing food. In addition they made pots for garden use, drain pipes for farmers, rough bricks and pantiles for the local builder and also harvest pitchers, watch-pockets and mantle ornaments. Some curious local names were used to describe the different capacities of the pots. For example large crocks used in the preparation of food were known as 'Great Crocks'; fish steins were 'Buzzards' and 'Gallons' and three sizes of pitchers were described as 'Penny Joogs', 'Pinch-guts' and 'Gulleymouths'. The pottery produced typically English slipware. A deep manganese brown glaze is found on many of the early pieces; a green was also in frequent use.

William Fishley-Holland, grandson of E. B. Fishley, left the Fremington Pottery following a family disagreement in 1912. He crossed the river Taw to help establish the Braunton Pottery and work as its manager. Initially the new pottery maintained the Fremington tradition; it continued to operate until 1971. Long before then, however, Fishley-Holland had moved to Clevedon Court Pottery in the present county of Avon. Fremington had ceased production shortly after he left it and Braunton's output was generally of sturdy, unpretentious character.

Towards the last quarter of the nineteenth century the demand for coarse-wares declined, but the more enterprising potters were able to turn to the creating of the so-termed 'Art Pottery' which, influenced by the Art and Craft Movement, became increasingly popular. The Fishley family had used the shape of the classic urn and shown some interest in other foreign designs and was to some extent experimenting with glazes. However, their work offered little serious competition to neighbouring Barnstaple, where the new style was adopted by three potteries.

Art Pottery is mainly identified with the last 30 years of the reign of Queen Victoria; the term indicates that the work is original and creative as opposed to repetitive routine output. In a sense it has something in common with the harvest pitchers and puzzle jugs, but a wide range of objects was produced and, in decorating them, coloured slips and glazes were imaginatively used. Mass-produced pottery was available by this date and could be afforded by almost everyone, but much of it was of inferior design. It would appear that in some quarters the classical inspiration of the late eighteenth century had been replaced by the mistaken notion that art is synonymous with ornamentation. The essence of the 'Art and Craft Movement', which William Morris stimulated to rectify the situation, was the employment of traditional methods in the production of simple, honest work. However, Art Pottery itself is ornate compared to the discreet decoration of some twentieth-century work. Art Pottery, and the movement in general, derived much inspiration from the art of the Far East which was coming into the European exhibition rooms for the first time; little homage was paid to the Gothic Revival which, it could be said, died through lack of support.

A good railway service linked north Devon to the London market and the holiday-maker was a welcome visitor. Customers were coming to the very doors of the potteries; it was no longer a problem of creating an export market. Couple this with the strong tradition of craftsmanship, which included the use of *sgraffito* decoration, and there is the foundation on which to build a thriving business. The enterprising owner of the Litchdon Street Pottery, C. H. Brannam, interested the fashionable London art retailers, Howell and James, in his work and they gave him advice on changes of style which would help to make it more saleable. When Charles Brannam employed highly skilled and talented designers, such as Dewdney and Baron of Doulton's, to work at his side and the Lauder Pottery provided articulate local competition, the stage was set for Barnstaple to make a contribution to the Art and Craft movement on a level the importance of which is only just beginning to be appreciated. When, in the early twentieth century, Art Pottery itself ceased to be fashionable the long, local tradition of craftsmanship was still sufficiently strong to enable Brannam's Pottery to survive.

In the Torquay area the history of the potteries is different. The discovery of a bed of fine red clay led directly to the idea of exploiting it through the establishment of potteries whose sole aim was to produce 'Art Pottery' in the form of terracotta sculpture, vases and urns based on classical models. Watcombe Pottery was established in 1896. The Torquay Terracotta Company and the Aller Vale Potteries were opened in the 1880s. As there was no local tradition, skilled potters were brought in from Staffordshire to get the concern started. The Torquay potteries had a considerable effect on each other. They rarely produced tableware, but most other articles were made. In the present century the potteries combined and produced work almost exclusively for the tourist industry with, in consequence, a lowering of quality to the point of triviality. However, the popularity of this trade stabilized the business and extended its life. This was the pattern, too, which evolved in the potteries of north Devon.

At Bovey Tracey the Indio Pottery was in operation at the end of the eightenth century, but it had probably originated at a much earlier date for good clays could be obtained close to the town. Unfortunately, although at one time 40 workers were employed, very few examples of its products have survived. It appears that the Folly Pottery, situated near the clay pits, was also in existence by 1809 and Lysons tends to confirm this by implying that clay dug at Bovey Heathfield was used at two potteries. Information concerning the Bovey Potteries is not copious, but a paper read by N. Stretton at the Wellcome Institute of the History of Medicine in 1970 adds considerably to knowledge of the Indio Pottery.

Apart from pottery, another branch of ceramics to which Devon has contributed is the making of porcelain. The key figure in the early development of this craft, William Cookworthy, was born of an industrious Quaker family at Kingsbridge in 1705. As a fifteen-year-old he had worked in a laboratory in London. In his early twenties he returned to the West Country and set up in partnership with a manufacturing chemist at Bristol. In the course of time he was appointed a minister of the Society of Friends. In this capacity he travelled in Cornwall where, at the mines, he saw the Newcomen engine in operation and studied the geology of the granite. He was inspired by the belief that he might find a material with which ceramic wares as fine as those being imported from China could be produced. Eventually he discovered kaolin near St Austell in 1758 and began experiments in porcelain-making at Plymouth; at the same time he was carrying out similar work at Bristol. Encouraged by his experiments he applied, in 1768, for a patent to protect his methods. Artificial porcelain was already being manufactured, but it is to him that credit must be given for producing England's first true hard-paste porcelain. Cookworthy opened a factory at Coxside, Plymouth, in 1796. In it some 60 people were employed, but the enterprise had only a short life before the work was transferred to Bristol. There is a collection of the work of this factory at Plymouth City Museum and Art Gallery. Some of the articles were decorated by Cookworthy himself, the glazes having what can now be described as a pleasing amateurishness. In the 1840s a deposit of china clay was opened at Lee Moor not far from the outskirts of Plymouth, on Dartmoor. Output from this vast reserve is still of considerable importance.

Much information concerning the early pottery of north Devon is given in *North Devon Pottery and its Export to America in the Seventeenth Century*, which was published in the late¹ 1950s by the Smithsonian Institution, Washington, D.C. The operation of the Fremington Pottery and related matters have been described by W. Fishley-Holland in *Fifty Years a Potter*, and further information about north Devon potteries is contained in *Strong's Industries of North Devon*. Both north and south Devon potteries are the subject of comment in *Victorian Art Pottery* by E. Lloyd Thomas, and *The Old Torquay Potteries* by the same author has recently been published.

Examples of north Devon pottery including harvest pitchers may be seen at Barnstaple in the North Devon Athenaeum and the St Anne's Chapel Museum, at Bideford in the Library and the Burton Art Gallery and also in the Exeter Museum, the Victoria and Albert Museum and the British Museum. Torquay Museum has a good collection of local pottery. The Fitzwilliam Museum at Cambridge has a collection of 38 pieces of traditional north Devon pottery including a number of harvest pitchers; they form part of the Glaisher Collection of pottery and porcelain. In America there are informative displays on the same subject at the Smithsonian Institution, Washington D.C. and there are other exhibits at the Colonial Museum Historical Park at Jamestown in the state of Virginia.

Bernard Leach who, more than any other individual is responsible for the reappraisal of the aesthetics of pottery which has occurred in Britain in the present century, established his pottery in Cornwall. Both his sons, together with many other 'studio potters' all of whom employ at the most only a few assistants, have set up their potteries near sources of clay in Devon. These prove, if proof be needed, that the craft of pottery is very much alive in the county today.

List of Devon potteries

(The place names, in alphabetical order, are followed by the title of the pottery or potteries which are or were situated there)

BARNSTAPLE ARTISTIC POTTERY, *c*1895-1938. This pottery was established by Brannam's former decorator, William L. Baron and it was housed in premises in Mill Road, Rolle Quay. His son, Frederick, who was also a decorator for Brannam joined him and gradually took over the running of the business. Production consisted mainly of 'motto' wares and grotesque vases many of which closely resembled other pottery being produced in the town at the time. On the death of F. Baron in 1939 the pottery was taken over by C. H. Brannan Ltd. MARKS: 'Baron Barnstaple' incised in script together with a code number; 'Baron N. Devon'; or simply 'Baron' with a code number.

BARNSTAPLE: BRANNAM'S POTTERY. Still flourishing in 1979 when it was taken over by the Newton Abbot ceramics company 'Candy Tiles.' Three separate potteries existed at Barnstaple during the early nineteenth century; one of these, situated in Litchdon Street, was owned by a potter named Lovering, and the others, one situated on the Strand and the other in Potter's Lane, were run by a Mr Rendle. Among the workers in these establishments was a journeyman, James Brannam, who was later to take over Rendle's Pottery in Potter's Lane which lies near the Civic Centre between the Castle Mound and the North Gate. This pottery was making domestic earthenware until mid-nineteenth century. Brannam later acquired an interest in the Litchdon Street Pottery which, until then, had been producing local *sgraffito* wares. In 1851 James Brannam achieved some success at the Great Exhibition in London. He sent his son Charles Herbert to study at the Barnstaple School of Art. As a result of this Charles Herbert began to experiment with 'Art Pottery' in the late 1870s. In 1879 the Litchdon Street Pottery was purchased. C. H. Brannam made himself responsible for the design of each piece of work. In due course his pottery became widely known and it found favour with Howell and James, the London art dealers, and later on, with the famous house, Liberty and Company. The firm benefitted from royal patronage and from 1885 the Art Pottery was retailed as 'Royal Barum Ware.' On his business trips to London C. H. Brannam made drawings of the pottery at the British Museum. The style of his work may be described in consequence as a composite of Japanese, Persian and Classical motifs. For many years, in addition to designing the shapes, Charles Brannam threw and decorated the articles himself and each piece was signed and dated. The ideals of the Arts and Crafts Movement were embodied in this work, which contrasted greatly with the commercial pottery of the period. The standard of decoration was high and at a later date was entrusted to John Dewdney and W. L. Baron who had previously worked for Doulton's of Lambeth. The association of Brannam's with Liberty and Company continued into the Art Nouveau period, when the forms of the pots became elongated and the methods of decoration lent themselves to the emphasis on linear design. MARKS: 'C. H. Brannam' incised in script with date and 'C. H. BRANNAM BARUM WARE' with number incised. Other decorators used monograms as follows:— Arthur Bradden— AB; Frederick Baron—FB; William Baron—WB; John Dewdney—JD.

BARNSTAPLE: THE LAUDER POTTERY, *c*1876-1914. Formerly 'Lauder and Smith', then known as the 'Devon Art Pottery', and, according to the directory, from 1897 as the 'Royal Devon Pottery'. It was started by the Barnstaple architect, Alexander L. Lauder, a man of wide knowledge and practical experience in the arts who also had local interests in the lime and manure trade with premises at Fremington and Pottington. Until 1873 he owned clay-pits on the site on which Rock Park now lies. In 1876 he obtained a lease of the clay deposit at Pottington and the pottery was built in its vicinity. At first bricks, tiles, architectural earthenware and drain pipes were produced, but when Mr Smith left the firm experiments were begun with the intention of making Art Pottery. Vases, jugs, plant pots and umbrella stands were produced, but architectural modelling in low-relief continued to be made. Some examples of architectural terracotta work still to be seen incorporated in façades in the town came from this source. Technical difficulties due to the inexperience of the staff were overcome by the 1880s, at which date three kilns were in operation and a maximum of 40 people were employed. The style of the work reflected that of the Brannum Ware of the period; it involved the use of coloured slips and glazes in combination with *sgraffito* decoration. Production varied and included, for instance, grotesque features in the form of heads of fish for spouts. The white clay of Peter's Marland was at times used as slip. MARKS: Early period, 'Lauder & Smith' incised followed by 'Lauder' with 'Barum' or 'Barnstaple' incised. The date and code number were sometimes given. The names of Lauder's decorators are not known.

BIDEFORD. In a paper published in the *Transactions of the Devonshire Association* in 1906 T. Charbonnier stated that Crocker's Pottery, established in 1688, survived until 1896. The street now known as North Road was formerly Potters' Lane and was the site of several potteries. Before the construction of the present west river embankment 'the Pill' lay not far from North Road and this made the task of delivering clay from Fremington relatively easy. Another Bideford pottery, active until 1916, was situated in

Old Torrington Lane in the East-the-Water district of the town. An old photograph of Green's pottery shop in the High Street reveals an extensive stock, most of it of local manufacture.

BOVEY TRACEY: THE BOVEY POTTERY, ?-1957. The history of the potteries which were situated in or near the town is vague and complicated. As the last owner simply called his premises the Bovey Pottery this title is used for convenience. A pottery known as Folly Pottery was active in the early nineteenth century and was evidently quite a large concern. It produced blue and white earthenware in imitation of Wedgwood. However, at the present time, few of its products can be identified. Bovey coal was used for the biscuit firings, and Somerset coal, because it generated greater heat, was used for subsequent firings. Between 1836 and 1842 the pottery, then described as the largest in the West of England, was for sale and at a later date was purchased by a Captain Buller and J. Divett and the name Bovey Tracey Pottery Company was used for the first time. In 1894 it had virtually closed again and in the following year was taken over by the Bristol Pottery Company. In 1930 the rights of the Fife Pottery of Gallatown near Kirkaldy, the source of the well-known 'Wemyss pottery', were bought; this has produced some problems of identification. MARKS: From 1894 onwards a series of printed and impressed marks usually incorporating the words BOVEY POTTERY were used.

BOVEY TRACEY: THE INDIO POTTERY (Sometimes spelt Indeo) ?-1843. Knowledge of this pottery is, unfortunately, incomplete, but it is reasonable to suggest that its origins lie a long way back. Josiah Wedgwood visited the business in 1775 and recorded the fact that its attempts to produce porcelain were unsuccessful. Even so, a year later it was beginning to manufacture salt-glazed wares, and later on, during the first half of the nineteenth century, blue and white wares were being produced. The site of the pottery was near the centre of the present town and fragments of plates, bowls and mugs decorated with deep yellow glaze have been unearthed. Only a few examples of the work of this pottery have survived; of these, two are tea caddies in private collections. MARK: 'Indeo' impressed.

BRAUNTON POTTERY, 1912-1971. This was established when W. Fishley-Holland left Fremington pottery and was asked to found a Braunton pottery and become its manager. The intention was to use clay dug near the premises, but it was found that it was just as convenient to transport Fremington clay to Braunton. Most of the early work of the pottery consisted of coarsewares for farm use and they were as a rule left in their natural biscuit colour. Table-wares glazed entirely in blue, green or white formed the bulk of the later production; further decoration, if any, was confined to a few words as, for example, on Jubilee mugs. At its period of greatest output the pottery, situated in Station Road, employed seven local men. In an advertisement, in a 1925 edition of *The Studio*, the pottery described its work as 'Hand-made Peasant Art Ware in rich colours and glazes.' The pieces possessed an honest simplicity and were sold throughout the United Kingdom and in countries overseas. The pottery closed on the retirement of F. C. Luscombe, the head potter and part-owner of the establishment. MARKS: Early, 'Braunton' incised in script together with the date; later 'BRAUNTON POTTERY DEVON' impressed.

EXETER: THE EXETER ART POTTERY, 1891-97, and THE DEVON ART POTTERY, 1896-1920 (Not to be confused with Lauder's 'Devon Art Pottery' at Barnstaple). The earlier of the two potteries was situated in an old malt house at the top of Napier Terrace close to the Mary Arches Street multi-storey car park. Little is known of this venture except that two of the potters employed there, William Hart who came from the Aller Vale Pottery and Alfred Moist who was trained at Bovey Tracey, teamed up and founded the Devon Art Pottery at St Thomas. By the turn of the century it was a thriving concern, producing Art Pottery and work in the Art Nouveau style and using clay from the Monks Road pit and also white clay from Bovey Tracey. A wide range of wares, including slip painted vases were made; the designs were very similar to those produced by the Aller Vale and Brannam Potteries. MARKS: 'HM Exeter' from 1897-1920.

FREMINGTON: FISHLEY POTTERY, c1790-1912. Was owned by several generations of the Fishley family whose history has been sketched by W. Fishley-Holland in *Fifty Years a Potter*. The building was situated close to Muddlebridge on the main Barnstaple-Instow road near beds of clay. The pottery was a remarkable example of the progression of a truly rural tradition into the early twentieth century. Typical north Devon pottery, including harvest pitchers, puzzle jugs, cloam ovens and other table and coarse wares were produced, so, in addition, was Art Pottery. MARKS: Many of the articles have the Fishleigh signatures such as 'E. B. Fishley Fremington

N. Devon' incised in script. Pieces such as watch-holders sometimes have 'FISHLEY FREMINGTON' together with a date impressed on their fronts.

HONITON POTTERY. Still flourishing in 1979. Samuel Ford is known to have been working in 1763. Towards the end of the eighteenth century two other potters, Flood and Hussey, established separate potteries. They all used locally-dug clay in the production of coarse-wares for home and farm use. Several changes of ownership have taken place in the last hundred years during which the surviving pottery has been in operation on its High Street site. Because of this position it is no longer possible to continue to used the bed of clay which lies at the rear of the buildings. Mould-made work now forms much of the output, but individually-thrown pieces are still produced and Honiton remains the only south Devon, nineteenth-century pottery to continue working today. MARKS: Early pieces probably unmarked. From 1918-47 'COLLARD HONITON ENGLAND' printed or impressed. At present 'Honiton, Devon, England' impressed.

PLYMOUTH POTTERIES. According to W. G. Hoskins there were three potteries in operation in 1815 and one of these continued to function until the last quarter of the century.

TORQUAY: ALLER VALE, 1887-1901. Originally known as the Phillips Pottery and later to combine with the Watcombe Pottery. In 1897 a small Art School was established at Kingskerswell beyond the outskirts of Torquay on the Newton Abbot road. A patron of the school was J. Phillips, whose pottery was burnt down in 1881. Undismayed, and influenced no doubt by the success of the other potteries in the Torquay area and the fact that suitable decorators were available through the school, he decided to rebuild with the intention of making terra-cotta wares. 'Aller Vale Art Pottery' was adopted as a name in 1887 to emphasise the character of the work produced. By the end of the century about 60 people were employed. Production was confined to small table-wares most of which were thrown on the wheel; figures and busts such as those made by the other Torquay potteries did not form a part of the Aller Vale output. A style was evolved which was to become typical of most Torquay pottery in the twentieth century. Its characteristics were large areas of coloured slip in cream, blue or green over which simple decoration in colour slip was superimposed; finally, the pieces were inscribed in *sgraffito*. The pottery was taken over by Watcombe in

1901, but production continued at Kingskerswell until 1918 when Aller Vale was closed and all production was transferred to Watcombe. MARKS: 'Aller Vale Pottery' plus a code letter and number scratched on the base.
TORQUAY TERRA-COTTA COMPANY LIMITED, 1875-c1905. Founded by a Doctor Gillow to exploit a deposit of clay discovered at Hele Cross little more than a kilometre from the Watcombe Pottery, whose success and high artistic standards it was intended to emulate. More figures were produced than at Watcombe and at the onset Italian artists were engaged. A very precise outline and a smooth surface were imparted to vases and jugs of classic shape by finishing them on a lathe; however, they were not embellished with modelled figures in the manner of Watcombe. The terra-cotta work included bird and animal groups and in addition the firm produced 'Art Pottery' from 1882. MARKS: Until 1890 'TORQUAY TERRA-COTTA CO. LIMITED' impressed or painted. Sometimes a monogram combining a double 'T' and a 'C' was used. Decorators from Stoke-on-Trent were employed, but it was not their practice to sign their names.
TORQUAY: WATCOMBE POTTERY, 1869-1962. Known initially as the 'Watcombe Terra-cotta Clay Company' and later as the 'Watcombe Pottery Company', it became the 'Royal Aller Vale and Watcombe Pottery Company' in 1901. G. P. Allen of Watcombe House had discovered a rich bed of clay alongside the Teignmouth Road in 1869 and the company was formed to extract and sell it as a raw material. When it was decided to commence production of pottery in 1871 skilled potters from Staffordshire were employed as there was no local tradition. As early as 1872 about 90 people worked at the establishment the products of which were displayed in the same year at the International Exhibition in London. Two periods can be distinguished in the output of the pottery. In the first high technical and artistic standards were set. The clay proved to be very suitable for terra-cotta and simple forms contrasted by small areas of decoration were characteristic of the pieces; vases and figures based on Classical and Renaissance originals are typical. The second period lasted from 1884-1900 when strict adherence to the original aims was abandoned and a combination of influences often resulted in the red body being covered completely with decoration. After merging with the Aller Vale Pottery in 1901 Watcombe remained in production until 1962. The buildings were demolished in the following year. MARKS: 'WATCOMBE TORQUAY' impressed with a code number or, in late work, simply 'TORQUAY' marked. A circular trade mark was also used.

CHAPTER SIX

Devonian Artists and Their Work

This chapter is concerned mainly with the paintings of the eighteenth and nineteenth centuries, but it may be interesting to note the works of art which would have been seen in this part of the country in the earlier periods. Many of the objects concerned were made elsewhere and brought to Devon by invaders and traders. The examples by which they are now represented are few in number. No paintings survive in Devon, or anywhere else in Britain, from before the medieval period except when they appear in manuscripts.

The most satisfying piece of art-work of the Roman era which has come to light in this county is a small bronze found on the beach at Sidmouth in 1840 and now included in the collections of the Rougemont House Museum at Exeter. It appears to represent the young Achilles riding a centaur which is being attacked by a wild animal. In the past decade another notable specimen of Roman craftsmanship, part of the polychrome mosaic, has been uncovered during the excavations in the Cathedral Close at Exeter.

It can be assumed that, as elsewhere in northern Europe, creative effort was concentrated on the applied arts during the turbulent centuries following the Roman withdrawal and this continued until the Saxon settlement and Norman conquest. Decorated weapons and articles of personal adornment, which could easily be hidden or removed in time of crisis, were the types of objects on which the artist-craftsmen exercised their skills. Some examples have been discovered. For instance, the bronze sword-guard found in 1833 below the foundations of a house in South Street, Exeter, and described in detail in the *Victoria History of the County of Devon*. A gold bracelet of the Viking period has recently been found in the sand of Paignton beach by a young woman who was staying at the resort on her honeymoon. The bracelet, consisting of three twisted strands of almost pure gold, realised £7,150 when it was auctioned in London during 1979.

Even when considering the medieval period, examples of paintings are scarce. The few which survive are fragmentary and too often in a poor state of preservation. These are the mural paintings which formerly decorated the walls of many Devon churches and the painted panels of the lower part of the rood-screens. The carved wooden rood-screens are a feature of the churches and it is clear that it was characteristic of their wainscot panels, with their vertical format, to be used as the support for paintings depicting the saints. Though primitive in execution it must be assumed that they were painted in the late fifteenth or early sixteenth centuries.

The best among the surviving examples are to be seen at St Michael's, Upper Ashton, in the Teign valley. Both sides of this rood-screen and the adjacent parclose screen were painted and much of it remains in a fair state of preservation. The front of the rood-screen consists of eight bays divided into 32 panels in each of which a polychrome figure is depicted on alternatively red and green backgrounds. The screen of the small, light-filled church of St John the Baptist, Plymtree, near Cullompton, has nine bays. Of these, the two most northerly have only three paintings each and are of a slightly different style from the 28 paintings which occupy the remaining seven bays. The latter have tighter drawings and their backgrounds are filled in with dark green. The six, in a rather looser style, have alternating backgrounds more in the style of Ashton. These screens and their paintings are very similar to the remnants surviving in many Devon churches. Some of the best are to be seen at Bradninch, Ipplepen, Kenton and Torbryan. The only north Devon examples are at Combe Martin. Few are as complete, or have quite the standard of craftsmanship, as those at Ashton and Plymtree. In Exeter Cathedral there are some similar paintings on stone. These are on the screen of St Gabriel's Chapel and adjacent to the tomb of Bishop Bronescombe; the tomb itself, situated in the Lady Chapel, is a good example of the way in which effigies and their surrounding stonework were painted in the late thirteenth century.

The paintings on the back of the screen and also on the sides of the parclose screen Ashton are more remarkable. For every four vertical panels on the front of the rood-screen, there is one square panel on the reverse, and panels having the same proportion occur on the wainscoting of the parclose screen. Seven of these square paintings appear to have been scrubbed off, but ten remain in good condition. They each depict the upper part of the body of a prophet, supported by scrolls. The bay forming the reverse side of the doors to the Chudleigh chapel depicts the Annunciation. All these paintings have a background of red ochre—one wonders, can this have been derived from the local red earths? The prophets and scroll-work are in tones of black, grey and white. The design throughout is bold and the drawing and technique are as good as any Devon example of this period.

Two churches situated in the South Hams have, on some of their wainscot panels, decorative motifs of Renaissance origin instead of representations of the saints. In the church of St Nicholas and St Cyriacus at South Pool, these motifs consist of heads surrounded by scrolls and balloon-like festoons. They are carried out in a linear style on a pale ochre background. The church of St Sylvester, Chivelstone, has some very similar panels in which the shapes are blocked-in and the designs are more cohesive.

Apart from the screen paintings usually executed in an oil-bound paint on a wooden support, there is evidence in a number of widely-separated Devon churches of the remains of mural paintings. These also originated in the medieval period and the technique was fresco, though one suspects that a distemper-like paint was applied to dry plaster rather than these being examples of *buon-fresco*. Ashton again provides an example. It depicts Christ and the cross with a ladder and other instruments of the Passion against a background colour of red ochre. It should be made clear that this work is in a state of dilipidation and that this applies to many similar fragmentary murals in other Devon churches. Bratton Clovelly is interesting in that the fragments extened over a large area of the nave walls. Similar examples are to be seen in the church at Branscombe, Weare Giffard and at Littleham, near Bideford, where a painting of St Swithin is preserved in a small recess. Two more-ambitious compositions from this period survive in Exeter Cathedral; these are the painting of the Resurrection situated over the chapel of Sylke in the north transept and the Assumption and Coronation of the Virgin on the outer wall of the Lady Chapel and dominated by the Renaissance monument imposed on the wall immediately below it. Although both works have much more content and involvement with pictorial values than the examples in the parish churches, they too have obviously deteriorated in condition. Conservation of both paintings was carried out by E. W. Tristram in 1930 and he prepared copies of the originals which are now placed near the actual works in positions convenient for viewing. One of the main causes of the deterioration of mural paintings in Devon is the existence of damp within the walls on which they are painted. It is only in the drier parts of Europe that fresco paintings survive well. It must also be remembered that many murals were destroyed, or at least whitewashed during the Civil War period.

Devon should be seen in relation to the main cultural trends of the time. The region was on the periphery as far as the best models of panel painting and illumination are concerned and it appears that the perfection of continental counterparts was rarely attained by English artists. This country developed later than the European centres of art; William Hogarth (1697-1764) is often taken as the first characteristically English artist, but it is interesting to note that the achievements of the great sea captains of Elizabethan Devon were not entirely without parallel in the visual arts.

John Shute born at Cullompton early in the sixteenth century is a some-what shadowy figure as a 'limner', or what we would call a painter of miniatures, for no work of his has been authenticated. According to the records, he was held in high repute by his contemporaries and he had more than one interest, being sent, by his employer the second Duke of Northumberland, to study under the best architects in Italy. The title of the work which he published in 1563 is worth giving in full—*The First and Chief Groundes of Architecture, used in all the Auncient Monyments, with a Farther and more Ample Discourse upon the same than Hitherto hath been set out by any other.*

The best-known miniature painter of that age and founder of the English miniature school, Nicholas Hilliard, was born in Exeter during 1547. Like the sea captains, his achievements were great; he was the eldest son of an industrious goldsmith and a leading Protestant in the city, and after Catholic Queen Mary came to the throne it is believed that young Nicholas may, at the age of ten, have been sent to Calvin's city, Geneva, to receive his education. At the age of 14 he was apprenticed to Robert Brandon, a prominent member of the London Goldsmiths' Company and goldsmith and jeweller to the new queen, Elizabeth I, but W. G. Hoskins has questioned whether or not Shute could have been his earliest teacher. Trained as he was in these fine crafts Nicholas was able, when he turned to miniature painting, to compress into an area of luminous colour often less than ten square centimetres an expressively-drawn face or figure and significant accessories. He conveyed, both to his contemporaries and to later generations, the spirit of the age in which he lived. By the time he was 25 years old he was attracting subjects from the Court, including the queen herself. Eventually he became goldsmith, carver and limner to the queen. So Hilliard was a national figure. He lived most of his life outside Devon, though the fact that his father, on his death in 1594, left him land in Exeter may suggest that he maintained contact with his county. A privately-owned Hilliard miniature of Queen Elizabeth still exists in Devon. The National Portrait Gallery contains his portrait of his fellow-Devonian Sir Walter Raleigh, but the best place in which to see examples of his work is the Victoria and Albert Museum.

Though most of the painters who were Devon-born, or who worked from Devon subjects, were active in the eighteenth and nineteenth centuries, Exeter and Plymouth attracted travelling artists in earlier centuries. As soon, in fact, as the English gentry established themselves in country houses in Tudor times, travelling painters would have begun to call on them. The paintings of the Elizabethan sea hawks, Drake and Hawkins, owned by Plymouth City Museum and Art Gallery, may possibly come in this category. M. Gheeraerts of Bruges worked in England between 1568 and 1577 and the two portraits of Sir Francis Drake are attributed to him. It is thought that the Italian, Federigo Zuccaro, made the half-length painting of Sir John Hawkins which is usually exhibited by the museum at Buckland Abbey; however, Federigo's sojourn in England in 1575 was not lengthy and the painting was probably executed in London. The painter of the portrait of Queen Elizabeth I, also at Buckland Abbey, is not known with certainty; it has been attributed to both Zuccaro and one or other of the Gheeraerts family.

Some pen and wash drawings of Plymouth, housed in Plymouth Museum, show the area comparatively unaffected by the works of man, as it appeared in the second half of the seventeenth century. These may be the work of Wenceslaus Hollar (1607-77), born in Prague. He spent most of his working life as an illustrator and topographer in England and produced some etchings of Devon subjects. The famous Dutch marine artist, Willem Van de Velde (1611-93) possibly accompanied by his son with whom he co-operated in painting was in Plymouth in 1666. Plymouth Museum has in its collection a painting of his in which the Citadel, with its white bastions, is backed by wild uplands beyond the town whilst in the foreground naval vessels and smaller craft are shown.

Another Dutch painter, Gerard Edema (1652-1700) may have collaborated with Van de Velde in some marine paintings of Plymouth. Two paintings, 'A view of Mount Edgcumbe' and 'A view of Mount Wise', the latter being painted from the Mount Edgcumbe area, are to be seen in the same collection. Once again, an almost totally pastoral landscape is shown surrounding the house in each case. At about the same date Hendrik Danckerts (c1625-79), a Dutch painter who produced views of the royal palaces for Charles II, depicted Plymouth as a small town surrounding Sutton Pool and overlooked by the Citadel and St Andrew's church. No doubt other painters visited Devon and in the following two centuries what had started as a trickle became a stream.

When parts of the county were still remote, such visits were not all strawberries and cream. A melancholy side-light is cast by a letter published in the *Western Antiquary* of 1892. It describes events which were even then regarded as vague. An artist visiting Okehampton on his honeymoon left his wife in their lodgings and went up the West Okement valley to make some sketches. No trace was found of him until 21 years later a small metal document case which he carried was discovered in the bed of the stream in proximity to some human bones. It was supposed that he slipped between two large masses of rock and could not extricate himself. Another description concerns the Lynmouth area. Whilst attempting to cross a stream an artist got his foot caught between two boulders. Night was coming on and he was obliged to stay where he was and when, as a result of a heavy thunderstorm, the water level rose suddenly he was drowned. If these stories derive from the earlier part of the nineteenth century it is surprising that they are not better documented, but improbable as they seem, the hazards to which they refer are very real.

One of the earliest Devonian artists about whom we have good records is Francis Hayman, who was born at Exeter in 1708. Whilst still young he went to London as a pupil of the portrait painter Robert Brown. Hayman became one of the leading exponents of that type of group portrait, usually with a domestic background, known as the 'conversation piece' and he was largely responsible for introducing a French rococo element into English painting. This is best illustrated in his 'Francis Hayman and an Unknown Person' to be seen at the National Portrait Gallery. However, he was involved in various types of work some of it on a large scale. The manager of the Drury Lane Theatre employed him as a scene painter and he worked on some of the painted decorations at the famous Vauxhall Pleasure Gardens. He is also recorded as having produced a number of ceiling paintings. At the other extreme he was employed as an illustrator of Shakespeare and other English classics. Hayman was acquainted with Hogarth and was a well-known figure in London society. It was natural that he should have been chosen as chairman of the committee of artists set up to plan the Royal Academy; and later he was to become the Academy's first librarian.

The first quarter of the eighteenth century had almost passed when the child who was to become one of England's greatest artists was born at Plympton St Maurice—Joshua Reynolds. His career and achievement are to a great extent bound up with his place of birth for it was through his contacts with naval captains that he was able to travel to Italy; and furthermore, naval officers and their wives provided him with subjects when, for a period, he established his studio at Plymouth Dock, as Devonport was then named. The scholarly background created by his father, who was the schoolmaster at Plympton Grammar School, gave him extensive knowledge without which it is doubtful if he could have achieved the wide-ranging view of art which enabled him to move among the intelligentsia in both Devon and London.

Before the significance of Reynolds is examined more closely it is worth considering some other issues. During the eighteenth and nineteenth centuries there was no scarcity of Devon-born painters or painters born elsewhere who visited Devon, but no one has referred to a 'Devonian School.' George Pycroft whose *Art in Devonshire with Biographies of Artists born in that County* is a source of information on Devonian painters, draws attention to the fact that after Middlesex, including London, which heads the list, Devon appears to have been the birthplace of more artists than any other county. However, the inter-relationship of these artists was fairly loose and there was nothing similar to the internal cohesion which one finds for instance in the Italian local schools.

It is interesting nevertheless to note the spirit of neighbourliness that drew Devonians together when they moved to the capital city. Thomas Hudson's place of birth is not exactly known, though Northcote refers to him as a Devonian and he was very closely associated with the county. He was a fashionable portrait painter to whom Reynolds was sent as an apprentice in London. Hudson was also responsible for training Richard Cosway of Tiverton who became one of the best miniature painters of the eighteenth century. Three Devonians were influenced in different ways by Reynolds: Ozias Humphrey born at Honiton, William Payne whose actual birthplace is not known but who is traditionally regarded as a Devon man; and James Northcote, a Plymouthian. Northcote encouraged another Plymouth-born artist, Samuel Prout, who had attended Plymouth Grammar School at the same time as Benjamin Haydon, also Plymouth-born. When Haydon went to London he, too, sought out Northcote to whom he had a letter of introduction. 'Northcote being a Devonian, I felt a strong desire to see him first', wrote Haydon in his memoirs. Charles Eastlake, who eventually became President of the Royal Academy, was also born at Plymouth and when he went to London he studied under Haydon. Another part of this network of friendships and influences can be traced through Cosway and Humphrey mentioned above. They were close friends of the Exeter painter Francis Towne who, in his turn, took Exeter-born John White Abbott as a student. Abbott became important as a landscape painter on a regional level. Without doubt there were other links which have not been recorded by biographers.

It was Reynolds who, with Wilson and Gainsborough, elevated the portrait and landscape painting in England as a whole by infusing it with those elements of design and composition that had been originated and developed by the Old Masters. In the case of Reynolds, and Wilson too, this took place after a period of study in Italy. Following this visit, Reynolds returned to London where he became the leading portrait painter, challenged only by Gainsborough.

Though Reynolds is a cornerstone of English art and spent much of his life in the metropolis, it was his Devon birth and connections which enabled him to achieve his position. Born in 1723, the year in which Wren died, he was the seventh of the eleven children of the Reverend Samuel Reynolds, master of Plympton Grammar School and sometime fellow of Balliol College. The little town of Plympton, superior in importance to Plymouth in the early middle ages, lies in a valley which slopes gently to the headwaters of the Plym estuary. This was important because on the opposite side of Plymouth Sound at Mount Edgcumbe, now part of Cornwall, lived the Earl of Mount Edgcumbe, who was closely identified with Plympton and used his influence to help its inhabitants.

At the age of 16 Reynolds was apprenticed to Thomas Hudson who had recently moved from Devon to London. Hudson was the son-in-law of Jonathan Richardson, one of the founders of the influential St Martin's

Lane Academy. Though Hudson's work sometimes appears to be dull compared to Reynolds at his best, he was the most fashionable portrait painter in the 1740s. A considerable number of his portraits remain in Devon. He is said to have been helped by his student Reynolds in the unusual series of 30 portraits of local worthies of Barnstaple, 29 of which are still held by the town; but it appears to be more likely that the apprenticeship began shortly after Hudson completed the series. Reynolds left Hudson at the end of his third year of apprenticeship, feeling, it is suggested, that he could then paint as well as his master.

Reynolds returned to Devon to set up his studio at Plymouth Dock on the first floor of a shop in which, on the ground floor, his sisters carried on a millinery business. During these years, 1743-49, he alternated between Devon and London. The Edgcumbes introduced him to Keppel, then a young naval commodore who eventually became First Lord of the Admiralty. It was through knowing Keppel that he was able to travel to Italy by sea in 1749. He went with the intention of learning all he could from what he saw and he made many rapid sketches and drawings of non-laborious type, rather than complete copies. Northcote states that on his return from Italy in 1752 'his health was in such an indifferent state that he judged it prudent to visit his native air'. In the following year he moved into his studio in Great Newport Street, London, where his sister Frances went to act as housekeeper and hostess, he did not marry. Later in the year he was introduced to Dr Samuel Johnson whose circle of conversationalists Reynolds joined. It was about this date that he painted the self-portrait which may be seen at the National Portrait Gallery. Two years later Reynolds painted the three-quarter length seated portrait of Johnson which shows 'the great if overbearing conversationalist' in a relaxed mood; the work hangs in the same gallery.

By 1760 Reynolds was increasingly successful; he moved to a new studio in Leicester Square and became closely bound up with the literary and social life of the day. Two years later Doctor Johnson accompanied him on a holiday in Devonshire. The Royal Academy was founded in 1768 and Reynolds became its first President at the age of 45. It was in this capacity over a period of years that he delivered his *Discourses* which were, in effect, a summary of several centuries of debate on academic ideals. Because they are concerned with such basic concepts as the nature of art and questions of style, they have an enduring significance. On their publication Reynolds used to send copies to his friends such as the Mudge family in Devon. A portrait of Zachary Mudge, vicar of St Andrew's church, Plymouth, was painted by Reynolds after his return from Italy; it now hangs in the Prysten House at Plymouth. The attractive portrait of the Parker children, John aged seven and Theresa at the age of four, still hangs in the position in the morning room at Saltram House to which it is originally allocated when completed by Reynolds in 1779.

Soon after the second Royal Academy exhibition Reynolds was on holiday in Devon again, visiting old friends and participating in country activities. His mother's family, the Potters, lived at Great Torrington in north Devon and one of his sisters, Mary, married John Palmer who built Palmer House in New Street, Torrington, where both Reynolds and Dr Johnson stayed. The house, completed in 1752, still stands. The Palmers' daughter, Mary, was Reynolds' favourite niece and when he returned to London in 1770, she went to live with her uncle. Towards the end of his life Sir Joshua's sight deteriorated and he painted his last picture in 1789. 'I commend my soul to God, in humble hopes of his mercy, and my body to the earth,' wrote Reynolds in his Will. His niece inherited the bulk of his £100,000 fortune together with the pictures in his studio.

It has been suggested that Reynolds found it difficult to communicate verbally, particularlly when as a teacher of painting it came to passing on advice. But his friendship with known conversationalists seems to prove that he was verbally at ease. The four family portraits in the possession of the Plymouth Museum tell us much about the man and his feelings about other people. They are portraits of two of his sisters, his father and a self-portrait, and one can be certain, therefore, that they are entirely of his own hand rather than the combined work of Reynolds and his assistants. Of the four, the one of the youthful Fanny is the most appealing. That of his father shows a patient and intelligent face and expresses more than words can convey. But his portrait of his sister Mary is perhaps the most revealing. In it he has depicted the prominent birthmark on her right cheek near her eye, together with other blemishes. It is an indication of the extent to which Reynolds was a realist. As a group these portraits, with their fresh handling, help us to understand the reputation of Joshua Reynolds; it is reassuring that there was such downright honesty in Plymouth in the eighteenth century. In the portrait of Charles Rogers, the founder of the Cottonian Collection now housed in the museum, Reynolds uses even more lively brushwork than in the family portraits. The museum also has the custody of the painting stick and palette which he used.

Of those painters who came under the influence of Reynolds, pride of place must be given to James Northcote, who went to London by walking from Plymouth with ten guineas in his pocket. Unlike Reynolds he did not embark on a career as a painter until he was 25 years of age, when he entered Reynolds' studio as an assistant and lived in his house. Until then he had been apprenticed to his father's trade watchmaking in Plymouth Dock. Following his master's example he was able to travel to Italy in his thirty-first year and he remained there for three years studying the work of the Old Masters, especially Titian. Northcote had always been skilled in portraiture even before joining Reynolds and his reputation rests partly on this aspect of his output. Plymouth Museum contains his 'Portrait of Dr Yonge' which shows his ability to produce sound traditional work. His 'Self-Portrait' in the same collection is, like all self-portraits, more revealing. He depicts himself as a greying man with a somewhat receding forehead and prominent nose, seated before a reading desk. The Royal Albert Memorial Museum at Exeter has two more paintings in which his self-portrait appears, firstly 'Self-Portrait as a Falconer'—he was reputed to be very interested in falconry—and secondly 'Sir Walter Scott, Bt., and James Northcote Painting his Portrait'. The latter work was produced towards the end of his life and provides a glimpse into his studio.

By this time Northcote had made his name in a field other than pure portraiture—the 'history painting' then in vogue. The Exeter collection includes 'The Entry of Richard and Bolingbroke into London'. It is based on Shakespeare's Richard II—a huge oil painting on canvas showing Richard and Bolingbroke mounted; the design verges on the Baroque. Northcote also turned his hand to writing and his interesting but slight satirical biography of Sir Joshua Reynolds was well received.

He left a legacy of £1,000 in order to commemorate himself by means of a statue. This was carved by Sir Francis Chantrey, better known as the source of the 'Chantrey Bequest', and it may be seen in the north transept of Exeter Cathedral. The inscription reminds us that Northcote distinguished himself in the fine arts and literature for a period of 40 years.

Honiton-born Ozias Humphrey was a miniature portraitist who used a crayon as his medium, though he also worked on a larger scale. Reynolds took an interest in him and when his sight began to fail in later life Humphrey read the newspapers to him. Humphrey's own sight failed suddenly in his last years. The miniature remained popular in the eighteenth century and there was at that time a revival of interest in portraits in crayon and pencil. It was in this field that Humphrey worked. He became 'Portrait Painter in Crayons to his Majesty' shortly after his election to the Royal Academy in 1791. Exeter Museum has a 'Portrait of a Lady in a Mob Cap' which is attributed to him; the pastel technique of this work is so fine that it resembles painting. Humphrey is represented by four works in the National Portrait Gallery.

Richard Cosway, a latter-day Hilliard, was born at Tiverton. His self-portrait in the National Portrait Gallery shows that he was capable of producing very beautiful miniatures. His 'Liberation of St Peter' in St Peter's, the parish church of Tiverton to which he presented it, is one of his four larger-scale works still to be seen in Devon. The exaggerated gestures of St Peter and the angel contribute to the dynamic composition of the painting. In contrast 'Christ Bearing the Cross' presented to St Michael's, Bampton, at present suffers from a layer of darkened varnish. Powderham Castle houses the other two paintings; both are portraits. One of these shows three of the Courtenay sisters. As a student in London Cosway worked in the studio of Thomas Hudson and came under the Neo-Classic influences of the time in which drawing underlies painting. He was patronized by the Prince Regent and was regarded as a 'vain little dandy', but his early successes were founded on ability and as his drawings reveal, hard work. He did much to raise the status of miniature painting and introduced subjects deriving from classical mythology. He painted in watercolour on supports cut from thin sheets of ivory. In 1801, after 20 years of married life, he and his artist wife, Maria Hadfield, separated because of his eccentricity and reckless extravagance. She entered a religious house at Lyons.

Francis Towne, the landscape painter, was probably born at Exeter and certainly was closely associated with the social life of the city though he lived the last nine years of his life in London. He was studying at Shipley's School in London at the age of 15 and became friendly with Richard Cosway and Ozias Humphrey. At the age of 37 he toured Wales with James White of Exeter and further travel in Italy, Switzerland and the Lake District followed. But it appears that during the greater part of his working life his base was Exeter, and indeed, in his lifetime his reputation was a distinctly local one. He worked in both oil and watercolour. His continental journey made a great impression on him and in particular the Swiss Alps, which he sketched on his homeward journey, seem to open up the possibilities of romantic art. It is this trend which makes his work interesting today. In his sixty-seventh year he married a younger dancer of French extraction and a few months later moved to London. When they had been married for only seven months, his wife died. There is a good collection of his work at the Exeter Museum.

Towne had many students in Devon. Among them was John White Abbott, an Exeter surgeon. Born in the Cathedral Close, Abbot has been described as a keystone of Devon landscape painting. Being a surgeon he had no need to sell his paintings. He studied the work of Gainsborough and made copies of the older masters. He was introduced to Reynolds and other artists in London. Abbott did not travel but he did go to the north of England. His style of painting was naturally based on that of his master and the work of both is best summarized by the term 'tinted-drawing' when compared with the landscape painting of the last quarter of the nineteenth century. His clean watercolour washes are nevertheless quite modern in their breadth; he almost always reinforced these washes with outlines. In the representation of foliage the outline is apt to be rather stereotyped, yet it was the means by which he grasped the essence of the forms of both densely-wooded and rock-bound parts of his county.

Little is known about the early life of William Payne, but the tradition is that he was a Devon man. Sir Joshua Reynolds befriended him. It is known that he was a civil engineer at Plymouth Dock and despite the lack of formal artistic training, he began to paint landscapes of the countryside around Plymouth. He exhibited with the Society of Artists in 1776 and continued to do so until 1790. After this date he started to build up a reputation as a teacher and made a series of tours throughout the country. At about this time he produced a number of etchings in which the main shapes were undeveloped; it is probable that they were intended for completion in watercolour and were produced in connection with his teaching activities. Scarcity of knowledge concerning his background and birth is compensated by the numerous examples of his work. A good place in which to see it is the Plymouth Museum, which holds a number of his local landscapes. He worked in watercolour, flooding on washes and, when dry, he built up textures by using his characteristic grey pigment in an almost calligraphic way. These textures give his work a sparkle that was an innovation in the topographic work of his time.

John Downman is another artist whose exact place of birth is not known, but he is thought to be a Devonian and was a contemporary of Cosway, Humphrey, Northcote and Payne. Several of his crayon portraits are to be found in private collections in Devon. Recognized as one of the favourite portrait painters of Regency society, he used chalk or crayon tinted with watercolour as his medium, but not exclusively because he also produced small-scale oil portraits on copper. The best of his work, with its fine linear basis, represents the decorative phase of Neo-Classicism. Though his patrons evidently regarded him primarily as a portraitist, he also produced some history paintings' and when he visited Italy he made a number of landscape drawings in the Albano area.

Samuel Prout came from an old Devon family; his mother being the daughter of an enterprising Plymouth shipping venturer. He began his career by producing topographic work of the south-western counties from 1805-11 before going to London where Rudolf Ackermann, the publisher employed him and, subsequently, he made many visits to the Continent and produced a series of very attractive representations of streets and churches which were much sought after. Encouraged by James Northcote he established a successful practice as a drawing teacher in London and in 1820 he was elected a member of the Old Water Colour Society. Plymouth Museum has many examples of his pen and wash drawings. They have a sparing use of outline supported by minimal, blocked washes, sometimes suggesting the work of a twentieth-century artist and even tending towards a certain abstraction. The subjects consist of views of Plymouth and its waters, Dartmoor Prison during construction and other architectural subjects which are carefully rendered. The Exeter Museum has two watercolours by him. Plymouth Museum holds a miniature portrait of Prout by his friend and fellow artist, William Hunt, who shows him with a high forehead, straight nose, direct eyes and wearing sideboards; he is attired in a white shirt and black caravat. He should not be confused with his nephew John Skinner Prout (1808-76), also born in Plymouth, whose work is far less firm in outline and texture.

Benjamin Haydon, like Prout, was the son of a local bookseller and was a fellow-pupil at Plymouth Grammar School. He went to London full of hope and enthusiasm in 1804 to become a student at the Royal Academy Schools and he exhibited at the Academy at the age of 21. After a brief period as a portrait painter in Plymouth, he became enthused by the wish to excel in 'history painting' and heroic themes on huge canvases appealed to him, but, it is suggested, their inspiration was rarely matched by their technique. The Roman youth, Curtius, who, mythology tells us, sacrificed himself by galloping his horse into a fissure which opened up in the Roman Forum, provided him with the type of subject in which he was interested. His oil painting depicting the incident may be seen at the Exeter Museum and can be described as melodramatic, but it requires only a slight shift of the observer's sensibility for it to become truly convincing. Some of the foreground brushwork is freely handled and it is perhaps easier to appreciate it today than it was in his own lifetime. The same can be said of the brushwork in his small 'Self-Portrait as the Spirit of the Vine' in the same collection. Plymouth Guildhall houses his 'Judgement of Solomon' which he painted in 1814. The 'Raising of Lazarus', 1823, is in the possession of the Tate Gallery, but being in poor condition is not available for the public, and the National Portrait Gallery holds his 'Wordsworth', 1842, in which he depicts the poet, deeply brooding, against dark, lakeland colours. In London Haydon sought out Northcote, who tried to dissuade him from his ambition of being a painter of ancient history and mythology.

In spite of the fact that he antagonized some of his influential patrons, he achieved fame and success which were, unfortunately, not to last. Subsequent rejection and neglect created difficulties which became insuperable and very discouraging. On three occasions he was confined to a debtors' prison. Finally after he had submitted schemes for the decoration of the Houses of Parliament, under a competitive plan which he himself had done much to stimulate, and they were rejected, he decided to end it all and committed suicide by cutting his throat. He wrote an interesting autobiography, published by his wife in 1847 and it is recognized by many readers to be more vivid than his paintings.

Charles Eastlake was born at Plymouth his father being a solicitor to the Admiralty. Prompted by the apparent early success of his fellow pupil at Plymouth Grammar School, Benjamin Haydon, he enrolled at the Royal Academy School in 1809 and later he studied in Paris; at the age of 21 he returned to Plymouth as a portrait painter. He made his name in 1815 when the *Bellerophon*, with Napoleon a prisoner on board, put into Plymouth Sound. Eastlake made sketches of Napoleon from a small boat and from these and from the uniform which Napoleon sent ashore so that he could draw it, he produced a large painting which now forms part of the collection of the National Maritime Musuem. With the proceeds of this successful picture—about £1,000—he visited Italy in 1816 and worked principally as a portrait painter. After a brief return to Plymouth he went to Rome again and, becoming deeply attracted to Italian culture, he stayed 12 years. Two landscapes which he painted at Rome have an affinity with the early work of Corot, but it was the classic influence which made itself felt in his work and was a guiding principle when he later became President of the Royal Academy and Director of the National Gallery. In these posts he undertook many official duties. A mezzotint engraving after a painting by Eastlake, owned by Plymouth Museum, depicts the Reverend John Bidlake who was head of the Plymouth Grammar School from 1780-1810. Among his pupils were several who later became artists: Eastlake himself, Haydon, Johns, Prout and Rogers.

Among the more famous artists who visited Devon in the late eighteenth century was Thomas Rowlandson, whose Devon work is represented at both Exeter and Plymouth. Thomas Girtin was in the county in 1797 and the Courtauld Institute has in its collection a watercolour which he made of Exmouth.

There is a strong tradition, based on the fact that his grandfather and father were born there, that one of England's most important painters, J. M. W. Turner, was a South Molton man. This can be discounted because shortly after young William's date of birth, his father, a barber of limited means, is known to have been working in Maiden Lane and it seems likely that the baby was born in London for his christening is registered at St Paul's, Covent Garden. As Turner's rise to fame does not depend on his Devonian connection, like that of Reynolds, general comment on him does not form part of this work. But it is interesting to note that he made extensive tours of both north and south Devon in 1811 and 1813 and it is recorded that during these visits Turner got in touch with his relatives in both Barnstaple and Exeter. He was able to cover long distances on foot and in due course he became familiar with some parts of Devon. Many stories, not all of them complimentary, were told of him. An anecdote relating to one of these tours appeared in the *Western Antiquary* of 1884. Turner, Prout and Varley (it does not state which Varley) were said to be touring and working together. Coming to a ferry Varley had no change and Turner reluctantly advanced him two pennies. The next morning Varley and Prout, taking the early Exeter coach to London, and leaving Turner behind, were surprised and gratified to find him apparently waiting to see them off, but 'No,' said Turner, 'it isn't that, but you forgot to give me back the two pence I lent you yesterday.' At this date Turner was making money fast and accumulating it.

His tours were purposeful affairs and in 1813 he maintained his prolific output accompanied by Cyrus Redding, a journalist, and assisted by his Devonian friends such as the Plymouth painter A. B. Johns. It is worth noting that Redding did not find Turner to be niggardly in money matters. The young Charles Eastlake was still under tuition in London at the time and his letters of introduction helped considerably. Turner was to stay with Eastlake's aunt on the Cornish bank of the river Tamar, at Calstock; it is possible that Eastlake was also there at the time. This visit was to have important results for one of Turner's more famous paintings 'Crossing the Brook', which hangs in the Tate Gallery, was the culmination of drawings made whilst he was there. The bridge in the painting was identified as one of two bridges spanning the Tamar in that district. It would be wrong, however, to expect the work to be a mere transcript of the Devon scene because Turner infuses it with the Claudian system of composition; but there can be no doubt that his visit to Devon provided the inspiration for it. Several Devon paintings by Turner were exhibited at the Royal Academy. Many engravings from his originals of Devon were produced by William and George Cooke, to whom Turner sometimes gave instructions on how a particular effect was to be achieved, for these works were imbued with his feeling for visual drama and his appreciation of strong atmospheric effects.

It should not be forgotten that, by this date, topographic painters and print-makers and sellers of prints were in competition. Many readers will be more familiar with the prints than they are with the paintings. The peak period for their production was from the beginning of the century until the Great Exhibition of 1851—it was also the year of Turner's death. Printing from wood-blocks or from engraved metal plates has a long history and, as has been mentioned, Wenceslaus Hollar produced a few etchings depicting Devon subjects in the mid-seventeenth century. As the Napoleonic wars had induced the English to seek refreshment in the south-west of their own land in substitution for a blockaded Europe, so they indirectly encouraged the burst of print-making in the peaceful period following the end of hostilities.

The considerable number of etchings and engravings of Devon owe much to non-Devonian artists and engravers. Aquatints were made from about

1780, and, as far as Devon subjects were concerned, lithography first came into use about 1820. It was the general rule for prints to be gathered together as a series and bound in a book; some of Turner's views of Devon for instance, appeared in *Picturesque Views on the Southern Coast of England* in 1826; but a large proportion of the later examples could also be sold singly. Among the earlier prints of Devon subjects are some engravings in the series of *Antiquities* produced by the Buck brothers early in the eighteenth century. Their work is representative of the period before the picturesque characteristics of English landscape were fully appreciated. Among their Devon subjects, Exeter Cathedral, Okehampton Castle and Frithlestock Priory all illustrate the slightly archaic style of the brothers and the emphasis on buildings which was typical of the period.

William Daniell, the aquatint engraver, set out from Land's End in 1814 to sketch the coastal scenery of Britain. Each winter he returned to his London home with his drawings and notes from which he worked. His north Devon views were included in his first folio of *A Voyage Round Great Britain.* They are elegant interpretations of the coastline at Hartland, Clovelly and Ilfracombe. Ten years later on his return journey he passed along the south Devon coast and left work of similar quality showing the Exe Estuary, Torbay, Salcombe and other places.

The work of some artists lost its conviction on being translated into engravings, and early in the period it is obvious that the engravers sometimes worked 'second-hand' from other engravings rather than from specially-made drawings or paintings. On the other hand some artists both drew and painted direct from nature and then used the work as the basis of their prints. The lithographs of north Devon produced by W. Gauci exemplify work made in this way. The bulk of the prints recorded the Devon scene as it was before the age of the railways. The artists found an echo, in the distinctive features of the landscape, of the romantic influences of the time and when these were allied to a good sense of design the results were often exquisite. Many examples of Devon topographic print-making at its best were made from the drawings of Thomas Allom and W. H. Bartlett and published in *Devonshire Illustrated* with historical and descriptive accounts by J. Britton and E. W. Brayley in 1829. George Campion should also be mentioned as a topographic artist whose drawings of both north and south Devon were attractively engraved in the 1830s and Laetitia Byrne, the daughter of an engraver, was responsible for the etchings of Devon subjects which appeared in Lysons *Magnum Britannia.*

Towards the end of their period of greatest popularity prints often took the form of vignettes—small oval representations the edges of which were shaded off into the background space. They were produced in large numbers and could be sold comparatively cheaply. The most important Devon publisher was Henry Besley and Company of Exeter. Three artists are particularly associated with the firm: George Townsend, J. W. Tucker and S. R. Ridgway. Engravings from the drawings which they made were produced in London and they were put on the market by Besley in the form of sets of views. They are now described as 'Besley Ovals'; many will be found in *Views of Devonshire*. The earliest were the work of Townsend, a drawing master. He ceased to be employed by Besley in 1860. The work of William Willis is also typical of the vignette period and he both drew and engraved. His somewhat prosaic prints were usually published in the form of small albums containing about 20 engravings of a particular area.

By the end of the third quarter of the nineteenth century the work of the topographic artist, whether painter or engraver, was in competition with the new craft of photography. The earliest photographs produced in Devon go back to the very beginnings of the age of photography, for W. H. Fox Talbot stayed at Mount Edgcumbe near Plymouth and a few of his calotypes of the area survive from the mid-1840s. Later in the century other typographic photographers of national importance, such as Francis Bedford and Francis Frith, made photographs of Devonian subjects which were reproduced on a large scale. Close on their heels came Devonian photographers, for example: R. Burnard, W. J. Chapman, A. W. Searly and J. Stabb, each important as a pictorial journalist on a regional level.

The long line of visiting artists continued to grow in the nineteenth century. Samuel Palmer, an important influence on modern English painters, worked in the Lynmouth area as a young man and he returned to the county to paint at various times during his life. Perhaps the most famous painting ever made in Devon is 'The Boyhood of Raleigh'. Sir John Millais, one of the founder members of the Pre-Raphaelite Brotherhood, came to Budleigh Salterton in 1871 and rented the ground floor studio of the 'Octagon' close to the sea front. In doing so he was establishing himself within two kilometres of Raleigh's home and in a locality where as a boy he would certainly have 'pottered'. The setting of the picture is almost identical to the view that Millias had from the Octagon. Apparently the painting is the only work which he produced in Devon.

Sir Edward Burne-Jones, who was less-closely associated with the Pre-Raphaelite Brotherhood, is represented by two paintings and two stained-glass windows in the church of St John at Torquay and also by glass in several other Devon churches. The paintings, on the chancel walls of the church, depict the 'Holy Family' and the 'Shepherds and the Magi led to the site of the Nativity.'

Among the many visiting painters of the first half of the twentieth century was Robert P. Bevan of the Camden Town Group, who spent the summers of 1912-15 in east Devon. His 'Green Devon', in the possession of Plymouth Museum, is remarkable for its beautiful blue and purple. Mark Tobey the American known for the esoteric qualities of his paintings, came to Devon in 1931, aged 41, at the invitation of Dorothy and Leonard Elmhirst of Dartington Hall. He stayed until 1939, having worked during that time as a painter and art teacher in the Dartington Arts Department and community. In 1934 the Elmhirsts sent him to Japan for a year's refreshment and it was after his return that he developed his so-called 'white writing'.

Mark Tobey's life story illustrates how cosmopolitan influences are at work in Devon today. The mixture of cultivated and wild countryside, historic towns and varied coastlines, all enjoying comparative freedom from the uglier aspects of industrialization, can be expected to attract visiting artists from outside the region in future as it does at present. On the other hand the direct responses of painters with roots in their local environment are likely to retain their vitality.

List of painters

Abbreviations:

ARA	Associate of the Royal Academy
CMAG	City Museum and Art Gallery, Plymouth
NG	National Gallery
NPG	National Portrait Gallery
PRA	President of the Royal Academy
RA	Royal Academy or Royal Academician
RAMM	Royal Albert Memorial Museum, Exeter
TG	Tate Gallery
VAM	Victoria and Albert Museum

ABBOTT, John White, 1763-1851, *b*Exeter. A surgeon. Student of Francis Towne. Painter in watercolour and oil. Exhibited at RA between 1793-1822 in the honorary section. Travelled in England and in 1791, Scotland. Sometimes signed his work with a mongram. Examples may be seen at CMAG, RAMM and VAM.

BROCKEDON, William, 1787-1854, *b*Totnes. Subject and history painter also produced some sculpture. 1809 student at RA schools. Exhibitor at RA 1812-41. Travelled on the Continent and published works dealing with the Alps and Italy, etc. In his later years he worked on various inventions. 1830 assisted in founding the Royal Geographical Society. 1831 he founded the Graphic Society. Reredos painting at St Saviour's Dartmouth, other work at VAM.

CONDY, Nicholas, 1799-1851, *b*Plymouth, of Cornish ancestry. Served in the Peninsular War when he studied Napoleon's collections in Paris. On return, painter in Plymouth; oil and watercolour, coastal and marine subjects. Exhibited at the RA and British Institute 1830-45. Died a few months after his son's early death, it is said of grief. There are examples of his work at the CMAG.

CONDY, Nicholas Mathew, *c*1817-51, *b*Plymouth. Son of Nicholas Condy. Oil painter of ships and marine subjects. Exhibited at the RA. His work may be seen at CMAG.

COSWAY, Richard, RA, 1740-1821, *b*Tiverton. Miniature painter usually on ivory or bone. Student at the school of William Shipley. First exhibited at the RA 1768, elected ARA 1770. Painter-in-Ordinary to the Prince of Wales. His miniatures noted for their delicacy and charm. He introduced subjects from classical mythology. His wife Maria Hadfield an artist, had been brought up in Italy. He collected drawings by the Old Masters. Examples of his minatures may be seen at the NPG, VAM and the British Museum; a few easel-paintings by him exist in Devon.

DOWNMAN, John, ARA, 1750-1824, *b*Devon. Portrait draughtsman and miniaturist but he also produced some landscape drawings. Crayon and coloured chalks, watercolour, oil on copper. One of the favourite portrait painters of Regency society. In Italy 1773-5; often in the West-country, studio at Exeter 1807-8. There are works by him at Saltram House,

Powderham Castle, RAMM and in London at the Wallace Collection, NPG, TG and VAM.

EASTLAKE, Charles Locke, PRA, 1793-1865, *b*Plymouth. Director of the NG 1855. Educated at Plymouth Grammar School, Charterhouse and RA Schools 1809. Later in Paris. Oil painter of portraits and genre. He lived and worked in Rome for 12 years. Examples at CMAG, TG and VAM.

GANDY, William, *c*1650-1729, *b*Plymouth (?). Son of James Gandy a portrait painter and member of an old Exeter family after whom Gandy Street is named. Painter in oil. Examples at RAMM and the Royal Devon and Exeter Hospital.

GENDALL, John, 1789-1865, *b* and *d*Exeter. Varied career as a draughtsman and painter in watercolour and oil. Worked for R. Ackermann the fine art publisher in London. Returned to Exeter *c*1830. Produced many lively topographic drawings and etchings of Exeter which he seldom signed. Exhibited landscapes at the RA 1846-63. Associated with the establishment of RAMM and was one of its first, joint honorary-curators of paintings. Examples in the Ashmolean, British Museum, West Country Studies Library, RAMM and VAM.

HAINSSELIN, Henry, 1820-92, *b*Devonport. Painter in oil. Genre paintings of a slightly satirical type. Emigrated to Australia in 1852. Examples at CMAG.

HAYDON, Benjamin Robert, 1786-1846, *b*Plymouth. Educated at Plymouth Grammar School; student at the RA Schools 1807. Portrait painter in oil and later a 'history painter'. Propagated the idea that patronage of the arts was socially desirable. Committed suicide. Examples at Plymouth Guildhall, RAMM, NG, NPG and VAM.

HAYMAN, Francis, RA, 1708-76, *b*Exeter. Oil painter, scene-painter and illustrator. Introduced a French rococo element into English painting. Noted for his 'conversation pieces'; painted decorations for Vauxhall Pleasure Gardens. Foundation member of the RA; first librarian at the RA from 1771. Friend of Hogarth to whom he has been likened. Gainsborough may have studied under him. Examples at RAMM, NPG and VAM.

HILLIARD, Nicholas, 1547-1619, *b*Exeter, *d*London. Famous miniature painter, one of the first English artists about whom much is known. Eldest son of a goldsmith. A Swiss source appears to show that he was in Geneva at the age of ten. At 14 apprenticed to Robert Brandon, goldsmith to Elizabeth I. Eventually Hilliard became carver and 'limner' to Queen Elizabeth. Portraits, also full-length figures. Designer and producer of fine jewellery. Examples in London in the Royal Collection, NPG and VAM; in Cambridge at the Fitzwilliam Museum and in a private collection in Devon.

HUDSON, Thomas, 1701-79. Described as a Devonian by James Northcote. *d*Twickenham. Leading fashionable portrait painter in oil after the death of Kneller in 1723. Ran a successful practice with assistants and pupils, among them Joseph Wright of Derby and Joshua Reynolds. Many examples to be seen in Devon: at Barnstaple and Exeter Guildhalls, the Royal Devon and Exeter Hospital, RAMM and in many private collections; he is also represented at NPG, TG etc.

HUMPHREY, Ozias, RA, 1724-1810, *b*Honiton, *d*London. Portrait miniaturist and draughtsman in crayon and pastel. Studied in Italy, 1773-77 and worked in India 1785-88. His work may be seen at Exeter, RAMM and NPG.

JOHNS, Ambrose Bowden, 1776-1858, *b*Plymouth. Topographic work of Devon especially Plymouth area. Drawing teacher. Accompanied J. M. W. Turner when he visited the area. A few examples of his work survive in private collections in Devon.

LEAKEY, James, 1773-1865, *b* and *d*Exeter. Miniature painter, he also produced landscapes in the oil medium. His 'Head of Christ' may be soon in Exeter Cathedral. Other Examples at Exeter Guildhall, the Royal Devon and Exeter Hospital and RAMM.

LEE, Frederick Richard, RA, 1798-1879, *b*Barnstaple, *d*South Africa. Oil painter. Landscapes of the Devon scene with figure groups also many seascapes. Much time spent aboard his yacht; he eventually settled in Cape Colony. A portrait of Lee by H. P. Briggs RA hangs in the North Devon Athenaeum. Examples of his own paintings may be seen at CMAG, RAMM, TG, NG and VAM.

LUNY, Thomas, 1759-1837, *b*London *d*Teignmouth. Served in the navy until 1820. Settled in Teignmouth 1810. Sea battles and coastal scenery of mellow almost monochromatic colour, in a style reminiscent of the Dutch School. His work may be seen at CMAG RAMM and Torre Abbey.

NORTHCOTE, James, RA, 1746-1831, *b*Devonport. Follower of Reynolds in his portraiture, also a painter of 'history subjects.' Son of a watch-maker. Studied in London for four years, including work as an assistant to Reynolds. Portrait painter in Plymouth. From 1777-80 in Italy, influenced by Titian. One of the great characters of his day. Publications include *Memoir of Sir Joshua Reynolds*, 1813, *Life of Titian*, 1830. Examples of his work at Saltram House, CMAG, RAMM, VAM and in private collections in Devon.

PATCH, Thomas, *c* 1725-82, *b*Exeter. Landscape and townscape painter and engraver influenced by the classic style. His caricatures, in the oil medium, were never so satirical that they could not be appreciated as portraits. From 1747 most of his life was spent in Italy where he made engravings from the Old Masters, first in Rome and then in Florence. Examples at RAMM and NPG.

PAYNE, William, *c*1776-1830, *b*Devon (?). Civil engineer at Plymouth Dock. Self-taught watercolour painter with distinctive style in which 'Paynes grey' played a prominent role, he also painted in oil. Exhibited with the Society of Artists from 1776-90. Extensive tours of the country combined with work as a drawing master. Many examples of his work at the CMAG, RAMM and VAM.

PROUT, Samuel, FSA, 1783-1852, *b*Plymouth, *d*Denmark Hill. Topographic artist and teacher. Subjects drawn from the south-western counties and after 1818 from the Continent and published for instance as *Sketches at Home and Abroad*. Examples of his watercolours, in which pencil outline is supported by minimal, blocked washes, may be seen at CMAG, RAMM, TG, and VAM.

REYNOLDS, Sir Joshua, PRA, 1723-92, *b*Plympton St Maurice, *d*London. Seventh child of the Master of Plympton Grammar School. Apprenticed to Thomas Hudson in London at the age of 17. As a portrait painter at Devonport his naval contacts enabled him to travel to Italy, 1749-52. He worked in Rome, Florence and Venice. His ultimate achievement was the assimilation of the style of the Old Masters and its infusion into the English tradition. A national figure who maintained contact with his Devonian roots. His publications include his *Discourses* as first PRA. He experimented with technique, some of his paintings tend, therefore, to be in a dubious condition. Examples may be seen at Exeter Guildhall, Saltram House, RAMM, CMAG and in private collections in Devon and, in London, in the NG, NPG and TG.

ROGERS, Philip Hutchins, 1794-1853, *b*Plymouth, *d*Baden-Baden. Oil and watercolour paintings of the Plymouth area. After 1818, travelled widely. Much appreciated in Austria and Germany where he worked. Some of his landscapes were influenced by the classic tradition and demonstrate his sensitive treatment of light. He produced a dozen etchings for Carrington's *Dartmoor*, 1826. Examples may be seen at CMAG.

SHUTE, John *fl*1550-70, *b*Cullompton. Records show that Shute was in the service of the second Duke of Northumberland who sent him to Italy in 1550 to study the work of the masters. In 1563 he published *The First and Chief Groundes of Architecture* in the introduction of which he describes himself as a painter and architect. Although he was held in repute by his contemporaries no known works of his remain.

TOWNE, Francis, 1740-1816, *b*Exeter (?), *d*London. Painter in oil and watercolour, lived much of his life at Exeter. Exhibited at most of the exhibitions of the Society of Artists from 1762-73 and at the RA after 1775. Continental journey 1780-81. The Swiss Alps made a great impression and led him towards a romantic interpretation of landscape which has only been appreciated in modern times. Examples of his work may be seen at CMAG, RAMM, NG, TG, VAM and the Walker Art Gallery, Liverpool

TRAIES, William, 1789-1872, *b*Crediton, *d*Exeter. Painter in oil. Sometimes known as the 'Claude of Devon', but more likely to have been influenced by Wilson. Many of his finest works depict the Topsham area. Examples may be seen at the CMAG, RAMM and in private collections in the county.

TUCKER, John Wallace, 1808-69, *b*Exeter. Oil painter, sometimes on wood panels. He recorded, on the back of each of his Devon landscapes, the date and location. Examples at RAMM.

WIDGERY, Frederick John, 1861-1942, *b*Exeter, son of William Widgery. Educated at the Cathedral School, Exeter School of Art, South Kensington

Museum Schools and the National Art School in Antwerp. Oil painter who followed the style set by his father. Dartmoor subjects dominate his work; he illustrated *A Perambulation of Dartmoor* by Rowe, *Devon* by Lady Northcote, etc. Much involved with public life in Exeter; Mayor of the city 1903-4. A prolific painter represented in many Devon collections.

WIDGERY, William, 1826-93, *b*North Molton. Plasterer and stone mason, son of a labourer. Moved to Exeter, painted in his spare time. Self-taught painter in oil, etc. Prolific painter of Devon landscapes, also marine subjects. Visited Italy and Switzerland. Represented in many Devon collections including RAMM and Torre Abbey.

WILLIAMS, T. H. *fl*1798-1830, christian names and place of birth unknown. Painter in oil, etcher. Exhibited views of Devon at the RA 1801-14. Travelled in England and Wales and made numerous etchings to illustrate topographic books such as *Picturesque Excursions in Devon and Cornwall*, apart from that rarely left Devon. An example may be seen at CMAG.

WILLIAMS, William, 1805-95, *b*Cornwall. Exhibited at the RA, etc. Painter of landscape and coastal scenery. Usually signed work 'W. Williams Plymouth'. Represented in private collections in Devon also in RAMM.

CHAPTER SEVEN

The Principal Towns

The four main centres of the population of Devon have clearly defined characteristics arising from the land-forms on which they are built and from the diverging occupations and aspirations of their inhabitants. Exeter's historic status as the ecclesiastical centre of the south-west, and its increasing cultural importance, have led many to refer to it as the 'Capital of the West'. Plymouth on the other hand, in the extreme south-west corner of Devon, is ideally placed to serve, as a distribution area, the needs of Cornwall; but it is unlike Exeter in that it was created by the amalgamation of three separate burgeoning towns.

Communications between north Devon and Plymouth and Exeter are not made easier, even today, by direct roads of the type which many smaller, less hilly counties have been able to construct. The tract of country which is drained by the rivers Taw and Torridge and their tributaries is large enough to be a sub-region and has Barnstaple, for many centuries the third largest town in the county, as its focal point. Torquay, Devon's most important resort, is comparatively recent in origin, having been expanded from a fishing hamlet to meet the sophisticated requirements of the families of naval officers when the fleet used the bay in the eighteeenth century. The building of the railways produced further opportunities which have resulted in the rapid development of this climatically-favoured part of the county.

Exeter

Not only the city itself but many of the market towns and villages of the south-west as a whole consider Exeter Cathedral to be their mother-church. The rich collection of secular buildings in the precinct is grouped in such a

way that it has a very satisfactory relationship to the Cathedral. On the
south side of the Close some buildings have been demolished since 1942
with the result that from certain positions St Mary and St Peter's is now
seen to better effect. The narrow, medieval alleys, by which the Close is
reached survived the air raids and modern approaches too, foster an element
of visual contrast.

The Cathedral contains many treasures of which one of the most precious
is the *Exeter Book* which was written before A.D. *c*975. It was presented to
the Cathedral by its first bishop Leofric and contains the largest single
collection of poems in the English language known to exist. The library
which houses it also contains the *Exeter Domesday Book*. In the Close, the
statue of a studious man, with a book on his lap and books underfoot,
represents Richard Hooker (*c*1554-1600), the Exeter-born theologian. He
is remembered for his work *Of the Laws of Ecclesiastical Politie* in which
he defended the Church of England as it was established in the reign of
Elizabeth I. Another famous Elizabethan Exonian, Sir Thomas Bodley,
founded the Bodlian Library at Oxford.

Among the buildings of the Close, Mol's Coffee House and the 'Ship',
nearby, are reputed to have been popular with Elizabethan sea captains. St
Martin's church, next to Mol's, is not the most interesting of the many
medieval churches in the city centre.

About a half a kilometre from the Cathedral the river Exe could be crossed
by ferry or bridge. Rivers are the means of approach for foe as well as friend
and it is not surprising that farther along the coast, at Zitherixon Clay Pits
on the river Teign, the remains of a Viking ship was found under a deposit
of mud in 1898. The Exe gave access to the Danes when in 1003 they
sacked the city. At that date the religious centre was Crediton, 11 kilometres
(7 miles) to the north-west. The see of Crediton had been established in the
year A.D. 909. Crediton, overshadowed since then by Exeter, stands in the
angle formed by two rivers, the Creedy and the Yeo, a tributary of the Exe.
The town was less accessible to intruders, but was not as good a centre of
communications. So when, after centuries of neglect, the Roman wall of
Exeter was made good the city became the bishopric in A.D. 1050. From
then until 1877 the Exeter see included Cornwall in addition to Devon.

As this change was made so moves which were eventually to lead to a
great strengthening of Exeter as the cultural centre of the two counties
were being set in motion. The Great Exhibition of 1851 created the right

mood for the establishment of the Exeter School of Art in 1855. After the death, in 1862, of the Prince Consort a wish was felt to establish a memorial to him; this eventually led to the founding of the Royal Albert Memorial Museum in 1865. Gradually the scope of these two establishments developed, and they functioned at times in the same and then adjacent buildings. At the end of the century the Exeter Technical and University Extension came into being. A college was opened in 1911 and, in 1922, it was incorporated under the title of 'University College of the South-West'; during the same year a presentation of land north of the city centre was made; the first building on this splendid site, the Washington Singer Building, was completed in 1931.

In 1955 Exeter University was granted its Charter and, in the following year, Queen Elizabeth II unveiled the foundation stone of Queen's Building. In its first quarter of the century the University, together with the Northcote Theatre situated on the campus and opened in 1967, has had an increasingly invigorating influence on the city and the region as a whole. It is probably because of this that Exeter still has the lingering feeling of being the centre of a whole province. It is also the place in the South-West with the longest commercial history; one compounded essentially of distribution, marketing and administration. Large industrial intrusions have never ruptured its gradual and continuous growth.

As a result of the way in which Exeter has developed most of the interesting architectural features lie either within or just outside the wall. Indeed, the city and the wall which encloses it have always been slightly apart from development outside owing to the configuration of the ground. A series of pleasant open spaces reach two-thirds of the way round the centre. The Longbrook valley, a natural feature modified by infilling and best seen from the western corner of the wall at St Bartholomew's Terrace, was connected to two greens, the Northenhay and Southernhay. The former is now laid out as a park overlooked by the walls of the Rougemont Castle which forms the north-east corner of the city. After being interrupted by buildings near the site of the former East Gate, the open area is continued by the Southernhay—a good example of Georgian planning. Modern replacement buildings, necessitated by war damage, retain the window-spacing of the original.

A walk through the centre of Exeter still reveals the many building periods involved in the making of the city. Apart from the wall none of the Roman structures survive above ground. The medieval churches and houses indicate the increasing wealth and importance of the area as a result of the woollen trade. High Street, and its westward continuation, Fore Street, make a nearly straight line—once an Iron Age track—to the river-crossing. The line is transected by South Street and North Street and the other main junction is formed by Queen Street.

In the High Street, the Guildhall, with its arcade straddling the pavement, is the oldest municipal building in England. Beside it stands the fifteenth-century 'Turks Head' and nearby Parliament Street, a mere slot between the buildings, is claimed to be one of the narrowest streets in the world. On the north side of Fore Street, the street known as the Mint gives access to the Priory of St Nicholas which was originally a small Benedictine establishment. In Queen Street, an essentially Victorian development, the portico of the former Upper Market has recently been cleverly integrated with the new Guildhall Shopping Centre. Close at hand is the Royal Albert Memorial Museum, the façade of which incorporates a pleasing range of stone and marbles.

After the bombing of Exeter in World War II, Dr Thomas Sharp was employed to produce an outline plan for re-building. His recommendations, published in 1946 in the form of a book titled *Exeter Phoenix*, were imaginative and thorough. He accepted the fact that many areas, though not actually damaged by bombing, were in a state of delapidation and should be cleared. He put a strong case for the balanced development of the shopping, administrative, ecclesiastical and industrial functions of the city and argued that the aim should be renewal, not restoration. He suggested that the shattered High Street should be retained, but made the sensible suggestion that there should be ground floor arcades along the part of the street which was to be renewed. A new pedestrian precinct, the Princesshay, was proposed for the area where Bedford Circus had stood. New views of the cathedral which had appeared during the bombing were to be preserved by new street alignments. Traffic was to be discouraged from using the city centre. It was a foward-looking plan parts of which were put into effect with some loss of the former intimate scale. But, unfortunately, many of the new elevations seemed to be uninspired adaptations of Georgian proportioning. A correspondent's article in a national newspaper in 1962 was able to claim that the city had wantonly thrown away many of the opportunities, worthy of its site and history, with which it had been presented.

However, in a second surge of redevelopment in the 1960s and 1970s more of Dr Sharp's proposals have been realised: the exposing of the walls for the whole of their length; the clearing of the blighted areas including Exe Island; the re-directing of traffic in the heart of the city and the building of the Guildhall Shopping Centre in which shoppers are protected from the vagaries of the Devonshire weather.

To return to the survey of the centre of Exeter. Fore Street leads to the Exe Bridges constructed in the late 1960s. Before crossing the river it is instructive to turn first to the left and then to the right. At the foot of Stepcote Hill there are a few half-timbered buildings which together with the church of St Mary Steps form a picturesque group. Turning back to go to Frog Lane there is a four-storied Tudor house the conservation of which earned a European Architectural Heritage Award for the builder who carried out the work in 1975.

The bridges form part of a busy road junction. St Edmunds-on-the-Bridge is now isolated on a traffic island; the river was much wider in medieval times than it is today. Some of the arches of the old bridge had always been visible in the crypt of the church. Clearance of the semi-derelict area presented the opportunity of revealing the sub-structures of the medieval bridge. The construction of the edifice was instigated by Nicholas Gervase, a wealthy merchant who was four times mayor of Exeter; when he died about 1259 his son carried on the work. Their bridge was 183 metres long and consisted of 17 or 18 arches which ran diagonally across the river. The eastern abutment and the first arch can still be seen next to St Edmund's tower. The church and chantry chapel were built on the specially-shaped cut-waters of the bridge. The two buildings, with the carriageway passing between them, must have been an attractive sight in their hey-day. On the west bank of the river, paths now extend both upstream and down for some considerable distance. Flooding of these low-lying parts occurred in 1960 and new embankments have been constructed and trees have been planted in keeping with the proposals put forward by Dr Sharp.

A few minutes walk downstream from the bridges, with the city in view on the east bank, is the quay where the river may be crossed by ferry. This area retains the atmosphere of trade and commerce. The fine seventeenth-century Custom House, together with two handsome Victorian warehouses, dominate the east bank. This was the port of Exeter during the periods when the river could be freely navigated. For a long time its use was prevented by an obstruction, Countess Weir, made, it seems, with the intention of crippling Exeter's trade. Eventually the city fathers constructed a canal on the west bank where there is also a nineteenth-century canal-basin. A collection of ships, of world-wide origin, has been assembled here to form the Exeter Maritime Museum. Above the quays residents of Colleton Crescent, built in the Georgian period, can look out across the Exe valley to Haldon Hill and the foothills of Dartmoor; it is a prospect which enhances many parts of this attractive city.

Plymouth

It is worth trying to imagine the promontory between the estuaries of the Plym and Tamar before it became covered by the works of man. This virgin territory, afforested with oak and alder, thinning naturally in places to gorse-covered heaths, was the home of a few simple families who lived by fishing. The land ended then, as it does today, at the range of low, limestone cliffs behind the Hoe, which, even in the reign of Elizabeth I, should be visualized as an open down covered with greensward. Similar cliff-tops still exist beside other parts of the Sound.

The Hoe is the open heart of Plymouth and its region. In the foreground of a panorama which is full of interest lies Drake's Island, formerly known as the island of St Nicholas. The waters of the Sound lie roughly four-square but extend, in the west, into Cawsand Bay. As far as the eye can see, Penlee Point to the west and the cliffs near Wembury Point to the east, the shores consist of rocks rising here and there to cliffs. Mount Edgcumbe House and its parkland, no longer a part of the county of Devon, forms a gracious, eighteenth-century background. Though not visible from the Hoe, Saltram House and its park near Plympton lies within easy distance.

To the immediate east and west of the Hoe two rivers, the Plym and the Tamar, flow into the Sound. Their respective lower reaches, the Cattewater and the Hamoaze, provide natural and almost impregnable harbours of superlative quality. Their entrance channels are little more than 500 metres wide. The Plym estuary reaches back three kilometres and originally ended under the very walls of Plympton Castle. The narrow at Devil's Point is the entrance to a substantial drowned-river valley which branches into a dozen inlets and gives access to both the Devonian and Cornish hinterland. In some places the Tamar's banks rise steeply from the waters' edge, in others they take the form of extensive salt-marshes, whilst elsewhere oak woods still drape the banks. The site of Plymouth is, therefore, lapped by deep water on three sides and, furthermore, many inlets intrude on the central promontory on which the city is now situated: Sutton Pool, Mill Bay, Stonehouse Creek and Western Mill Lake were formerly considerably larger, having been the subject of much in-filling, but it can still be said of this land and water—they interlock. No city in Britain enjoys a visually more interesting site.

Many different trains of thought can be set in motion by all that the Hoe has witnessed. Here the Elizabethans might enjoy a game of bowls at the edge of their flourishing town and, at the same time, could keep an eye on the horizon. Since those days the Hoe has often been used as an assembly-area by the people of Plymouth—a splendidly situated stage on which many historic parades and ceremonies have taken place.

Below the stage lies the Sound, the great naval arena, to which since the 1840s protection has been given by the breakwater. Across these waters, in 1403, came a force of 30 Breton ships with 1200 men who ravaged the town, leaving it in flames. The area beside Sutton Harbour which the Bretons occupied has since been known as 'Bretonside'. To the Sound in 1667 came a Dutch fleet to threaten Plymouth and challenge English sea power. Here in 1815, Napoleon spent several days as a prisoner aboard H.M.S. *Bellerophon* attracting considerable attention and some sympathy. A painting of the scene by Jules Girdet, in the collection of the City Art Gallery and Museum, shows small boats so crowded around the ship that a child has been jolted overboard. The authorities were given cause for annoyance when hundreds of small craft followed the ship as she set off to transfer Napoleon to H.M.S. *Northumberland* to continue the voyage to St Helena. One dinghy was accidentally rammed by a gunboat and some of the passengers were drowned.

The port is well known as the place from which many of the Elizabethan expeditions departed. But Plymouth saw many other embarkations including those of the Black Prince, the emigrants who founded New Zealand, Captain Cook, bound for Australia, and, above all, the *Mayflower*—a reminder that no other British city has stronger links with the New World.

The Hoe is the site of several memorials, among them a nineteenth-century statue of Sir Francis Drake which was modelled by J. E. Boehm, the Viennese sculptor who received several English commissions of the day. Two bronze casts were made, the first being ordered for Tavistock, Drake's birthplace, by the Duke of Bedford. He granted Plymouth's request for the second cast. Four years after the unveiling of the statue the foundation stone of the National Memorial, situated nearby, was laid on the three-hundredth anniversary of the sighting from the Hoe of the Spanish Armada. It was paid for by public subscription and designed by W. C. May, sculptor, and H. A. Gribble, the architect who was responsible for the Brompton Oratory.

The largest monument is the Naval Memorial which was erected by the Commonwealth War Graves Commission. It honours the Navy and the memory of the men of Plymouth and their comrades of the Empire who 'Have no Grave Other than the Sea'. A committee recommended that each of the three Home Ports of the navy should have a memorial which, whilst carrying the names of the dead, should also serve as a 'leading-mark' for ships entering the port. The three monuments are identical, being obelisks of Portland stone, supported, at the four corners of their bases by buttresses, and the designer was Sir Robert Lorimer. The shafts are crowned by large copper spheres supported by allegorical figures and ships' prows. Two low-relief bronzes, one on the east and one on the west face of the shaft, represent the Naval Air Arm and the Submarine Service respectively and are strong designs of their period.

The extension which commemorates the dead of the 1939-45 war spreads sideways in the form of two semicircular arms enclosing a garden; the design for this extension was made by Edward Maufe RA. The Plymouth memorial is unique in that, at the wish of the countries concerned, it names the members of the naval forces of the Commonwealth countries who were lost at sea during World War II. The monument to the Royal Marines of the Plymouth Division is situated on the part of the Hoe near the Citadel; and the Army memorial will be found at the Lockyer Street entrance to the Hoe.

Smeaton's Eddystone Lighthouse is also on the Hoe. For a hundred years it stood on the hazardous reef of the same name and was only rendered unsafe by the undermining action of the sea on the rocks on which it stood. The upper part of the structure was taken down, stone by stone, and re-erected on the Hoe in 1882 when the new, taller Eddystone Lighthouse, often visible on the horizon, was built.

Many are the celebrations which have taken place on the Hoe. In 1897, for instance, a *Feu de Joie* was performed in honour of Queen Victoria's Golden Jubilee. The militia were stationed at arms' lengths along a 14-

kilometre line around the Sound. If, as it appears, the rifles had been primed so that puffs of smoke were produced as they were discharged into the air in precise succession, the effect, of the visibly-extending white wreath accompanied by the sound, undoubtedly produced a grand, panoramic spectacle.

The heart of medieval Plymouth was Sutton Prior, north-east of the Hoe beside Sutton Pool. St Andrew's, the parish church, marked the upper, western edge of the town. The Barbican was a sixteenth-century extension rather than the centre of the town, an outcome of Elizabethan enterprise. Some of the older buildings have been swept away in the enforcement of slum clearance policies which failed to promote conservation, and some were bombed. But there are still many buildings of character and this is the part of Plymouth to which visitors return time and time again because of its vitality and historic associations. Here the old mercantile framework of warehouses, quays, Custom House and Fish Market jostles with small shops, inns, colourful fishing vessels and sleek modern yachts.

The Old Plymouth Society rescued number 32, New Street in 1926 and it is now owned by the city. The thresholds show the wear of centuries, the floors sag. This home, and many others in what was a brand new street, was convenient for work and comfortably furnished and probably contained exotic objects which had been brought back from the Tropics and the Americas. The bedroom windows with their mullions and leaded-lights extend from one side of the room to the other. Across the street the façade of a similar building, jutting out on its carved corbels, may be seen. There is still a faint smell of creosote and salt water in the air; the shouts which drift in from the Barbican might be of an earlier English. From the window, the masts and rigging at the end of the street can be seen to respond to the regular movement of the water....After musing for a few minutes in surroundings such as these, time ceases to have a meaning and the feelings of the age in which England stood on the brink of world conquest can come very close—how constrained those pioneering Devonians would find the sedentary lives of their twentieth-century descendents!

The original township was protected by various castles. Much has been made of the fact that the Citadel was designed to threaten the town as much as deter attack from the sea—Plymouth had been a bulwark of the Parliamentary cause in the Civil War. But the essence of any citadel is that it dominates, as well as protects, its city.

To return to the Naval Memorial, a broad prospect, Armada Way, part pedestrian precinct, part roadway, carries the eye into the centre of the city which has been reconstructed after its destruction in World War II. Armada Way crosses Royal Parade, the new east-west spine road beside the Civic Centre and the restored Guildhall and St Andrew's church. At this point a left turn brings the walker to Derry's Cross where, continuing in the same westerly direction, it joins Union Street which Foulston laid out in 1815. Looking westwards along this street the Devonport Column can be discerned in the distance. Erected in 1824, to Foulston's design, it marked the year in which George IV changed the place-name 'Plymouth Dock' to 'Devonport'. The town owned its foundation to the nation's need for a naval base in the south-west to balance the growing threat posed by France in the seventeenth century. The Devon bank of the Tamar was chosen as the site for the new dockyard in 1690. This is now known as the South Yard and forms a small part of the vast 'Royal Naval Dockyards' which have kept pace with the changing technologies of the present day.

Plymouth Dock developed rapidly and, after a century, its population was greater than that of Plymouth. The finely-proportioned Town Hall with its associated buildings is described in Chapter Four. Civic pride led to friction with Plymouth even in the years leading up to the unification of the three towns in 1914. One of the few places in Devonport at which the Tamar may be approached by the public occurs at Ferry Road, which leads to Torpoint Ferry. By means of the ferry car drivers can quickly reach the Maker peninsula, and the Mount Edgcumbe Country Park, in Cornwall. Another place from which a view of the water may be had is a small public park on the cliff-top near Admiralty House. Here there is a memorial to 'Scott of the Antarctic'; it was provided by public subscription and was designed by A. H. Hodges RBS, architect and sculptor. Robert Falcon Scott, a captain in the Royal Navy, was born in Stonehouse and Plymouth was the port of embarkation for his voyages of discovery including his last.

Stonehouse, lying between Devonport and Plymouth, is now linked with them by the continuous development of the built-up area. It owes its growth to the overflow of naval and residential buildings from Devonport, being the site of the Royal Naval Hospital, the Royal William Victualling Yard and the Royal Marine Barracks.

Plymouth was one of the first war-devastated cities to stir into action. The City Centre is no longer recognizable as the place which existed there before 1941. *A Plan for Plymouth*, the report prepared for the City Council by Patrick Abercrombie in association with the City Engineer, J. P. Watson, in which the proposals for rebuilding were put forward, was published as early as 1943. The report noted that 'the present moment provides conditions especially receptive and favourable to planning.' It gave much space to both the inner and outer road systems and many of its proposals have been implemented. The need for an outer road to take through-traffic from other parts of England to Cornwall, by means of a road bridge across the Tamar, had been recognized before the war. The report put forward the concept of an inner ring-road within which a shopping centre, worthy of the whole region, would be developed. This was balanced by the idea that residential neighbourhoods, self-contained as far as social services were concerned, should be developed.

Royal Parade was opened in 1947. Narrow streets which had served their purpose for centuries were replaced by broad thoroughfares. 'Streets should be made sufficiently wide to permit continuous short-term parking without hinderance to the traffic flow', stated the report. Thus the first developments consisted of wide streets flanked by traditional shops. The resulting spaciousness, combined with the small scale of many of the buildings, failed to produce much aesthetic verve and it was not realised, at the time, that the automobile is not necessarily a civilizing influence. Rotterdam, the first European city to separate the car from the pedestrian, had not then risen as a model which was to guide others.

The traffic system has since been modified to accommodate a greatly increased number of vehicles. Taller buildings such as the Civic Centre, 1963, designed by the City Architect, now give contrast and greatly improve the general proportions of the centre; and in the latest developments road vehicles and pedestrians have been separated.

In addition to its many other assets, Plymouth is well endowed as a centre for outdoor recreation. There are many places on the shores of the Sound and the estuaries where there are good berths for ships, large and small, and north of the city, Dartmoor, with its opportunities for walking and horse-riding, is within easy reach. This, combined with the many places of historic and architectural interest, not only in Devon but in adjacent Cornwall too, make the city an excellent centre for residents and visitors alike.

Torquay and district

Between Teignmouth and Brixham the coast lies roughly from north to south. Two prominent headlands consisting of a hard limestone, Hope's Nose and Berry Head, protrude from the general line. Between these points, a distance of seven kilometres (four miles) the forces of erosion have removed a bight, Tor Bay, from the softer conglomerate rocks. This was once known as 'Torre Bay'. The word torre is French and it presumably referred to the existence in the district of towers of rock or 'tors'. It was to the ships which anchored in the bay that the growth of Torquay into Devon's best-known resort, enjoying an international reputation, was primarily due.

The coast, which may be visited at various places, is traversed by the South Devon Coast Path and is one of the many attractions of this sheltered and flower-bedecked district. Berry Head, a Country Park, has varied points of interest and good facilities for visitors. It is famous for its wild, lime-loving plants and sea birds; there is an extensive fortification of the Napoleonic era, and beyond this is the modern lighthouse. The Hope's Nose area was acquired by the municipality of Torquay in 1921 and the Marine Drive, from which it may be viewed, was constructed largely in order to provide work for the unemployed. It was opened in 1924. Farther east, at Babbacombe, an extremely steep lane descends from the residential area to the small cove. An easier descent may be made to the adjacent Oddicombe bathing-beach by means of footpaths or by using the funicular railway. In 1846, Queen Victoria in the Royal Yacht made one of her visits to the coast. Because of heavy rain she did not land as intended but went on to Brixham. Taken by surprise, Torquay managed only a volley from the Beacon, and it was not heard by the royal party. The Queen's comment was reported to have been that 'Torquay is the only sensible place on the coast'.

Today's car-driving tourists will probably notice that, but for modern by-passes, the last part of the route from Newton Abbot to Torquay would have passed through an almost continuously built-up-area. Within Torquay itself, now part of the greater Torbay administrative region, the urban character extends from Watcombe in the north to Churston 12 kilometres to the south. Then, after a break of only two kilometres another built-up-area hems in the seafaring village of Brixham. In this respect Torbay may be compared to Plymouth, for both places consists of an amalgamation of communities which were, at one time, separate. With one-way traffic arrange-ments, and the fact that the hills frequently cause the direction of the roads to bend, the visitor is to be excused if he finds it difficult to get his bearings. Torquay's waterfront is a good place from which to identify some of the main features.

Seen from the Inner Harbour, Braddon Hill rises directly behind the Strand and Waldon Hill is on the west and Park Hill on the east. Fleet Street passes up the valley on the left between Waldon Hill and Braddon Hill; underneath the street the Fleet Brook flows in a conduit. The street continues up the valley in the form of Union Street, the main shopping street of Torquay. About a kilometre from the harbour, at Castle Circus, stands the Town Hall. Further progress in the same direction leads to the main exit from the town to Newton Abbot.

To return to the harbour. On the right Torwood Street ascends the valley between Braddon Hill and Park Hill. At a distance of less than half a kilometre the Museum of the Torquay Natural History Society stands on the left. The road is also an approach to Ilsham where Kent's Cavern lies; the cave is described in Chapter Three. The earliest scientific investigator of the cavern was the Cornishman, William Pengelly. He was a founder member of the Torquay Natural History Society and the musuem is famous as a repository of his finds. Among other scientists associated with Torquay the following three are worth mentioning: William Froude, the naval architect; Oliver Heaviside, discoverer of the 'Heaviside Layer' of the upper atmosphere; and Philip Gosse, the naturalist mentioned in Chapter Two. As a matter of interest the road which has led to the musuem, if followed for a distance of 12 kilometres, leads to Teignmouth.

On the opposite side of Torquay Harbour a narrow road was constructed at the foot of Waldron Hill in the 1840s. The way was then opened for the building of a coast road linking Torquay and Paignton. It resembles parts of the French and Italian Rivieras and, like them, is spoilt by the noise and fumes of traffic. Rock Walk, on a higher level than the road, was laid out in the 1890s. The path, overhung with trees, traverses rocks adorned with wild and cultivated shrubs and climbing-plants, many of these being of sub-tropical origin. Pleasant glimpses of the harbour and town are obtained.

The hills and valleys on which Torquay is built are steep sided and of irregular disposition. Were it not for the fact that some of the valleys have been deliberately filled in they could be described as ravines. The enclosure of Fleet Brook has already been mentioned; other valleys too, have streams which have been enclosed in conduits. Part of the attraction of Torquay is a result of the varied inclination of its land surface.

The town's greatest period of growth occurred between 1840 and 1870. Fortunately, this development was consciously planned. The land-owners were the Palks and Carys; Sir Lawrence Palk in particular set out to develop his land with quality in mind. From the Inner Harbour there is a good view of the earliest of the terraces, Higher Terrace, erected in 1810. Oñ the left of the terrace is the nineteenth-century church of St John — with the exception of Torre Abbey most of the ecclesiastical buildings of Torquay are of Victorian origin. One of the most imposing terraces is Hesketh Crescent above Meadfoot Beach, some distance from the harbour. Both terraces were designed by members of the Harvey family, the architects employed by Lawrence Palk. Braddon Hill and Park Hill were among the first areas to be laid out, but development extended to Ilsham, Wellswood and Ellacombe districts and later to Marychurch and Cockington. Attractive villas arose and trees were planted in their gardens to replace the natural woodlands which had been cut down. Sensible roads, eventually to become tree-shaded, were set out along the contours. Palk continued to build terraces and lodging houses and started to reconstruct the harbour, a development which was taken over by the municipality when it obtained powers to do so towards the close of the nineteenth century.

Continuing development of the Torbay residential area in the present century has tended to obscure some of the landmarks which help to explain its origins. At the beginning of the medieval period, Torre Abbey, the hamlet of Torre Mohun, St Michael's chapel, and a small fisherman's quay, a mere corner of the present Inner Harbour, were the only man-made constructions. Torre Abbey was founded in 1196, by one William Briwere, as an offering in gratitude for the safe return of his son who was among the 67 hostages held by the Duke of Austria. Richard I of England had been kidnapped by the Duke on his way home from the Third Crusade and 150,000 marks was demanded as his ransom. As only 70,000 marks could be raised the hostages were sent as sureties for the remainder. The monastic establishment consisted of the church and other buildings grouped around the cloister; it was eventually handed over to the Premonstratensian Order. The mansion, which was the home of the Carys for 300 years, was built over parts of it and most of the remainder is in a ruinous state today. But a fine gatehouse of the fourteenth century survives and so does the tithe barn, known as the Spanish Barn.

Torre Mohun is no longer recognizable as a separate village. Even St Michael's, on a limestone outcrop and once equipped with a leading-light, calls for determination if it is to be visited. The parish church of Torre Mohun, dedicated to St Saviour and situated not far from Castle Circus, was thoroughly restored in 1849, but it still contains the tomb of Thomas Cary dated 1567. The wooden pulpit, also in the early Renaissance style, was moved to Cockington where it may be seen in the church dedicated to St George and St Mary. Cockington Mansion and the park in which the church is situated were acquired by the Torquay Corporation in 1935; it is a pleasant place to see early or late in the season after visiting the famous hamlet adjacent to it. Cockington has much well-kept thatch; even the Drum Inn built in 1934 has a thatched roof.

Three quays situated beside the bay at Brixham, Paignton and Tor Quay were probably in existence by the medieval period. The present harbours are enlargements of these fishermen's quays. The bay was well known to seamen as a reasonably safe anchorage, especially when ships became too big and 'unmanoeuvrable' to use Dartmouth. The Fleet, too, used it during the seventeenth and eighteenth centuries and it was this that prompted ships' officers to bring their families to Torquay, thereby creating a demand for accommodation. The Napoleonic wars at the beginning of the nineteenth century reinforced a development which had already begun.

The harbours were important to the subsequent growth of the three places. Paignton developed in the form of two setlements: a village beside the parish church, away from the shore, and the harbour with the homes of the fishermen. The old centre of Paignton, in the vicinity of St John's church, includes the tower of a palace which the bishops of Exeter established and a fourteenth-century stone dwelling, known as Kirkham House, stands nearby. The harbour lies in the shelter of Roundham Head. Seine net fishing, as distinct from the trawling in which Brixham specialized, could be carried out on the gently-sloping beach. The living quarters of the Paignton fishing people were built above the rooms in which the fish were salted, packed and stored; access to the upper floors was gained by outside flights of steps. Examples of these cottages survived until the 1950s. A modernization of Paignton Harbour was put under way in 1837 by Act of Parliament; the piers were built soon afterwards and, for a century, the Harbour Company enjoyed moderate prosperity. In 1931 the directors were called upon to deal with a new attraction in the form of the flying boat!

Brixham has always been much concerned with the sea. It was the leading

Devon fishing port until the 1870s when Plymouth overtook it. By that date some local boats were working as far away as the North Sea and landing their catches at east coast ports. The fishing fleet has kept up to date and facilities for the handling of the latest motor-trawlers and their catches are provided. The harbour originally extended farther inland beneath what are now low-lying parts of the town and in medieval times it was enclosed by a water-gate which trapped the seawater at high tide. Two tide-mills were powered by the controlled release of this water through sluices. The original Brixham settlement was not situated beside the harbour but was built in the vicinity of the parish church— a higher and safer place. The statue of William of Orange commemorates his unopposed landing, with his Protestant army, at this spot on the quay in 1688.

Barnstaple and the north-west

As the road into north-west Devon turns downhill for the last time, before entering the eastern outskirts of Barnstaple, an expanse of water, seemingly land-locked, may be noticed beyond the town. The illusion is produced by a meander of the river Taw, which, after rising amidst Dartmoor's crags, has flowed northwards. In this part of its course the river is wide and, when the tide is out, its bed is exceedingly muddy. It is well known that the configuration of the shores of the Bristol Channel sometimes create the phenomenon known as the 'Severn Bore'. No acute effect of tidal pressure is experienced on north Devon rivers, but the incoming current is among the most swift of the world.

The wide opening in the north Devon cliffs, through which the combined estuary of the Taw and Torridge passes into the sea, is visible from hill-farms situated many miles inland and can also be seen from Hartland Point. From the sea itself, the 'Bar' was the threshold sought by homecoming mariners making their way to Barnstaple, Bideford and the smaller quays of the two rivers. Some exceptionally broad, sandy beaches are associated with the estuary. The cliffs, of which the remainder of the coast is composed, are among the most spectacular of Europe. At night the beams of Hartland lighthouse sweep the sea and offshore Lundy and they are also noticed as a rhythmic flash along a wide arc of the mainland.

In the present century Barnstaple has been treated as the regional centre of north Devon. This is likely to continue as the need for centralization of services increases still further. The town was established well before Bideford, which developed under the Grenvilles, and they had obtained borough status for their town before 1217. A study of the two places reveals both similarities and differences. The hills slope up steeply from the banks of the Torridge at Bideford's 24-arch long-bridge and to this many be attributed the visual pleasure of the buildings rising from the quay, rank above rank.

At Barnstaple the hills stand farther back from the Taw and the whole of the shopping and commercial centre enjoys the advantage of a flat site. It is not at first sight an attractive town; almost all of its approach roads are ugly and, since the early 1960s, have too often been congested with slow-moving traffic. The considerable distance which separates it from the nearest large centres of population, Exeter and Taunton, has encouraged a spirit of independence and self-sufficiency in the inhabitants which is tempered by the bracing westerly-winds which sweep inland across the flatlands of the estuary.

Barnstaple and Bideford probably appeared to be more similar in the past than they do today: both were market towns built at the ends of fourteenth-century long-bridges, both were important ports separated from their common estuary by a few kilometres of tidal river, and—as sometimes happens with neighbours—a friendly rivalry developed. Whilst the estuary was the front door of the district, Bideford was able to compete because the deposition of alluvium gradually reduced Barnstaple's effectiveness as a port. The straightness of the river at Bideford kept the channel free of silt. With the arrival of the railways the orientation of north-west Devon changed. The first broad-gauge track was laid in the Taw valley and was opened in 1854. The direct line from Taunton was completed in 1873. These converged on Barnstaple. The estuary then became a mere side entrance the use of which diminished as bulk cargoes were consigned to the railways, causing the locally-owned and manned coasting vessels to go out of business.

Until recent centuries the high tides extended across riverside marshes, some of which are now built-up areas. The three largest man-made structures in north Devon, the Yelland Power Station, the Royal Air Force establishment at Chivenor and the covered yard of Appledore Shipbuilders, situated on the banks of the rivers, stand only a metre or two above high water. In both river valleys considerable areas would be under water at high tide, even today, were it not for the artifical embankments which confine the rivers to their channels.

The site of Barnstaple was the lowest at which it was possible to bridge the river Taw and the fourteenth-century long-bridge with its 16 arches is a fine example of the type. The carriageway has been increased in width at several dates, the most recent being 1963. This was a medieval pack-horse bridge as was that at Bideford. The pointed Gothic arches of the original, narrow structure remain intact and one of these may be seen at close quarters from the pedestrian under-pass at the north end.

In medieval times a long causeway was necessary in order to ensure a secure approach to the south end. The modern road is built on top of it. The original Barnstaple settlement, however, was probably not situated immediately at the end of the bridge. About a kilometre north-west there was a hill which was defensible. It was there that the Saxons had established Pilton, one of their four Devon boroughs, in the late ninth century. One view is that the man-made mound, near the Civic Centre, was not raised until the tenth century. Once a stockade or castle had been constructed on top of the mound a township and the river-crossing could have been defended and, on the slightly rising ground between the river and the line now marked by the High Street, the building of dwellings could be commenced. Alternatively, the castle may have been constructed to over-awe the rebellious inhabitants of a town which was already in existence. Though the river lies well away from the base of the mound today, this was not always the case. The site of the town was in fact surrounded on three sides by water. On one side there was the Taw, the Yeo lay on another, marshes oozed to the east in the vicinity of Litchdon Street and Victoria Road and, on the north-west, where the Yeo flows in an easterly direction, there was additional impassable ground. In order to make a direct approach to Pilton another causeway had to be constructed and this is still evident beside Pilton Park.

The sites of Barnstaple's four town gates, corresponding to the cardinal points of the compass, were marked, until recent years, by incised tablets let into the pavements. Knowledge of the gates lends support to the belief that, although there is no record of a 'grant of murage', the town was walled. The general line of the wall from the castle would have been through the North, East and South gates, returning to the river in the vicinity of the bridge. Boutport Street suggests the general direction taken by the wall, but the street itself lies outside the area assumed to have been walled. Excavations carried out in 1979 by K. W. Markuson appeared to indicate the foundations of a wall 3 metres wide and 24.80 metres west of the street frontage. Whether or not the wall was defensive or merely an enclosing wall is still far from clear.

Within the area defined on one side by the rivers and on the other by Boutport Street, many points of architectural, social and historic interest may be found. But it would be misleading to suggest that Barnstaple was ever an architectural treasure-house. There are many good features, and it can be claimed that the town is full of character, but masterpieces are lacking.

As indicated by the inclusion of 'staple' in the name, Barnstaple has probably been an important marketing centre for the surrounding districts for a very long time. There are separate markets for farm stock on Fridays, and foodstuffs on Tuesdays and Fridays. The 'Pannier Market' is situated in a building of handsome proportions in the centre of the town. Panniers are no longer in use for the transport and display of food, but it is the proud boast that if fresh, wholesome meat, vegetables, fruit and preserves based on these raw materials, cannot be bought in this market and the adjoining shops, then they are unlikely to be obtainable anywhere in the kingdom. It is a market where until a few years ago only the produce of farms and market gardens was offered for sale; now, a wider range of merchandise is available. The colour and fragrance of the vegetables and flowers, the movement and bustle of the customers in the market hall, which is nearly as long as the street itself, make an impression not easily forgotten. The famous Barnstaple Fair now begins on the Wednesday preceding 20 September it continues for three days, and it is still the occasion of age-old ceremony.

The market forms part of an example of the town planning of the Victorian period which was designed by the local architect, R. D. Gould, in 1855. The buildings at both ends of Butchers' Row, and those on the opposite sides of the adjoining streets, lie on the axis of the Row. The parish church, nearby, is situated in its former graveyard which now provides a useful space, similar to a small cathedral close. St Anne's Chapel, a fourteenth-century chantry chapel, stands beside the church; it was once used as the Grammar School and now serves as a museum of local history. The Cattle Market is situated in the open at the foot of the castle-mound and the buildings which hemmed it in for centuries have now been cleared away. The opportunity will, perhaps, be taken to replan this quarter of the town as an amenity and cultural precinct.

Unfortunately, in recent years a toll has been taken of the architectural heritage of the town as one corner after another has been rounded off to provide for the freer movement of the increasing volume of traffic. In World War II the Germans loosed only a few bombs on Barnstaple, but local apathy has produced similar results. For instance, four arches originally spanned the pavements near the ends of Butchers' Row. Without taking up much room, they had the effect of giving the street extra definition as an urban space and they served no utilitarian purpose. One day in the 1960s a lorry struck the supporting pier of one of the arches. Instead of it being repaired the three other arches were demolished by council workmen.

The tendency to condemn rather than conserve is not confined to the present age. Barnstaple was once a thriving Elizabethan town whose High Street was full of gable-end, half-timbered buildings; without doubt many of these were not worth preserving. But only two heavily-restored examples remain; they are number 80, the Three Tuns, and number 74. When the Three Tuns was modernized in 1947 some of the architectural features which were revealed by Bruce Oliver led him to conclude that the building was originally constructed in the mid-fifteenth century, but details of Elizabethan, Jacobean and Georgian date were also evident. Number 74 (Pickford's) stands at the High Street end of Holland Walk and its upper windows are still cantilevered over the pavement. Before leaving the vicinity it is thought-provoking to look across the street at number 36 (Lipton's) where, in 1685, the librettist John Gay was born. He is best known for his *Beggars' Opera* which produced a good profit; the sequel, *Polly*, which was banned, was even more successful.

The early seventeenth-century wealth of the town found an outlet in the endowment of alms houses and schools and produced stylish memorials in the local churches. In common with those of Totnes, the merchants of the town commissioned decorative plasterwork for their own homes. Many examples remained *in situ* in the earlier part of this century. The number has gradually been reduced, but a fine triple specimen still exists near the centre of the town at number 62 Boutport Street, the façade of which is of a later date. The removal of the intervening floor has made it easier to appreciate the decorative plaster ceilings, of the first floor, to advantage. The house is thought to have been the home of a Spanish merchant or his agent. Comment on the Queen Anne's Walk, the most important architectural example in Barnstaple, will be found in Chapter Four.

The Albert Memorial Clock tower in the Square, another design of R. D. Gould, is a reminder that the town saw several new developments in the Victorian period. Near the clock on a traffic island stands the town's only piece of public sculpture apart from the statue of Queen Anne; it represents the head of Charles Sweet Willshire, an influential local politician, who died in 1889. The head was modelled by the Barnstaple potter W. L. Baron and cast in bronze. Whilst Willshire was Mayor in 1878 the Square, where until 1847 the ruins of a lime-kiln were still in existence, was much improved. Continuing along Taw Vale Parade, the lamp standards of which are Coalbrookdale dolphin design, Rock Park is reached. The name is a reminder of an important benefactor, William Frederick Rock, who died in 1890 having made this riverside area a gift to his native town.

Another nineteenth-century landmark was a remarkable cast-iron railway bridge which carried the Ilfracombe line across the river and, in doing so, turned through ninety-degrees. If its southern approach causeway is included, the track was of reverse 'S' plan. It was designed by a Mr Galbraith, who was the engineer to the Barnstaple and Ilfracombe Railway which was opened in 1874; the downstream elevation of the long-bridge was obscured by the iron bridge until 1977, when it was removed.

Barnstaple now looks forward to the day when its traffic problems will be solved by the construction of urban relief roads. Being by-passes, these will have the effect of revealing and preserving the inherent human scale, and the considerable variety and charm, of the town centre.

List of towns

(The names of towns and some of the larger villages where the most interesting features are situated are given in alphabetical order. Lundy has also been included. The buildings are divided into the 'Main Sights', to be seen in the place itself and those which may be conveniently visited from it. These latter buildings or other features are placed after the sub-heading 'District.' The approximate distance by road is given in kilometres and the general direction is indicated by a compass bearing given in abbreviated form.)

Abbreviations:

DE	Department of the Environment
DTNC	Devon Trust for Nature Conservation
NT	National Trust

APPLEDORE see NORTHAM

ASHBURTON: former stannary town. Slate-hung elevations are a feature of the attractive centre. Charles Kingsley born at Holne 6km W. Main sights: church of St Andrew; Museum.

AXMINSTER: market and shopping town for an agricultural area. Carpet manufacturing centre. Main sights: town centre with St Mary's church. District: Shute Barton (NT) 5km SW; Loughwood Meeting House (NT) 6km NW.

BAMPTON: a small market town. October Fair famous for its sale of Exmoor ponies. Main sights: town centre with St Michael's church.

BARNSTAPLE: market town, centre of commerce and light industry. Annual Fair in September. Birthplace of John Gay. Main sights: church of St Peter and St Mary Magdalene; St Mary's church at Pilton; long-bridge; Queen Anne's Walk; castle mound; Butchers' Row and Market; Horwood Alms Houses; Penrose Alms Houses; North Devon Athenaeum; St Anne's Chapel Museum; Litchdon Street Pottery. District: Arlington Court (NT) 11km NE.

BIDEFORD: port and market town with a long history; associations with Sir Richard Grenville and Charles Kingsley. Main sights: the quay and long-bridge; market area, church of St Mary; Burton Art Gallery.

BRAUNTON: an ancient village and parish, now an expanding residential area. Main sights: St Brannock's church and Church Street; Museum. District: Vellator, tidal-creek, with Braunton marshes and the Great Field; Braunton Burrows a National Nature Reserve 1km W; Baggy Point (NT) 2.5km NW.

BRIXHAM: important, long-established harbour, home-port of a fishing fleet. Main sights: inner harbour area; Museum; Brixham Cavern; All Saints church. District: Berry Head Country Park with nature trail etc. 2km E.

BUCKFASTLEIGH: small town on the southern edge of Dartmoor, a one-time centre of the wool industry, old mill buildings remain. Main sights: church of the Holy Trinity; Farm Museum; Dart Valley Steam Railway. District: Buckfast Abbey.

BUDLEIGH, EAST: a large village formerly a port. Main sights: All Saints church and village centre. District: Hayes Barton, birthplace of Sir Walter Raleigh 2km W; Budleigh Salterton, an attractive small seaside resort with Fairlynch Museum 3km S; Bicton Gardens and Countryside Museum 2km N.

CLOVELLY: unusual adaptation of rural architecture to a restricted site. Main sights: High Street, harbour and lime-kiln. District: Clovelly Dykes 2km; Beckland cliffs (NT) 4km NW.

COMBE MARTIN: a village built on a 'spinal' plan situated in a mineral-rich locality. Main sights: church of St Peter in Chains; the 'Pack of Cards'; the cove. District: the Great Hangman, cliffs and moorland (NT).

CREDITON: a bishop's see from 909-1050 and in the sixteenth century was a wool town. Birthplace of St Boniface and General Redvers Buller. Main sights: church of the Holy Cross and town centre.

CULLOMPTON: a small busy market town. Main sights: church of St Andrew with the Lane aisle; 'Manor House'.

DARTMOUTH: ancient and modern seaport of importance. Main sights: South Embankment and the 'Boat Float'; St Saviour's church; Borough Museum and the Butterwalk; Newcomen Engine House; Henley Museum; Baynard's Cove Castle (DE); Dart Valley Steam Railway. District: river cruises; Dartmouth Castle (DE) 2km S; Little Dart cliff-walk (NT) 4km S.

DAWLISH: seaside town situated on the west side of the mouth of the Exe. Main sights: The Lawn (town centre); large cast-iron waterwheel; Museum. District: Dawlish Warren, sands and nature reserve, (DTNC) 3km NE; Powderham Castle 9km N.

EAST BUDLEIGH see BUDLEIGH

EXETER: County Town and Cathedral City. Main sights: Cathedral and Close; Guildhall; St Nicholas Priory; Tuckers' Hall; underground passages (entrance in Princesshay); Rougemont House Museum; Royal Albert Memorial Museum; Custom House, river quay, dock-basin and Maritime Museum; North Road Iron Bridge. District: Stoke Woods owned by Corporation, nature trail, 4km N; Killerton House, gardens and arboretum, (NT) 11km NE.

EXMOUTH: oldest seaside resort in Devon with harbour, situated on the east side of the river. District: La Ronde 1km N.

GREAT TORRINGTON see TORRINGTON

HARTLAND: An important village in a remote parish of considerable size. District: St Nectan's church at Stoke and, at Hartland Quay, cliff-paths and rock scenery 4km W; Hartland Point Lighthouse and, near East Tichbury Farm (NT), cliff-paths 6km NW.

HATHERLEIGH: a peaceful market town in a remote area. Main sights: church of St John the Baptist; examples of vernacular architecture.

HOLSWORTHY: a small but important market centre in a rural area. 'Pretty Maid' ceremony connected with Annual Fair in July. Main sights: church of St Peter and St Paul and market.

HONITON: developed because of its position on the former main road from Exeter to London. Main sights: town centre; Allhallows Museum; Honiton Pottery.

ILFRACOMBE: has the best resort facilities of the north Devon coast dating from Victorian times. Pleasure-steamer connections to Bristol Channel ports and Lundy. Main sights: harbour area with the chapel of St Nicholas; Museum; church of the Holy Trinity; Cairn Top (DTNC). District: Chambercombe Manor 1km.

KINGSBRIDGE: a small market town situated on a hillside overlooking an attractive estuary. Main sights: the quays and Fore Street; church of St Edmund; William Cookworthy Museum within Old Grammar School.

LYDFORD: Once a Saxon borough with its own mint, now much reduced in importance. Main sights: Castle (DE); gorge and woodlands (NT); St Petrock's church.

LYNMOUTH with Lynton: there was formerly a small fishing village beside the river mouth. Lynton, now a centre for the Exmoor National Park, developed on a flat site behind the hill which rises from the shore. In Victorian times the two settlements were linked by a water-powerd cliff-railway. Main sights: scenery; limekiln; Lyn and Exmoor Museum. District: Watersmeet Cottage (NT) 2.5km E; Woody Bay cliff-paths and woodlands (NT) 5km

W; Heddon Valley, woodlands and nature trail 8km W.

LUNDY: in the Bristol Channel, owned by the National Trust and administered by the Landmark Trust. The present port of embarkation for intending visitors is Ilfracombe. Main sights: church of St Helena, Old Lighthouse 0.5km from church; North Lighthouse 5km from church; Marisco Castle; cliff scenery.

MOLTON, SOUTH: market town with light industries. Access to Exmoor National Park. Main sights: The Square; Guildhall and Borough Museum; church of St Mary Magdalene.

MORETONHAMPSTEAD: a small market town within the eastern quarter of the Dartmoor National Park. Main sights: church of St Andrew, Almshouses. District: Chagford another attractive moorland town 6km NW; Castle Drogo (NT) 8km NW; Fingle Bridge 10km N.

NEWTON ABBOT: Founded by Torre Abbey about 1200, now one of the south-west's most important markets. Main sights: St Leonard's tower; market area and Rope Walk; Bradley Manor (NT); District: Stover Canal.

NORTHAM with APPLEDORE and WESTWARD HO! a village with a long history and a growing modern residential area. Main sights: the centre with St Margaret's church; 'Bloody Corner', the site of a battle the details of which have long since been forgotten. District: Appledore at the confluence of the rivers Taw and Torridge with its shipyards, vernacular architecture and Maritime Museum 2km NE; Westward Ho.! a modern settlement developed by a company in the nineteenth century, associations with Kingsley and Kipling, beach and pebble-ridge 3km long.

OTTERY ST MARY: formerly the site of a college of secular priests. Birthplace of S. T. Coleridge. Main sights: St Mary's church; tumbling weir. District: Cadhay (Tudor house) 1.5km NW.

OKEHAMPTON: situated immediately beside the northern slopes of Dartmoor it is the centre for a wide area. Nearby is the military camp. Main sights: town centre; Castle (DE). District: Dartmoor National Park; Meldon Reservoir 4km SW.

PAIGNTON: formerly a fishing hamlet now a large holiday resort. Main sights: St John's church; Kirkham House (DE); 'Oldway' 1874; Zoo. District: Aircraft Museum at Blagdon 4km W; Berry Pomeroy (castle) 7km W.

PLYMOUTH: Devon's largest city with naval dockyard and substantial industry. Main sights: St Andrew's church; Prysten House; the Barbican with Custom House and Elizabethan House; Citadel; Aquarium; Devonport Town Hall; Royal Naval Dockyard; Royal Albert Bridge. District: Saltram (house) (NT) 4km E; Plym Bridge Woods (NT) 7km NE; Burrator Reservoir 16km NE.

PLYMPTON ST MAURICE: situated beside its castle mound the town is less important today than it was in the middle ages. Birthplace of Sir Joshua Reynolds. Plympton St Mary is situated a short distance away along the former main road. Main sights: castle remains; Grammar School and Guildhall; churches of St Maurice and St Mary. District: Saltram (house) (NT) 2km W.

SIDMOUTH: a quiet seaside town on the site of a former fishing village. Main sights: church of St Nicholas and St Giles; museum at Hope Cottage; Royal Glen where Queen Victoria stayed as a baby, and other examples of Regency architecture. District: Sidmouth Cliff (DTNC); coastal and inland walks.

SOUTH MOLTON see MOLTON

TAVISTOCK: the town grew up beside the monastery where the first printing press in Devon was set up. It was a stannary town and it has a market. Main sights: church of St Eustace; Abbey ruins; Bedford Square with nearby riverside walks; Tavistock canal; Drake's statue; nineteenth-century industrial housing. District: Buckland Abbey (NT) 8km S; Morwellam Quay, industrial archaeology centre 8km SW; Wheal Betsy engine-house (NT) 8km N.

TEIGNMOUTH: the town has a long history as a port and market, second only to Exmouth in age as a Devon seaside resort. Main sights: the 'Den' and harbour area; St Michael's and St James' churches; Keats' House, where the poet stayed in 1818.

TIVERTON: a long-established market and manufacturing town, regional centre for east Devon. 'Waterbailing' ceremony every seventh year. Main sights: St Peter's church; Castle; St George's church; town centre; Old

Blundell's School where R. D. Blackmore was educated; regional Museum; John Heathcote and Company textile mill. District: Grand Western Canal; Knightshayes Court (NT) 3km N; Bickleigh Castle 7km S.

TOPSHAM: a seaport of some importance from Roman times. Main sights: a number of gable-end houses in the Dutch style; Museum; river scenery.

TORQUAY: Devon's largest resort. Main sights: harbours, Princess Gardens and Pavilion; Torre Abbey; Museum; Kent's Cavern. District: Compton Castle (NT) 5km W.

TORRINGTON, GREAT: long-established market town enjoying a commanding position overlooking the Torridge valley. Main sights: the Square; church of St Michael; Palmer House, Dartington Glass Factory; Castle Hill Common.

TOTNES: a Saxon borough, architecturally one of Devon's most interesting towns. Main sights: Fore Street and High Street with merchants houses; St Mary's church; Museum; Castle (DE); Ramparts Walk; medieval Guildhall; the bridge. District: Dartington Hall with its gardens, schools and the Devon Centre for Further Education 3km N.

WESTWARD HO! see NORTHAM

Index